KEEPING TEAMS ON TRACK

What to Do When the Going Gets Rough

KEEPING TEAMS ON TRACK

What to Do When the Going Gets Rough

LINDA MORAN

ED MUSSELWHITE

JOHN H. ZENGER

with JOHN C. HARRISON

IRWIN
Professional Publishing®
Chicago • London • Singapore

Times Mirror
Higher Education Group

Library of Congress Cataloging-in-Publication Data

Keeping teams on track : what to do when the going gets rough / Linda
    Moran . . . [et al.].
        p.   cm.
    Includes bibliographical references and index.
    ISBN 0-7863-0475-8
    1. Work groups.   2. Industrial management.   I. Moran, Linda.
    HD66.K44   1996
    658.4'036—dc20   96–12057

Printed in the United Sates of America
1 2 3 4 5 6 7 9 0 BP 9 8 7 6 5 4 3 2 1 0

To our clients, colleagues, and friends who strive to make organizations better for people through teams—and make teams more effective in their organizations.

PREFACE

It is almost a foregone conclusion that today's progressive organization will employ teams in some capacity to achieve its objectives, and most organizations can point to some part of their operation in which teams already play an active role. The impetus has come from many directions: increased competition, downsizing, and the trend toward a flatter, more flexible organization. As organizations look for ways to work smarter, they are recognizing that those closest to the work are in the best position to improve it.

Over the last few years, a steady stream of books has appeared on various aspects of team building. Because teams in organizations are a relatively recent phenomenon, most books on the subject have explored such subjects as how to determine whether an organization is ready for teams, how to get the teams launched, and how to clarify the various team roles—all topics related to the front end of a team rollout. With only a short track record to draw on, however, very little has been written on what it takes to *keep* the teams going.

Keeping Teams on Track carries the story to the next level. It is based on a wealth of information generated over the last five years as the authors have observed the outcome of many different team initiatives. As members of one of the nation's largest organizational training and consulting firms, we have been able to look beyond our hypotheses to see how roles and responsibilities actually have changed once teams were launched.

This book is a detailed look at what it takes to sustain teams after they've been launched. It offers information from several broad research studies conducted by Zenger Miller, one of which is in conjunction with the Association for Quality and Participation (AQP), a professional association dedicated to promoting quality and participation in the workplace. The book also reflects what we've learned from a series of detailed interviews with senior managers at major U.S., Canadian, and European organizations, interviews that explore the personal histories of successful and unsuccessful teams.

In addition, the book draws on years of experience gained through consulting with and conducting training for hundreds of organizations.

The authors have worked with small and modestly sized organizations as well as the biggest names in the Fortune 500. This experience has given us an excellent vantage point to observe why some implementations have been effective and why some have not.

The audience for this book consists of anyone who is working with teams or who may be struggling to improve how teams operate in his or her organization.

Executives will better understand how to lead teams through the politics and the resistance to change, how to expand teams beyond their initial sites, and how to evaluate whether to continue pumping money into the teams for training, meetings, and resources.

Managers will find the book useful in understanding the different organizational challenges faced by the four basic kinds of teams.

Team leaders will learn how to manage with minimal casualties during the transition period and how to elevate team performance in an environment of traditional policies, procedures, and management practices.

Internal and external consultants will gain a deeper understanding of the long-term consequences of various policies, procedures, and practices.

The book is divided into four sections. The first section, Problems You Can See from the Launch Pad, addresses early decisions and practices that can be anticipated even before the teams are launched. What executives and managers decide here will point the teams in a particular direction and have a direct bearing on the success of the teams as they mature. Section 2, Dealing with the Unexpected, looks at the broad range of problems that are more difficult to anticipate that arise as people struggle to adapt and function in an unfamiliar environment. Section 3, Putting It All Together, offers a detailed and in-depth interview with ABB Power T & D, a company that has successfully instituted teams. The section ends with concluding observations.

Finally, in Section 4 you will find 18 useful tools and techniques covering a wide range of team activities. These tools will help you determine the appropriate levels of teams for your organization and whether you should redesign the work processes. You'll also find useful tools and techniques for contracting with team leaders and facilitators, preparing new team managers, and coaching executives, as well as assessment instruments, sample training plans, and measurement tools.

The movement toward teams is still in its infancy, and it is obvious that the full potential of teams has yet to be explored. We hope this book will significantly further your knowledge and understanding of what works and will open up new opportunities that lead to successful team implementations within your organization.

Linda Moran
John H. Zenger
Ed Musselwhite

ACKNOWLEDGMENTS

We have written this book to summarize our learnings gathered from a wide range of businesses and industries. Reported are not only our direct experience with teams but the shared learnings of many Zenger Miller colleagues. Our consultants are on the front line with these implementations, and we want to thank them by name: Bob Hughes, Jerry Smolek, Judith Richterman, Dee Hoffman, Roy Blitzer, Jan Latham, David Williams, Seth McCutcheon, Joyce Thompsen, and Jerry Hogeveen. They worked with us to capture these learnings and worked with clients through complex team implementations.

Kathleen Hurson directed us through early drafts to focus on writing a book that's clear, and practical. Darlene Russ-Eft, Lilanthi Ravishankar, and Susan Muttart made it possible to capture team trends through their state-of-the art research. Caryl Berry provided key feedback as we defined the best way to share our learnings. Anne Farrell deepened our understanding of strategic and tactical measures and how they link team performance more tightly to business results. Michael Shuster, Todd Zenger and Patricia Haddock led us through the complex world of team compensation. Bill Johnson and Jill Heiden opened their plant to show us a model of an effective transition to teams. Jan Styles went beyond copy-editing to refine our tools and techniques so that they are clear for practitioners. John C. Harrison took random thoughts and insights and organized and synthesized them to help us see the holes in our thinking and create a clearly written book that's fun for even us to read. Leahandah Soundy designed our cover, managed our production process across three time zones, and transferred our notes into the manuscript.

Most of all, to our clients: Thanks for your trust. We value your partnership, respect your courage, and admire your tenacity. Because of your efforts, we can share learnings. You truly are making people for people and people better for organizations.

Linda Moran
Ed Musselwhite
Jack H. Zenger

C O N T E N T S

Chapter 8

Managing Stress   119

Chapter 9

Keeping Team Members Motivated   127

Chapter 10

Is Your Compensation Plan Working for or against You?   141

Chapter 11

Keeping Cross-Functional Teams on Track   155

⑥ TEAMS ARE NOT A WALK IN THE PARK

In [Mary Parker Follett's] view, managers and those they managed were of the same ilk, individuals governed by a mixture of reason, feeling and character. People behaved as they did because of the reciprocal response that occurs in relationships.

Pauline Graham

At 7:30 A.M., Cyra Bradberry settled down behind her desk at Caswell Manufacturing to begin another day in her role as director of Operations. So far, it had been a hellish week. As Bradberry sipped her morning coffee, she pondered the last in a series of recent problems that had arisen around team operations in her division.

"Why are these problems showing up?" she wondered. "We've already dealt with our start-up issues. I thought they were all worked through."

Indeed, the early days of the team initiative had been tempestuous at times as the teams were organized and members assumed new roles and responsibilities. During the first few weeks, endless snafus occurred as people struggled with unfamiliar assignments. Some team members appeared uncomfortable with their added duties, and some managers resisted letting go of control. But over time, as team members negotiated the early difficulties of working together, the problems associated with the launch diminished.

People began to show initiative and do more than was expected. Already the department had eliminated certain redundancies in the manufacturing process, and because the teams seemed to be spending less time and money to get things done, Bradberry had started to believe that she could stop spending so much of her time on team matters and could turn her attention to other business.

Then came the week from hell.

PEELING BACK THE ONION

Caswell Manufacturing specialized in producing nonstandard windows for offices and homes. On Monday morning, a representative from one of the company's largest customers called Bradberry. In an uproar, he told her that an order promised for the previous week had still not arrived although the invoice for the order had been received right on schedule.

"This is the third consecutive time an order's been late," the customer shouted at the other end of the line.

And, yes, he had called Customer Service for help.

In the old days, Customer Service could always provide callers with quick answers about when orders had shipped. But now the manufacturing team itself determined shipping dates.

When Bradberry checked with Jane in Customer Service, Jane explained that she had tried to call the team, but its leader had been busy with production issues and couldn't come to the phone. Undaunted, Jane walked over to manufacturing to look into the matter personally, but the team leader, who was trying to troubleshoot another problem, had brushed her off with, "The order's in the pile. I'll get to it when I can."

So now Bradberry was involved. As she set out to track down the order, she began to see why she'd been lulled into a false sense of security. Up to now, the teams had processed existing orders set up by supervisors under the old system. That explained why things seemed to work smoothly at first. It was when the teams started processing new orders that the system began to break down.

On the floor, Bradberry found piles of orders at various work stations. With no apparent logic or plan of organization, she could find no way to locate the information she needed. Nor was the team helpful. Team members were locked in an all-morning meeting to discuss their own departmental issues.

Each time Bradberry peeled back one layer of problems, she found another—like peeling an onion. Over the course of the next few days, Bradberry uncovered a series of weaknesses:

• *No access to critical data.* The team didn't know what to do with an order when incoming materials were late or when production schedules fell behind. The team didn't have the necessary tools, resources, and computer access codes to (1) pull up data on the screen and see what raw materials had been received, (2) update the status of orders for Customer Service, or (3) flag orders that were lagging.

• *The manual didn't cover everything.* Previously, when a supervisor learned that an order would be delayed, he'd advise Billing to hold off on the invoice until the order was actually shipped. From experience the supervisor had known that the invoice should go out 30 days after the order was received, but this information was never passed along to team members when the supervisory positions were eliminated. In fact, team members never had a clear idea of exactly what the supervisors did, and because nobody bothered to ask, many supervisors became miffed and refused to help the teams get up to speed.

• *No customer contact.* Teams never talked to customers directly and had little understanding of their problems.

• *Poor interface with other departments.* Now that the supervisors were gone, departments that hadn't organized into teams didn't know whom they should call in manufacturing when they had questions.

• *Status conflicts.* Managers of other departments who traditionally talked only to other managers resented having a team member from manufacturing bother them with questions.

By Friday, Bradberry was feeling the heat, especially from Frank Parkinson, vice president of Operations. From the start, Parkinson had been skeptical about the team initiative.

"If you want to try it, go ahead. It's your thing," he had said. "Just don't let things slip. And don't complain to me if things don't work out."

Well, thought Bradberry, things wouldn't have slipped if Parkinson had put the pressure on other departments to lend their support. But he hadn't. In fact, he hadn't really done much at all to support the team initiative. Many team members knew about this lack of interest among senior management, and they resented it.

By Friday night, Cyra Bradberry was starting to believe that perhaps Parkinson was right. Perhaps the team initiative had been a mistake all along. Management wasn't happy. The teams weren't happy. And the customer certainly wasn't happy. As Bradberry snapped her briefcase shut, turned off the light, and left her office, she found it easy to believe that the team initiative was out of control and just too much trouble. Managing teams was like trying to build a mobile. Just when you thought you had it balanced, something changed and threw the whole system out of kilter.

OUR SHRINKING WORLD

Were he still around, 1920s efficiency theorist Frederick W. Taylor would certainly have wondered why Bradberry was subjecting herself to so much stress. Back in the '20s, Taylor's theories were the current rage, and it was his followers who called the cadence in a well-functioning organization. Emphasis was on breaking down each process into clearly defined increments and performing each increment in the fastest, most efficient way.

Managers never shared information except on a need-to-know basis. Nearly everything seemed clearer then. Bosses set rules; workers followed. Ambiguity and angst were the domain of philosophers. "Real" people's roles were clearly defined, and whether or not someone actually *liked* his or her job was not an issue. Job satisfaction was seldom considered.

This focus on procedure rather than people arose in part from infatuation with technology that was new and exciting. If you invented a better ice box, an inexpensive Model T, or a better can opener, the world *would* literally beat a path to your door. Subtle product differences and the furious competition characteristic of the modern-day marketplace had yet to emerge. Markets shifted, but only gradually, and terms such as "60-day turnaround" were still decades into the future. If it took a full minute to make a trans-Atlantic call and Telex service hadn't even been introduced yet, how quickly could change occur?

Not until the latter part of the century would world events provide an answer to that question, and when the answer did come, it was shocking. The world could change *instantly*. As any modern manager can tell you, in a business environment where ideas and plans can be exchanged almost instantly by fax or over the Internet, success and failure are determined not by feet or inches but by millimeters.

Cyra Bradberry inhabits this new world, and it has metaphorically shrunk to a fraction of its original size. Consider how quickly Federal Express can deliver a package to almost any remote destination. Consider, too, how Bradberry must manage a workforce that can be remarkably diverse, yet required to work in careful concert. Quick turnarounds mandated by aggressive competition require managers to move at a rapid pace. If managers have found themselves, like circus performers, trying to keep several dozen plates spinning at once, it is not surprising that they sometimes become bottlenecks.

All of this has put undue pressure on the modern manager, and it has forced senior management to rethink how best to conduct business. For many, the solution has been a move to the use of teams.

PUBLISHED SUCCESSES LEAD TO
FALSE ASSUMPTIONS

Like the miracles at Lourdes, news of organizational transformation travels quickly to the farthest reaches of the business community. Over the last two decades, senior management across the United States and beyond has been regaled with published accounts of dramatic performance improvements wrought by the introduction of teams to the workplace.

We tend to become starry-eyed by these dramatic successes. This causes us to overlook what doesn't work—in this case, the roughly 50 percent of all teams that fail to provide viable answers or perform to expectation and are disbanded.

If there is one thing that has been learned, it's that a team is not a self-contained motor that continues to whirl smoothly as long as you supply the fuel. A team is composed of individuals in a dynamic relationship, both with one another and with their immediate environment.

The Dynamic Structure of Teams

Different metaphors have been used to describe the team environment. One metaphor is that of a delicately balanced mobile. Make a change in one part of the structure, and the entire mobile is thrown out of kilter.

Perhaps a more useful analogy is that of a polygon with interlocking points. As the following diagram indicates, each point affects and is affected by all other points, so if you change a system, a structure, or a measure, you may experience reciprocal changes in the culture, the team values, or any of the other points on the system.

The Team Environment

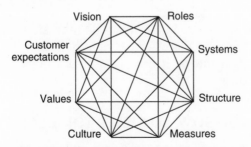

In the interactive team environment, changes in any aspect of the system are likely to be felt throughout the entire system.

Seth McCutcheon, a consultant at Zenger Miller, a consulting, training, and education company, describes the team environment this way: The concept of team forces us from simple linear cause-and-effect thinking to dynamic system thinking. Not only is each point acted upon, but each in turn acts upon all other points. It is like dropping a single droplet of water into a spider's web and watching the entire web respond to absorb the impact. All points are points of leverage to impact the whole, but the key question is, 'Which point do we need to push upon to have the desired impact?'

McCutcheon's response is, "The answer to this question, seemingly simple in linear cause-and-effect relationships, becomes extraordinarily difficult in a dynamic system. In truth, the simple linear cause-and-effect relationships never existed to begin with. Teams are merely a structural manifestation of the dynamics that were always at work. The team is, in fact, a multidimensional response to the multidimensional reality faced by organizations in today's turbulent global environment. This multidimensionality can hardly be managed by a single dimension manager."

This new paradigm can lead to considerable frustration for the executive in charge. In a traditional system it is relatively easy to determine who is accountable for any part of the operation. If things aren't working right, an executive can put pressure on a department, a person, or a loophole in the system to get done what is needed. In a team environment, team accountability makes it difficult to point a finger at any single individual, and executives may feel very tentative about precisely how to act. Questions such as "Do I step in, or do I wait?" and "How exactly should I intervene?" will not have neat, concise answers.

For executives with a low tolerance for ambiguity, the lack of guideposts can be psychologically painful and anxiety provoking. Many wrenches can wreak havoc with the team's smooth-running machinery, and executives and managers who are not well schooled in team building or who cannot fall back on natural team-building skills have a certain proclivity for gumming up the works.

Nevertheless, a well-functioning team does create synergy, and when established in the right place for the right purpose with the right members doing the right things, it can perform at a higher level than most people would expect.

WHAT YOU SOW, SO SHALL YOU REAP

The seeds for success or failure are sown in how teams are conceived and launched. Consider the dramatic turnaround of Tultex, a 6,500 employee manufacturer of cotton fleece clothing. In January 1993 the company's stock had hit an all time low and the plant in Virginia was carrying a $104 million inventory. Eighteen months later, however, the company showed the following results:

- 10 percent reduction of costs on the same volume.
- 25 percent improvement in inventory turns.
- $25 million reduction in inventory overhead.
- 75 percent reduction in meeting time.
- $13 million increase at the bottom line.

Though management could point to teams as a major cause of the success, in truth, Tultex was doing a number of things correctly to support its team rollout.

Management's objectives were to recreate Tultex as an organization that focused on delighting customers through value-added service and responsiveness. Additional goals were to shorten cycle times, lower costs, improve inventory turns, reduce inventory overhead, and improve customer acquisition and retention. During this time a foundation was being laid for total quality management (TQM), and the plant was undergoing a realignment of organizational structure and policy.

With the help of outside consultants and trainers, Tultex instituted teams and focused on fundamentals in all key areas. Executive support became active and visible, and leadership provided commitment, focus, and direction. Management also designed and managed an improvement plan, and an executive was appointed at the senior level to champion the change. The company's vision and values were clarified and communicated, and the company made a major commitment of time, money, and other resources.

The truth is, a team lives within a broader corporate culture that can either help or hinder it. The team is impacted by the type of team it is, its environment, the makeup of its members, the degree of management support it receives, and a number of other factors. In the case of Tultex, the company was consistent in supporting the teams at all levels.

Teams are often started, however, for less than durable reasons. Perhaps the most classic mistake of all is to roll out teams without solidly anchoring them to the business plan. This immediately places the team initiative at risk because it has not been built on a solid foundation. We have come upon some team rollouts over the last decade that were obviously destined to fail. The following are several scenarios that are not uncommon today.

BUILDING A HOUSE OF STRAW

One classic mistake is to introduce teams simply because the organization has undergone a downsizing. After the ranks of managers and supervisors have been thinned, someone looks around at the flatter organization and says, "Gee, we've created a *de facto* team environment. Let's move to teams." This strategy is unlikely to be successful. The decision to introduce teams needs to be rooted in the overall business strategy of the organization as well as in the nature of the work the team does. Unless there is a substantial reason to justify a team environment, all efforts to make it succeed will probably fail.

Sometimes, senior executives who have had previous successful experiences with teams assume that the experience is directly transferable, presuming that "if teams worked at my other company, they should work here, too." But to quote George Gershwin, "It ain't necessarily so," much to the chagrin of those recommending the change. Although outward circumstances may resemble what the executive experienced with a previous team, much under the surface may be different, and unless one is willing to take a sounding and check for rocks, diving off the cliff into the inviting lagoon may lead to less than satisfactory experiences.

Then there's the ambitious executive who's casting about for The Next Challenge. Being the forerunner in the company's team initiative can clear a path to increased recognition and earn the executive a conspicuous stripe. But pushing through a team initiative at the inappropriate time or under the wrong circumstances may be a greater invitation to losing a few stripes if things don't work as planned. At the very least, it puts undue stress on those unfortunates who must serve on a team whose leaders are more concerned with their own career path.

Corporate renegades often introduce teams to channel their energies and/or maverick ideas in more acceptable ways. However, the manager may adopt an adversarial, in-your-face attitude toward the organization in which being different is more important than working on common organizational issues. Such a manager may *not* want to champion teams that succeed in other parts of the organization but simply to put together a team that fills a special slot, much like a corporate SWAT team that has special powers to put out fires. This kind of exclusionary thinking is certain to place unusual strains on team members.

Teams can also be on shaky ground for any of the following reasons:

- Expectations are unclear.
- No team purpose has been established.
- It's the wrong kind of team, or the wrong configuration for the job.
- People have underestimated the amount of time, resources, and angst needed to get the team up and running.
- Although the team satisfies internal needs, it isn't aligned to the needs of the external customer.
- A conflict exists between the roles of team leader and team manager.
- The level and type of decision making are unclear.
- One or several team members have never bought into the team concept.

Considering all the factors that bear on a team, it is not surprising that one of every two team initiatives fizzles and dies. Teams that do get their ducks a row, however, can accomplish extraordinary increases in overall performance.

A team environment in the '90s calls for a substantially broader set of skills than that of the days of Frederick Taylor when an executive wanted nothing more than employees who were punctual, obedient, and hard working. Today's managers and executives are called upon to address questions that would make no sense to Taylor, such as these:

- Should work processes be redesigned?
- What are the most common hang-ups and frustrations of team members?
- How can I avoid being too strong?
- Should we turn back or keep going?
- How can I best share information with the teams?
- How can I protect the teams while they're struggling to establish their identity?

For those who have grown up in a traditional organization, maneuvering in a team environment can feel like exploring a strange and unfamiliar land. The questions are different. The language is strange. The customs are foreign. Nothing seems predictable. For many, however, the experience of traveling in an unfamiliar world is exhilarating. There is a sense of adventure and a promise of substantial reward. It's what drew the early European adventurers to the New World. This same willingness to explore will open up the enormous possibilities and challenges of a team culture.

PROBLEMS YOU CAN SEE FROM THE LAUNCH PAD

1

⑥ EARLY PROBLEMS AND CONCERNS

We trained hard, but it seemed that every time we were beginning to form up into teams, we would be reorganized. . . . I was to learn later in life that we tend to meet any new situation by reorganizing, and a wonderful method it can be for creating the illusion of progress, while producing confusion, inefficiency and demoralization.

Pet Renious, Arbiter, 210 B.C.

Questions Addressed in This Chapter

- How do teams differ?
- What rollout strategies are available?
- What problems should show up early?
- How can long-term success for a team be ensured?

Imagine for a moment that you've signed up for a wilderness survival course. All your life you've lived in a comfortable suburban community. You've had a spacious home, electricity, indoor plumbing, and paved roads. You've bought your food in supermarkets, shopped local stores for clothing and other essentials, and interacted with your neighbors at the occasional barbecue and PTA meeting. It's a world with which you're totally familiar. You know how everything fits.

Now you're about to be thrust into a radically different environment with a group of people, most of whom you know only casually and some not at all. Your familiar ways of running your day will no longer apply. Surviving in this environment calls for a different set of skills: how to catch and fry a fish, how to dig a sanitary latrine, how to provide shelter. You will also need to know something about the others in your group: how they think, how they act, what their values are. Most important, you will need to know how to support the group and bring out everyone's best qualities and strengths. Your survival—in fact, everyone's survival—depends on it.

It would be foolhardy to think that the "survival skills" you developed in your everyday community were all you needed to thrive in the wilderness. Yet, this kind of expectation shows up all the time when organizations move from a hierarchical to a team environment. People forget that when they move to teams, they are entering a different world—a world that will challenge them on many different levels, one that will test their strengths, weaknesses, skills, values, and many of their beliefs about "how things are."

How successfully teams fare in the new environment is significantly affected by decisions made even before the transition begins. In the wilderness, if you point yourself in the wrong direction or misjudge your mission or the composition of your team, you're headed for tough times. The same is true when an organization moves to teams. Many problems that teams experience can be directly related to decisions that were made before or at the time of the launch.

One of the first things you'll need to understand is the "lay of the land"—the kind of "terrain" the teams will be traversing. Will it be the beginner's course, or will they will be setting out on a path that is likely to present more compelling challenges and difficulties? You'll also need to understand fully the kinds of teams you'll be managing.

HOW DO TEAMS DIFFER?

Although people *think* they know what they mean when they say "team," there is often a discrepancy between the person's conception of the team and the actual reality. Mention "team" to a sports fan, and he's likely to conjure up a professional sports franchise or his daughter's team in the local soccer league. "Team" means something else, however, within an organizational setting. Unfortunately, our tendency to categorize may lead us to mentally group all teams together and not pay attention to the differences that exist among them.

There are four types of teams that are most prevalent in today's organization:

Intrafunctional teams allow people to share information and best practices. These teams make decisions about the day-to-day tasks they perform, processes they use, and challenges they face in their functional areas.

Problem-solving teams bring members together on a temporary basis to address specific problems and recommend solutions. Management usually retains decision-making authority. These teams are usually disbanded after the original problem is solved.

In *cross-functional teams,* team members typically focus on process improvement. These teams bring together people from across the organization. The teams make decisions about how to reduce cycle time by eliminating non-value-added steps. They recommend how the work will flow, and they look at ways to minimize variances and handoffs to reduce the opportunity for error. Often these teams have their recommendations approved by management and then are empowered to actually implement the improvements to the process. Cross-functional process improvement teams are usually ongoing groups that continue to monitor the process and make regular improvements.

Self-directed work team members have the authority to make day-to-day operating decisions about the way they accomplish their work and how they can improve it. These teams are usually organized after the process is examined, and their assignment is to eliminate non-value-added activities, minimize variances (the inconsistencies or errors in a process), and find ways to optimize the process. Self-directed work teams are given decision-making responsibility over the day-to-day steps of the process, and, as such, are a permanent part of the basic organizational structure through which work is done. Their greater decision-making authority gives them flexibility and speed in meeting customer expectations.

To assess which types of teams would be most useful for your organization, see Employee Involvement Tool on page 209.

Since each type of team evolves differently, you'll create unnecessary difficulties and limit their effectiveness if you ignore the differences between them. For example, you wouldn't want to provide a team infrastructure that is more appropriate to another type of team. To remind yourself of these differences and to make sure you're not lumping all teams together, here are some useful questions that will start you thinking in the right direction.

1. *How long will team members be together?* If the team will be together only a short time, it will usually require less infrastructure because team members will be off on other assignments before they have to deal with the consequences of interpersonal problems. On the other hand, if a long tenure is projected, the team may require a more exten-sive infrastructure to deal with a broader variety of issues that are sure to arise.

2. *What kind of responsibility will the team have?* Responsibili-ties can vary significantly, even among the same kinds of teams. You can see an example of this by examining process improvement teams at two different levels.

At the *bottom level* is the problem-solving team created to improve an individual segment of the process. The team is defined by the scope of the department in which it functions, and once its work is done, it is disbanded.

At the *top level* is the process im-provement team that looks at an entire process from beginning to end. This team's responsibility is to consider changing any segments that will make the process more effi-cient. The team will be composed of members from more than one department, and its goal is to standardize, measure, and improve the process by reducing the number of handoffs or standardizing procedures and measures. Managing a top-level team will be more demanding than managing a bottom level one.

3. *What types of decisions will the team be making?* Initially, decisions will be made jointly with the manager, but as teams mature, there will be a desire for more independent decision making as team members develop the necessary skills, knowledge, and authority. Will their decisions concern only day-to-day activities? Or will they impact an entire department or function? Decision making differs from one kind of team to the next. In *intrafunctional teams,* the team members make decisions. In *problem-solving teams,* the decision-making respon-sibility is usually retained by management. In *cross-functional teams,* team members make decisions about what non-value-added steps are necessary to the process. In *self-directed work teams,* the members are given decision-making responsibility over the day-to-day steps of the process.

To see if the team is ready for more independence, see the Mature Team Index Tool on page 294.

4. *To whom will team members owe their allegiance?* If members come from the same department, their loyalties will be to that depart-ment. If they come from different departments, however, their loyalties will be split, and they'll have to decide where their priorities lie. If the second situation prevails, it will be necessary to know how to handle those kinds of conflicts.

5. *How will the team go about meeting customer needs?* Who will decide what customer information the team needs and how will it get that information to be able to initiate or recommend changes? This will depend on the experience, sophistication, knowledge, maturity, and developmental level of the team as well as the kind of team you're managing.

For assistance in defining team development-related issues, see Planning the Team's Development—on page 252.

6. *What level of team development will you be addressing?* The level of employee participation to which you commit will determine how much development is needed. Self-direction demands more training and support than lower levels of involvement. Remember that needs change with time. Team leaders and team facilitators must be closely involved with the teams until they are more experienced in problem solving, leading meetings, and resolving team issues.

7. *Will you need to have team facilitators in place?* This will depend on the skills of the manager as well as the size of the rollout.

8. *Will formal training programs be needed to develop team-building skills?* The amount of training needed will depend on what levels of skill the teams already possess and how far along they are in the development of the team process.

9. *Will it be necessary to redesign the work process?* This will be influenced by the level of team rollout taking place.

10. *What launch strategy is being pursued?* This factor alone is worth paying extra attention to because it affects so many aspects of the team experience in the months that follow.

WHAT ROLLOUT STRATEGIES ARE AVAILABLE?

Pocket Strategy: The Small Rollout

There are three basic approaches to launching teams. The most popular is a pocket strategy. Management picks a little pocket of the organization—a single process, department, or function, nothing too risky—and installs a team to see how it works. The team is set in motion by a manager who is committed to establishing a higher level of worker empowerment in his or her immediate area. Managers frequently choose this strategy because they want their people to become more involved and efficient.

See Predicting Organizational Orientation toward Teams Inventory (POOTT) on page 230.

Because the risk is small, the initial team is often approached as a "living laboratory." Are teams functional? Will they work in this organization? A pocket strategy becomes a good way to test the waters without having to redesign or reexamine the work process. If the team succeeds here, perhaps the experiment will be repeated elsewhere.

A pocket strategy has both an up side and a down side. The up side is that not much is lost if things don't work out—a few bruised feelings, perhaps. The down side is that experimenting with a team in one small area may not really be giving the team a fair shake.

Normally, a team leader can expect some resistance from team members who are struggling with new and unfamiliar ways of managing their work relationships. What is often unexpected, however, is the ill will that is generated outside the group. The team can easily find itself a cultural island surrounded by hostile neighbors. The manager may detect negative feeling from peers who aren't crazy about the prospect of change and would really prefer that the experiment fail. Similarly, team members who have been empowered to take on more responsibility may be crushed by the resistance they encounter from internal customers and suppliers outside their immediate area. Resistance is common when these customers and suppliers are threatened by the team's assertive, independent behavior. In such situations, management may not be able to make an accurate appraisal of the efficacy of teams.

To give the team breathing room, the manager needs to create a protected environment in which team members can take on responsibility and build self-confidence. During this time the manager runs interference for the team within the larger organization by helping to facilitate requests for materials and setting up communication channels to the team from other parts of the organization. The manager may also spend time reassuring the next level up that the rumblings it hears from the team are simply part of the growth process. If the team is getting resistance from the outside, the manager may directly confront other managers or areas and help them understand that the team fulfills a legitimate business purpose and that their lack of support will hurt them as well as the team. Another useful assignment for the manager is to build allies in key support areas by showing those individuals how important their role is in the success of the team process.

The Dangers of a "Hothouse" Environment

Although it is necessary to protect the team during the early stages of development, one drawback to creating a safe space is that this does not give the team a dose of the real world. In fact, a manager can be so eager to have the team succeed that he or she creates an unrealistic environment, and the team never learns to function without the constant hand-holding it enjoys in the early stages of team development.

Consultant Sue Easton of Easton Associates recalls a client who had a pilot team in place for a year and a half. This team consisted of nine people in a population of 180 employees.

The HR director wanted to prove to the operations manager that teams would be successful, so he became the supervisor of the pilot team, and for a year and a half this was his baby. Not surprising, the team was very successful, and he was able to make a case that self-directed teams are a great option and the way to go.

What the people at the top didn't realize, however, was how much the other employees resented this one team because of the special privileges it was accorded. The HR director was supposed to be fair, but because he was so eager to have the team succeed, he constantly gave it preferential treatment.

"It's a situation I've seen before," says Easton. "Let's say a manager wants to prove that moving to self-directed work teams can help on-time delivery. If the manager has any clout in the organization, she can go down to the test room and request that her team's products go through first or ask the people in QC to pay more attention to the team's problems and concerns. In the end, the team does perform better, but it's not a fair judge of the team's effectiveness.

"In this particular case study I was called in a year and a half after the pilot began and there were a lot of bad feeling in the organization from the rank and file. The HR director knew how to make this one team successful. His approach was very paternal, very caring, very affec-tionate. He really loved those people. But he didn't understand work design, and he didn't understand how to approach the changes in the work flow and the other basic elements that were needed to support a team rollout."

Overprotection notwithstanding, in the early stages the team will benefit from special managerial support, such as always having a facilitator present to keep team meetings on track. The manager can also help by expediting requests for material and supplies through the organization. However, these and other jobs will at some point have to be taken over by the teams.

The Larger Rollout: Separate Section Strategy

The second approach is the separate section strategy. The manager in a larger team rollout must learn how to balance resources as well as manage multiple teams that may be developing at different rates. With a separate section strategy, a larger unit—a product line, a separate facility, a new business line—undergoes the transition to a team environment.

Instead of one team, there are many. With multiple teams interacting, new levels of coordination and support are required. In addition, it takes more time to communicate with people and give them the necessary skills and know-how so they can use the larger organization to best advantage. The separate section strategy is usually initiated by a middle- to upper-level manager, perhaps the director of a division. Although many of the start-up issues are similar to those found in a pocket strategy, additional problems can surface.

Déjà Vu

Imagine how a manager feels when Team C raises the very same problem that he or she just spent hours working through with Teams B and A. Having to do it all over again can leave the best managers feeling irritated and impatient. They may resent having to spend additional time and may come to believe that teams are by nature difficult. They're right, of course. Teams *are* difficult, at least at this juncture. Previously, managers would have assigned these jobs to supervisors who would have dealt with the situations themselves and then reported back. Now managers have to deal with each team directly.

Boundary Issues

In a pocket strategy a team deals with a process that has clearly defined beginning and end points. In a separate section strategy, the beginning and ending points may be clear for the entire section, but various teams will often find their boundaries fuzzy. It is up to the manager to clarify this.

Narrow Point of View

Perhaps the most challenging problem for the manager is to persuade all teams to identify with an overreaching strategy rather than focus only on their own localized issues. The manager must teach the teams how to share resources, address processes with overlapping points of responsibility, and create ways in which each team can teach itself what it needs to know. This self-learning may take the form of a learning network of best-practice forums in which teams have an opportunity to share the practices they have found to be most successful.

The Total Rollout: Go-for-Broke Strategy

The third rollout option is often referred to as the "go-for-broke" strategy because management bets everything by switching the entire organization to teams. Frequently, this takes place after management has tried unsuccessfully to solve persistent problems in other ways. So somebody says, "Nothing else has worked. Let's see if teams are the answer."

This is a high-risk strategy because everything is on the line. It requires great courage and a high level of commitment. The risk here is that management hasn't been realistic about the time and resources needed and the emotional turmoil that the transition engenders. Also, with more people involved, the potential for resistance and sabotage increases. If the transition is not managed properly, both the old and new system can grind to a halt. On the other hand, when there is strong enough commitment, thorough preparation, and sufficient skill development, this process can produce dramatic results in a relatively short time.

Organizations often experiment with the pocket and separate section strategies before committing resources to "go for broke" because that approach seems less risky. Over the long haul, however, the go-for-broke strategy has proven to be the one most likely to succeed.

Senior management generally initiates a go-for-broke strategy since it involves the organization as a whole. Though many of the issues are common to all three strategies, there is one major distinction. In a smaller rollout only one person acts as leader and spearheads change, but in a go-for-broke strategy, the change process can no longer depend on a single person. That approach makes the entire rollout too vulnerable. Consequently, executives must do several things:

• The first item on the list is to build an infrastructure so that everything does not rest on one person's shoulders. Other people must become involved in helping the teams develop. Otherwise, the viability of the process becomes at risk.

See Managing and Planning Checklist on page 240—for a list of items needed for this infrastructure.

• Managers must find ways to change the organizational culture to sup-port teams. In a smaller rollout, this could be a simple change of procedures. Now, because so much is at stake, managers have to look for ways to change the culture, norms, and values. In a smaller rollout, people recognize the experimental nature of the team environment and are often not surprised when the bottom falls out. After all, teams were never part of the organizational culture. But in a go-for-broke strategy, if the teams don't work out, the damage to employees is potentially severe. Taking the entire organization back to a hierarchical environment with lower personal involvement is usually devastating, and the loss of empowerment often leaves employees apathetic and ready to seek employment elsewhere.

• Managers need to enlist multiple champions to fight for the teams because one person can't accomplish such a significant cultural change singlehandedly.

• Managers must address large organizational issues such as the measurement, compensation, and review systems. In a separate section strategy, these systems may not initially need to be changed, but ultimately, for the teams to continue growing or to spread to other parts of the organization, changes will be necessary. In the meantime managers may have to improvise solutions to immediate problems by looking for loopholes and ways around the traditional systems.

To gauge team morale, see Evaluating Team Morale on page 264.

Although thinking through every potential problem in advance may seem like a more prudent way to enter into a team environment, there is a certain advantage to jumping in with both feet. Jim Lawler, manager of Organizational Development at Union Camp, believes that one attempted team rollout at a 20-year-old plant would have benefited from a more aggressive approach.

During the introduction of work teams into this plant, the design team spent endless hours going through the preparation phase. In addition, management did not succeed in communicating the business rationale for the effort. Ultimately, the teams had little success, and the effort was postponed to focus their energy on a major capacity expansion.

"The design team spent too much time overdesigning and getting caught up in the fine details," Lawler recalls. "We didn't need to dot every i and cross every t. It would have been better to create momentum by getting teams up and running quickly and then trusting ourselves to work out whatever loose ends came up. In retrospect, I would have blitzed the conceptual phase and would have come up with the design using concentrated effort in a short period of time. It could have been done in a matter of months without sacrificing quality. Others have successfully used large group interventions for similar initiatives. As it was, we met only once a month and relatively little occurred between meetings."

WHAT PROBLEMS SHOW UP EARLY?

Once the teams get rolling, it may be difficult to identify and understand what the team's rallying points are since the manager has to deal with multiple complex changes taking place simultaneously. At times the manager may feel as though he or she is trying to hit a moving target, especially if teams also are being integrated into other organizational change initiatives. There *are* various problems that are common to most team rollouts, however, no matter what the size and scope. The following are some of some of these early problems and the strategies for addressing them.

The Wrong Systems Are in Place

You can't build a compensation system before the teams are formed, nor can you predetermine the metrics for things such as quality standards and absenteeism. Team systems such as hiring practices and communication plans can be developed only after the teams are in position. Only after the team launch takes place will it be time to determine what system characteristics are important to the teams, whether the current systems are limiting them, and what you need to do to remove those limitations.

Customer-Team Relationships Are Rocky

Developing closer ties between teams and customers is a good idea provided the teams are capable of gaining the customer's respect. Therefore, it's a good idea not to rush things. Give the teams time to mature and gain confidence before you allow them to interface directly with the customer. Because mature teams are exposed to data about the competition and the marketplace, they are better prepared to take customer calls and explore customer needs personally.

Team Members Are Not Committed

If someone is sitting on the fence, you don't want to oversell the team initiative so that the individual develops unrealistic expectations. The person first needs to know what the challenges are. You want the individual to enter into the team environment somber and realistic about what it takes to manage or function there.

Everything Rests on the Manager or Executive

You can't afford to build the team culture without also building the infrastructure. That's because you can't risk having the entire team effort rest on one person's shoulders—yours or anyone else's.

Words Are not Backed by Actions

If things aren't working smoothly, you can't simply complain and do nothing or order employees about. You need to discover how you can contribute to the team environment, even though you may be confused by what is going on. Also, effective team managers must resist pulling the teams back to a more traditional and comfortable setting at the first indication that matters may be getting out of hand.

HOW CAN LONG-TERM SUCCESS FOR A TEAM BE ENSURED?

On May 25, 1962, President John F. Kennedy electrified a nation by predicting that it would have a man on the moon by the end of the decade and return him safely to earth. Well before the actual launch took place, however, scientists and technicians had to invent an entire technology and set up a complex support system. They had to create semiconductors and microprocessors, exotic alloys, and new control technologies. NASA had to develop an extensive infrastructure as well as specialized training, not only for the astronauts but also for thousands of support personnel. A deep space, global communications network had to be built and a plan made to provide overall control of the Apollo program. All of this had to happen before *Apollo 11* and the lunar module *Eagle* could set out on the historic journey toward the Sea of Tranquillity.

Similarly, in the days and weeks directly after the launch, the situations the manager encounters will be tied closely to the level at which the rollout takes place and the kind of infrastructure that has been set up. For this reason, it is important to acknowledge the basic ways in which teams differ and to plan accordingly. If these issues are not properly addressed, the team might not get very far into the mission before problems cause it to abort. The result can be a waste of precious personnel hours and resources.

In particular, the manager needs to

- *Explore* whether the organization is able to support teams.
- *Prepare* an infrastructure to manage the transition to teams as well as to prepare managers for new roles.
- *Implement* the teams by rolling out the team strategy, changing or expanding roles, and preparing the handoff of tasks to the teams.
- *Maintain* the teams by changing systems to support the team structure.

On page 240 in the Tools and Techniques section, you will find a complete Planning Checklist covering all the issues you need to consider as you prepare to shift decision-making responsibility to the teams.

Whether managers are shooting for the moon with a go-for-broke rollout or actually attempting to put someone *on* the moon, they will have to look far beyond the launch if they want their team initiative to succeed.

CHAPTER

2

⑥ PUTTING TEAMS ON THE ROAD TO SELF- SUFFICIENCY

You cannot build character and courage by taking away a man's initiative and independence. You cannot help men permanently by doing for them what they should be doing for themselves.

Abraham Lincoln

Questions Addressed in This Chapter

- What stands in the way of teams becoming self-sufficient?
- What kind of training is required?
- How do facilitators provide a safety net?
- How can an effective leadership style be created for a team environment?

If you were shepherding a group of suburbanites through an outdoor survival training, you'd probably want to keep a close eye on them during the first few days as they built their confidence and became acclimated to the new environment. Then you'd want to begin weaning them from your constant care so they could build their own survival skills.

To check the maturity level of the team, see Mature Team Index—on page 294.

Teams in organizations need to be similarly weaned. Throughout the early weeks and months, a team basks in the special attention it receives, but after the first year, the considerations that team members have enjoyed start falling away, and the team finds it is having more difficulty functioning effectively. It begins to attract attention from those who are threatened by the team environment and who find subtle ways to undermine it. The team no longer enjoys the constant encouragement that previously came its way, even from the "friendly forces."

At this point the team has not been prepared enough to know what it needs and, left to fend for itself, it is likely to suffer the same fate as the fledgling that leaves its nest too early. Therefore, it is up to the manager to exert pressure on the team to begin taking over some of these support activities itself.

The next section presents some of the factors that prevent teams from becoming more self-sufficient.

WHAT PREVENTS SELF-SUFFICIENCY?

Insufficient Communication Skills

Team members may know very little about how to work together, but because the manager or a trained facilitator has always been there to move things forward, it's not likely the team recognizes its lack of skills. Thus, the team needs to be educated in how to facilitate its own meetings and resolve interpersonal issues. This task will fall to the manager or to someone brought in from Human Resources.

Little Knowledge of How to Work the Organization

Although the team is interdependent with the large organization, it may falter because it does not understand how to go after the resources it needs. Team members need to develop "corporate smarts." They must learn whom to talk to, how to negotiate, and how to work their way up the hierarchy if their needs are frustrated at lower levels. In the past the manager handled these tasks, but to be independent, the team members must understand the business of the organization and learn how to employ the formal and informal systems that make things happen.

Little Understanding of How to Protect Itself

Though the team may have enormous potential, it is defenseless and as vulnerable as a newborn fawn, especially to threats from managers and employees who have a vested interest in seeing the team fail.

It's easy to assume that everyone will recognize the opportunities that teams present. Unfortunately, many people are invested in a more rigid, authoritarian chain of command. If they're line workers, they may like the security of being told exactly what to do as well as the

freedom from personal responsibility that comes with rigidly defined tasks. If they're managers, they may secretly treasure the opportunity to wield authority. Often, such managers believe that they have
earned this power and resent "giving it away" to the teams. Such people
will resist change and will do what they can to prevent the team concept
from spreading.

Research conducted by Zenger Miller cites startling figures on how
prevalent and widespread team sabotage can be. According to a 1994
study, Team Members Speak Out, 35.5 percent of all respondents reported
the presence of strong resistance to and/or sabotage of their organization's
team initiative. Of these respondents, 70 percent cited resistance and/or
sabotage at the middle management level, 61 percent cited front-line man-
agers/supervisors, 45 percent cited nonsupervisory employees, 38 percent
mentioned executives, and 10 percent mentioned team leaders.

Even more startling is the impact of such sabotage. In organizations in which team efforts were being sabotaged, 29 percent reported
that team efforts, while progressing, were not meeting or exceeding
expectations. By contrast, in organizations without sabotage, team
efforts were either progressing (54 percent) or actually exceeding expectations (7 percent).

Exposing team members to failure before they've built self-confidence can be demoralizing if the journey gets too rough too early.
Consequently, until the team develops its own muscle, the manager must
function as the team's protector. It is his or her responsibility to keep the
team safe from any hostility or efforts at sabotage that come from other
parts of the organization.

The manager can help the team in this regard by setting boundaries
so that team members do not have to perform in situations that ex-
ceed their expertise, status, or decision-making capabilities. Without
such guidance and protection, the team may become at least partially
immobilized.

*A cross-functional problem-solving team was put together by a helicopter
manufacturer to look at various difficulties the group had been having.
One of the problems the team focused on was how to get the right material from vendors in the right quantities and configurations.*

*In one instance, the team found that the engineers had asked that a
particular part receive an extra coating to make it safer. The final assemblers knew that the additional coating would increase the thickness of the
part so that it would not properly fit without further processing, a costly
additional step that assemblers didn't want to take.*

But why didn't the assemblers speak up?

It seemed the engineers talked in a language that the assemblers on the team couldn't follow. The team members were self-conscious about not having the "right words" or knowledge and were unwilling to risk looking foolish by raising an objection. As a result, the assemblers never challenged the engineers on whether parts that were not sized to fit exactly should be specified.

Allowing team members to operate comfortably within their depth gives them time to build self-confidence. As team members become more self-assured, they'll begin to take bigger risks and start looking for greater challenges. They'll also be more able to withstand the ups and downs of organizational life.

To help you link the team to the organization mission, review the Team Chartering tool on page 245. This tool will help you define boundaries, identify team sponsors, and determine the resources available to the teams.

Lack of Technical Knowledge

Team members may not yet have all the technical knowledge required to do their job as defined. For example, they may not be aware of certain governmental regulations or feel comfortable interpreting the financial data and international client requests. Originally, the manager did this for them, or the manager may have prescreened the regulations and given the team only those that were standard or that applied to them. Now they'll have to consider all this material themselves.

Gaining the necessary knowledge may come from on-the-job training, or the manager may have to work directly with team members to help them understand what isn't obvious. In addition, the team may call in experts from HR or the legal department to get more background. Some companies place the needed information on computers that teams access directly. Such information might include directions on where to find specific data or checklists of everything the team needs to consider in undertaking a particular project.

WHAT KIND OF TRAINING IS REQUIRED?

In a team environment, all team members must be continually prepared to make competent business decisions as well as function in a leadership capacity when called to do so. This usually requires additional training to allow people to master the necessary skills.

Two areas should be considered when training strategies are planned. First, there's the technical training needed for such tasks as accessing inventory data on the company's computer system. The second area pertains to building problem-solving, communication, and team-building skills. Here the primary training skills include

- Listening.
- Giving feedback.
- Presenting ideas to the teams.
- Building a foundation of trust.
- Clarifying customer expectations.
- Participating in effective meetings.
- Making various types of decisions.
- Solving problems effectively.
- Resolving issues with team members.

Secondary training topics include

- Developing effective presentation skills.
- Giving and receiving constructive feedback.
- Interviewing a team member or manager.
- Conducting peer performance reviews.
- Disciplining a team member.
- Handling a dissatisfied customer.
- Negotiating for resources.
- Challenging team boundaries.
- Sponsoring team ideas.
- Resolving issues with other teams.

The manager helps the teams to become more self-sufficient by defining which competencies will assist them in handling their expanded responsibilities. Some of the first subjects to consider include setting expectations, resolving team conflicts, giving feedback to team members, and problem solving.

Who actually does the training? If only a single team has been set up, the department manager usually provides special coaching to individuals as needed. Some companies institute extremely comprehensive programs to train managers to be coaches. "At Eastman Chemical Company," says director of training Nic Clemmer, "we have a 14-week program that takes them through extensive team and interpersonal skills training. This program has been so successful that it's been classified company confidential—management perceives it as a competitive advantage. The only people who attend are first, second, third and fourth level managers."

> For a more complete list of skills that will be needed later, refer to Advanced Team Training on page 299.

The departmental manager often makes the best classroom instructor, since he or she is usually in a good position to demonstrate how the material can be tied to actual on-the-job situations. In a large department, training responsibilities must be shared with others. Generally, it is useful to have team facilitators in place to help prepare team managers to address tough interpersonal issues and conduct team meetings.

HOW CAN FACILITATORS PROVIDE A SAFETY NET?

Because team members generally lack experience in group process, they may not recognize that they have requirements for such things as materials, training, or additional physical resources. If a manager is responsible for a single team, he or she can look after team issues. In large transitions in which managers must support many teams, trained facilitators are usually necessary to identify weaknesses and provide strategies and direction.

There are also steps that a facilitator can take to help teams move toward self-sufficiency.

> To better understand how to assist new team managers, look at Assimilating a New Team Manager on page 291.

Keep Meetings from Bogging Down

A Zenger Miller survey indicated that the most recurrent criticism voiced by team members is that meetings go on forever without anything getting done. If every meeting feels like a stroll through a tub of molasses, it's not long before criticism of the group process starts making the rounds. A skillful facilitator can ask the right questions and prevent the team from going off on tangents. The facilitator can also mediate problems between individuals and help people see where they're off track or blocked.

For developing a team-specific development plan, refer to Planning for the Team's Development on page 252.

Advocate at Higher Levels

Another important role for the facilitator is to speak persuasively for the team at higher levels of management. Suppose the group is experiencing problems with the team manager—perhaps there's unspoken resistance or even out-and-out sabotage. The facilitator might sit down with the manager, interpret the group's needs in a nonthreatening manner, and offer some useful suggestions. If that doesn't work, the facilitator may then plead the team's case at the next higher level—for example, with the director of the division.

Provide Access to Other Functions

Let's say that team members have identified in the work process a non-value-added step they would like to remove—perhaps extra paperwork or unnecessary reporting. The team may not have the authority to simply revamp the workflow, but the facilitator can step in and check with other departments to determine whether removing that step will have any negative impact. If it won't, the group can then petition to have the extra step removed. On the other hand, if that step is really necessary, the facilitator can find out the reasons and explain them to the team in a way that encourages acceptance and understanding.

Identify Needs for Further Training

The facilitator can also identify areas where further training would be helpful and, in particular, help the team develop the necessary cross-training so the group can be more flexible.

Refer to Team Development Plan on page 252 for assistance in identifying areas that require further training.

Until the team develops its own body of skills and experience, it is unlikely that any large-scale team initiative can take place without at least a small cadre of facilitators to assist team members as they acquire new abilities and responsibilities.

HOW CAN AN EFFECTIVE LEADERSHIP STYLE BE CREATED FOR A TEAM ENVIRONMENT?

Typically, communication flows from the top down. Senior management tells middle managers, who tell team leaders, who tell team members. These hierarchical channels are particularly effective when one-way communication is appropriate and compliance is the expected response.

In a team environment, the values are different. Independence and individual initiative, not compliance, receive the highest recognition. This is fostered through a more personalized and interactive leadership style, one that builds the feeling in each team member that he or she is important.

Managers can encourage a deeper experience of involvement in team members and a higher level of personal participation in specific ways. These are some proven practices that bring it about.

Provide Personalized Briefings

One effective method to establish a close rapport with team members is to let them hear important news "straight from the horse's mouth." Though employees always get news through traditional channels such as company newsletters, bulletin boards, E-mail, and departmental briefings, they will feel more participative if the manager or executive briefs them personally. As Marshall McLuhan pointed out some years ago, "The medium is the message." In this case, the medium is the manager, and the message—that each team member is a partner in the process—is in the way the message is delivered.

Personal briefings are also an effective way to create team buy in for new programs and ideas.

John Aikers, former chief executive officer of IBM, has long recognized the need to personally touch base with people at all levels of the organization. Aikers does his share of selling corporate programs through planned presentations to management and employees. He also looks for opportunities to talk to any employee at any level of the corporation.

Consequently, you may often find him out on the floor of the plant, chatting with a manager or line worker, listening to concerns, and getting people enthused about the company's latest program.

What Aikers is doing is seeding the work environment with people who will champion his ideas and help persuade and excite others. Even though at any one moment he may talk to only a single individual, by enrolling that person in his vision, he is indirectly addressing everyone this individual will come in contact with by building a strong sense of personal participation. He could not have the same kind of impact by keeping his distance and communicating just through the printed word.

Look After the Politics

Because the team environment threatens the status quo, many nonsupporters find any excuse to undercut the effectiveness of the teams or to make life difficult for them. Unfortunately, there is no simple answer for how to address this. The organization may simply have to go through enough successful launches so that people begin to see the benefits of joining in. Meanwhile, managers and team members will have to lobby for the teams at every available opportunity.

To make sure you're getting the best person at the helm, see Interviewing a Team Manager on page 288.

If you're an executive, one way to create new supporters is to "pack the court," so to speak, by making sure that any new manager hired supports teams. You want to add people who are excited by the possibilities of a high-participation environment and whose focus is directed at creating greater customer satisfaction. You *don't* want people whose focus is entirely on how much they earn and whose ambition is to simply move up the ladder.

Listen to the Heartbeat of the Team

To be able to provide what teams want, it's important to know what teams *need*. Executives and managers can be quick to provide lip service to the team concept, but real support and trust building begin when they get out on a regular basis and talk with employees about their concerns.

Westinghouse Norden, a defense contractor, is one company that decided its executives should remain in constant touch with employees. After the team launch, the company published a master calendar of all monthly team meetings and assigned each executive specific meetings to attend. But the executives weren't showing up. They always seemed to have more pressing business to attend to and just couldn't find the time to sit in on meetings.

That wasn't good enough for the disgruntled teams. "You want us to take on responsibilities, but you're not interested in hearing what we're dealing with," they protested. It also wasn't good enough for Executive Vice-President Mike DeAngelo. He sent word to the executive staff members that even though they didn't want to attend the meetings, they were still expected to be there.

DeAngelo was clear that the executives attending the meetings were not to play an active role. He directed them to rein in their impulses and simply listen to get in touch with what people were feeling—not an easy task for take-charge executive types with a passion for fighting fires. What issues and concerns were team members struggling with? What were their difficulties? What were their successes? This was the kind of information with which DeAngelo wanted his executive staff to stay in touch.

Learn How to Listen with "the Third Ear"

The executives at Westinghouse Norden were being asked to listen on several different levels—a mode that can seem unfamiliar to those focused only on facts. Psychoanalyst Theodor Reik calls this "listening with the third ear" when your attention also focuses beneath the words to the subtext of the conversation.

What are people passionate about? Where is their pain? Are there potential conflicts being subtly expressed in the way various parties interact? What are the unspoken messages? Though you may not be up on the technology under discussion or understand the exact nature of the issues, you can still tune in to the team and gain important information by simply listening to the pattern of how people communicate. Even if you are a technical expert, you don't have to let your involvement in technical issues blind you to the subtext of the team interactions. The same holds true in your personal, one-to-one conversations.

Sue Easton of Easton Associates has an additional suggestion. She says, "Great listening requires great questioning skills." Often, this requires paying attention to what questions are *not* being asked by the team and then gently questioning it in ways that identify trouble spots that need to be addressed.

Listening with the third ear is a skill that does not come easily to many executives. If you are willing to make an effort to do so, however, you can often garner a wealth of useful information that otherwise might pass unnoticed.

Pay Attention to Your Nonverbal Communication

Executives are often more comfortable making a decision involving thousands of dollars than they are sitting quietly and listening to what team members have to say. This comes across in how they comport themselves during the meeting. It's not uncommon for executives to show up with a pile of mail and proceed to sort and read it while the meeting is taking place.

But imagine how that looks to a team member. His group is discussing an important issue, and over on the side the manager or executive is sitting there sorting mail. What message comes across? *Even though the executive may be carefully listening to every word that is being said, his or her body language communicates a totally contradictory message.*

If you're sitting in on a team meeting, especially one that relates to a crucial team event such as the team development plan, a progress review, a new member welcome, or the celebration of a major milestone, you must never lose sight of the fact that your body language speaks volumes. It says much more than your actual words.

Many executives believe that they're not earning their keep if they're not actually doing something. In this case they *are* doing something—something extremely important—*listening.*

Louellen Essex, Ph.D., a consultant in Minneapolis, offers another good example of a manager who communicated a mixed message. This executive was upset because her staff complained about how she was managing her unit, and she responded by saying to the team, "Okay, I won't manage you. I'm officially making you a work team, so now you're in charge of yourself. Now you'll see how hard it is to do my job."

On one hand, the manager was saying, "You can be autonomous." At the same time she was saying, "But once you become autonomous, you're on your own." This conspicuous lack of support said to the team that it was not being set up to succeed and made it difficult for it to develop any enthusiasm for the team process.

Mixed messages can also be given by something as basic as asking questions. Imagine being asked to swim in a river that you believed to be treacherous. Would you do it? Perhaps the first time, but not likely the second if you had a bad experience.

Yet, isn't this what happens when an executive encourages employees to speak out when they're not clear about something and then procedes to find fault with any questions that don't measure up? Team members aren't fools. If the water looks too deep or fast moving, that's one river they're not going to cross, and important questions may never be asked.

A more effective approach is to model the desired behavior yourself. For example, if you want to encourage question asking, then ask about something that *you* don't know. As an executive, it may be hard to admit that you lack all the answers, but by admitting publicly what you don't know, you'll not only be "talking the talk," you'll also be "walking the talk." You'll come off as more credible and human.

Restrain the Urge to Take Over

For the typical executive, being asked to simply sit back and listen without actually *doing* something is casting against type. The executive wants to say, "Have a problem? Great. I'll solve it." Blocking that impulse can lead to the fear that, in the words of one executive, "I'm just sitting here like a bump on a log, looking like a fool in front of the troops. I'm not leading."

> *Janis Sears, information systems vice president, Technology Services at Canada Life, recalls how compelling her own urge was to take over and run things. One day she found herself sitting in on a team meeting while members were struggling with an issue. For Sears, who prides herself on her technical competence, the solution was clear, and she wasted little time communicating her solution to the team. She told team members what to do and whom to contact and then abruptly got up and left the meeting to attend to another appointment.*
>
> *Sears had lapsed into her old management style of taking over, and as awareness of this gradually dawned on her, she realized that her behavior could not go unacknowledged. Consequently, she took it upon herself to apologize to those she had offended by her actions. She confided that she was still working on bringing her own behavior into line and concluded by reaffirming her complete confidence in the team's ability to manage its own affairs.*

Unfortunately, the kind of sensitivity and team support shown by Janis Sears is more the exception than the rule. In the Zenger Miller study, more than two-thirds (71 percent) of all respondents indicated that executives were only passively supporting teams. This lack of support can easily be read by team members as "you're not that important"—hardly a morale builder.

An executive's attitude typically has a direct impact on the success of the team initiative. The Zenger Miller study also indicated that less than half (49 percent) of teams were progressing satisfactorily in companies in which executive support was slack. When management provided strong support for teams, however, the report of satisfactory progress zoomed to 84 percent—over a 70 percent increase! Clearly, this high level of support also helps teams become self-sufficient.

Be Willing to Deal with Awkward Situations

Letting go of control is painful for many executives, especially when the team decides to take an action the executive finds questionable. Do I jump in and do the "right" thing, or do I let the team learn through trial by fire? Not an easy choice. Huey Greene of Baxter Health Care recalls a time when team members wanted to redesign their own work areas and came up with recommendations. "From an engineering perspective," Greene says, "what they were asking for didn't quite make sense. But I realized that I was being tested, and not accepting their recommendations would be a slap at empowerment. Ownership and accountability were something this plant didn't have, so I let them try it. Well, they made it work. It showed our commitment, but I'll tell you, it was tough. Letting go of those things took some getting used to."

An awkward situation of a different sort can occur when a particular site moves to teams, but the rest of the organization does not. What happens when the executive must function within conflicting cultures?

John Saunders, director of Operations of Binney and Smith's Canadian plant, found himself in just such a situation. Saunders had a broad charter from the company—find ways to increase the participation and involvement of employees—but little was spelled out as to how this should be carried out. Saunders chose to interpret this charter as liberally as he could. Instead of figuring out how little responsibility he could transfer to people, he capitalized on the opportunity to set up cross-functional teams that possessed a broad range of responsibilities.

But because one of Saunders' jobs as plant manager was to minimize overhead and nonproductive time, he found himself in the awkward situation of having to account for the extra time that teams were spending in planning meetings, an expense that was being flagged by the company's accounting system. Saunders resolved the situation by sitting down with the accounting department and explaining why the company's standard performance measures needed to be reexamined and why team performance might decline until the teams became more focused.

An awkward situation may also occur when an executive finds that people are producing excellent results but not doing so in a way that supports the team initiative. An example is an effective manager who continues to exercise aggressive, hands-on management to the detriment of team members. How do you say to such a person that you still encourage good results but no longer want him or her to follow the old, proven path? This is like asking Steffi Graf to revamp her tennis swing while she's at the top of the rankings. It hardly makes for a confident player.

If you ask the manager to relax control of team members to let them become more self-sufficient, you must be willing to create a safe space in which the manager can experiment with the new management style and not feel that he or she has to account for results on a moment-by-moment or even week-by-week basis. To gain this cooperation, you need to model the behavior yourself. Here are some ways you can do this:

- Admit when you're wrong. Be willing to show that you, too, make mistakes.
- Don't take yourself too seriously.
- Admit what you don't know or can't do.
- Acknowledge what other people *do* know.
- Create opportunities for others to shine. Don't hog all the glory for yourself.
- Don't hide out in your office or bury yourself in mountains of minutia or nonstop meetings.
- Stop trying to solve all the problems yourself.
- Stop taunting or putting people down. Avoid uncontrolled emotional outbursts.
- Don't rake people over the coals.
- Portray teams as an investment and make a commitment to use them in tough times.
- Sell the concept that "we're all in this together." Position teams as a common undertaking in which everyone benefits.

Support an Information-Rich Environment

Everyone loves to be special, and sometimes being special relates to what you have or what you know. As a child, you may have owned the best collection of baseball cards or Barbie dolls; as an adult, you may take pride in your Targa convertible or your friendship with a local celebrity. This what-I-have-makes-me-special thinking is where executives often get stuck. Knowledge represents power, prestige, and control. The 1920s management guru Frederick W. Taylor knew this only too well, which is the reason that he proposed that in the typical hierarchical organization, managers should share as little information as possible. According to Taylor, they should make data available only on a need-to-know basis. Many executives still subscribe to this principle.

For this reason communicating in a team environment takes getting used to. It's no longer appropriate to ask: How little information can I share and how infrequently? The question for executives in a team organization is: What other information can I share, and how quickly can I get it out?

Walk down the halls or corridors of a mature team environment and you'll see graphs and charts everywhere. People *want* to make information available so that others will know how things are going. Computers are located on the shop floor rather than behind managers' desks, and workers are skilled in accessing the data. There are few restrictions.

Rather than waiting to be told what's important, self-sufficient team members can then take it upon themselves to look up what they need to know. They no longer have to go through the manager.

This does, however, put an additional burden on employees because they now have to be not only savvy enough to know where to find the data but also sophisticated enough to understand what it means. One team member observed, "When we went to teams, what I lost was my information sorter. My manager used to organize the information into what was important and what wasn't. He'd keep me focused. Now I have to do it all myself."

From the executive's point of view, helping teams become self-reliant has decided benefits. Team members are compelled to become more knowledgeable. They have to know a great deal more about the issues at hand. Each person needs to understand not just his or her small piece of the pie but also the mission and direction of the entire organization.

The road to self-sufficiency is anything but linear, however. There is constant backsliding. Often it's a question of one step backward, two steps forward as teams try, stumble, and try again. Learning new skills goes at its own maddening pace, as does creating new norms and breaking old behavior patterns. At such moments, it is a common mistake for an executive to see the teams' struggle as an indication that the transition is not going well or that individuals are not cut out to function on teams.

During these moments, the executive might harken back to his or her own struggle in learning to ride a bicycle—the crashes, the skinned knees, the frustration at not being able to make it work. What ultimately succeeds is the willingness to persist until confidence builds and balance is achieved. Team members also need time to experience the struggle. They too must deal with frustration and failure as they work to achieve balance and functionality. For this reason, the executive must not judge them harshly but be willing to see the teams through the difficult times and give them enough room to master the skills they need.

3

⑥ SHOULD YOU REDESIGN THE WORK PROCESS?

When we give up myopic attention to details and stand far enough away to observe the movement of the total system, we develop a new apprecia-tion for what is required to manage a complex system.

Margaret J. Wheatly

Questions Addressed in This Chapter

- Does work redesign have to be a big undertaking?
- What guidelines should you follow in planning a redesign?
- How do you implement the work redesign?
- What does a successful work redesign look like?
- How do you determine which decisions and responsibilities should be passed to team members?

Although certain residual benefits such as improved communication accumulate simply by switching to teams, generally only after the work has been redesigned is it possible to streamline the processes and remove variances. That's when you begin to see less work in process, reduced cycle times, faster internal feedback, and lower rework and scrap.

Typically, work flows horizontally from one department to another, but communications channels are set up vertically. This means that peo-ple who facilitate handoffs between processes often have only minimal contact with one another. One of the major attractions of teams is that they allow people to communicate more easily about the work and the way teams can reduce the number of times the work moves from one department to another.

A pocket strategy usually calls for little if any alteration of the work process, operational structure, or organization. Instituting a multi-team environment in which groups of people—executives, managers, and front-line workers—manage entire strategic processes calls for confronting a different set of problems.

In planning the launch of a multiteam facility, organizations often make the strategic mistake of overlaying work teams on poorly designed work. Work has traditionally been organized around a single process— assembly, finishing, punch-press, word processing, claims adjustment. Teams, on the other hand, operate most effectively when the work can be designed not around batches or "chunks" but around customer-supplier chains.

Maximizing the impact of teams calls for developing a keen understanding of the customer-supplier chain and recognizing the ways to exert the greatest leverage on the work process. It means addressing questions such as these:

- Should we spend money in new equipment for teams and/or staff each team with its own production engineer?

- Should we tear down a wall? Build a wall? Build a new building?

- Should we give up a product line or farm out components to other facilities?

For help in appraising work redesign issues, see Redesign or Not?—on page 310.

To answer these questions, you must understand how the work flows from one link to the next. Only then can you begin to make decisions about whether the work process should be redesigned and, if so, how.

DOES WORK REDESIGN HAVE TO BE A BIG UNDERTAKING?

Many people believe that work redesign has to be a long, arduous, and technical process. Not so. It *can* be extensive if you're talking about a greenfield site or a major manufacturing installation. In these cases redesign may involve extensive analysis and design, major capital equipment investment, and substantial revisions of policies and procedures.

Most efforts are more modest. Beginning the process may involve little more than making a freehand map of the workplace and drawing lines to show how members move from one place to the next. It may even be as simple as assigning patient charts to clerks alphabetically instead of at random.

Work redesign should not be seen as a process that "once done, is done forever." In fact, work redesign is best regarded as an iterative process. As people gain experience, they begin to see new opportunities for further improvement. Thus, a team that starts by simply rearranging the furniture in a customer service area may later end up redesigning all the work processes that affect customer service.

WHAT ARE THE GUIDELINES TO FOLLOW IN A REDESIGN?

Planning the redesign requires looking at the needs of the organization. Most of these never show up on the organization chart, although their importance is prominent and critical to the success of the teams. These needs include the following:

- The strategic goals the work is intended to meet.
- The processes by which the work gets done.
- The people who do the work.
- The way these people interrelate.
- The customer.

In particular, the needs of the workers must be considered. To plan a proper work design, it's a good idea to talk directly with those who are actually doing the work. After all, they're the ones with the real insider information. They have the most intuitive feel for the requirements of the job on a daily basis. They're also the ones who have to buy into the redesign, so their input and participation are essential. Are the social and psychological needs of the workers being considered? Does the redesign give meaning and dignity to the work? The work should always be looked at from a "bottom-up" perspective—from the point of view of those who perform the work and from the perspective of the customer whose needs are always paramount.

Although the requirements dictated by technology naturally vary from one type of work to the next, the qualities that people look for in a job—any job—remain fairly constant. For the most part, people want jobs that

- Include a variety of tasks.
- Call for a variety of skills.
- Challenge them to learn new skills.
- Foster interaction with others.
- Change over time.
- Provide immediate feedback from their customers, co-workers, or others.
- Provide flexibility of movement.
- Allow opportunities for making decisions.

These items should be considered as essential ingredients when you are thinking through ways to make the work process more efficient.

Ten Useful Guidelines for Creating a Successful Work Redesign

What does it take to create a work redesign that delivers the greatest return on your investment in teams? These 10 guidelines, drawn from research by Geary Rummler and Alan P. Bache, and presented in their book, *Improving Performance: How to Manage the White Space on the Organizational Chart,* can help in planning the implementation.

1. Focus your initial redesign efforts around *strategic* issues. It's tempting to try to change everything at once—big mistake. At best, it will take longer to see results; at worst, by focusing on less strategic issues, you may never achieve the increased performance you're seeking. A more effective approach is to start with only those issues that have the greatest influence on your organization's major strategies, for example

- If you want to increase profits, you might look for ways to reduce paperwork.
- If you want to increase sales, find ways to get merchandise to the shelves faster.
- If you want to gain market share, see how you can improve customer service.

2. Identify the processes related to those issues. Say that you've chosen to direct your efforts at improving customer service. The processes you'll want to study include such things as ordering, tele-phone service, information systems, and training.

3. Organize work around a product that involves multiple processes rather than a single process. Since teams are a potent way to build involvement, you'll want to capitalize on this momentum by giving the team responsibility for *all aspects* of producing a product, not just for an isolated process. If you can, assign the team multiple process-es to provide a variety of work and minimize process handoffs. The notable exception is when the work is of necessity organized around a single process involving capital equipment, although even here, installing work teams can still be effective.

4. Be willing to expand job responsibilities. Look for ways to push down managerial-level, decision-making authority to employees who are one or more levels below. You allow people more autonomy when you give them authority to undertake such tasks as setting work schedules, solving problems, and dealing directly with people in other parts of the organization.

5. Create more feedback opportunities. Another way to stimu-late responsibility is to give people frequent opportunities to experience the impact of their actions. Typically, workers only hear about their per-formance from supervisors. A work redesign can provide additional feedback by giving employees closer links to customers, by allowing them to check the quality of their own work, and by giving them direct access to performance reports and meaningful measures.

6. Create support teams to back production teams. Support teams offer a quick response when team members need help. They also constitute a highly visible endorsement; their presence says to the team that "management wants you to succeed." The more technical the work, the more technical expertise the support team should be able to offer.

7. Move support functions as close to the production process as possible. Create plenty of opportunities for production teams and sup-port teams to communicate directly. You can facilitate this by moving the support team directly onto the production floor. Traditional thinking has always been that you want to centralize support services to effect a greater economy of scale. In practice what is true is that redundancy is often desirable because of the efficiencies gained through increased pro-ductivity, cost reduction, and team member buy in.

8. Identify the links in the customer-supplier chain. Make sure there's a way to know which people and teams make which products.

This way, if someone has a question about a part, he or she will know whom to talk to. Clarifying the links in the chain improves quality and makes problem solving more efficient.

9. Assign an executive "sponsor" to each major process being redesigned. A sponsor can help the work teams secure any resources they need. A sponsor can also let the teams know if the redesign they've come up with is practical and affordable.

10. Don't overdesign the work. Too much planning beforehand by the design team will discourage work team members from making contributions themselves.

HOW IS THE WORK REDESIGN IMPLEMENTED?

We began by examining ways to create a successful redesign. To implement the redesign, you'll need to look at how the work is performed and how team members function together to accomplish the tasks.

Begin with an *environmental scan.* This calls for accessing all those factors inside and outside the group that can have an impact on how work is carried out. In conducting this assessment, it is important to pay particular attention to customer expectations and competitive positions. Do you *really* know what the customer wants? Do you know your customer's considerations, standards, fears, and concerns? This is the step most often overlooked. People often assume that they have the answers and are unwilling to put in the time and effort to confirm that their information is correct.

The second step is to perform a *technical analysis.* This involves examining the work flow and identifying variances—those areas where inconsistencies or breakdowns in the process are most likely to occur. You may be surprised by what you find. Vice President Bob Horney reports that during the technical analysis at MDB Financial Network, an organization that provides hospital decision makers with ways to reduce risk and conserve capital, the design team was able to reduce the process steps from 144 to 41 and the number of transfers from 29 to just 2.

Step three is to *problem solve* ways to minimize or control these variances.

The fourth step calls for conducting a *social analysis.* This involves looking at what makes the work meaningful to the people doing it. These are questions you'll need to consider:

• Are workers still being left out of the responsibility loop?

- Is everyone empowered?
- Do workers believe they are really able to make a difference?
- What tasks are satisfying or dissatisfying?
- What do people find frustrating?
- What wastes workers' time?
- For how much of the total process do workers feel responsible?

The more you are able to build into the work a sense of dignity and meaning, the more likely you are to create buy in and improve your chance for success.

Finally, it's time to step back, survey your information, and develop the *work design plan*. Elements of this plan should include the following:

- A process map of the work process.
- Team configurations.
- Role responsibilities.
- Work area layout.
- Training plan.
- Task transfer (handoff) plan.
- Implementation plan.

Now is the time to be creative as you make everything function in concert. This calls for synthesizing all the data you've collected and then reconfiguring the work process in a way that balances the needs of the job with the personal needs of team members. The minimum critical specifications, which constitute the first part of the plan and are worked out in collaboration with team representatives, compose about 40 percent of the plan. The remaining 60 percent is worked out in conjunction with the entire team. Remember, do *not* overplan.

WHAT IS A SUCCESSFUL WORK REDESIGN?

To get a sense of what a successful workplace redesign looks like, let's look at this example from an electric motor company. Before the company was reorganized into self-directed work teams, the organization chart looked like this:

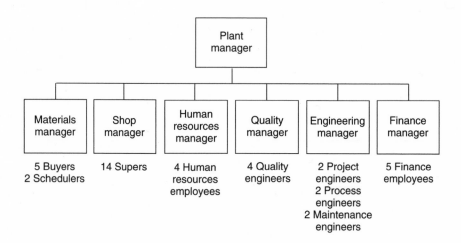

This is a schematic drawing of how the work was organized:

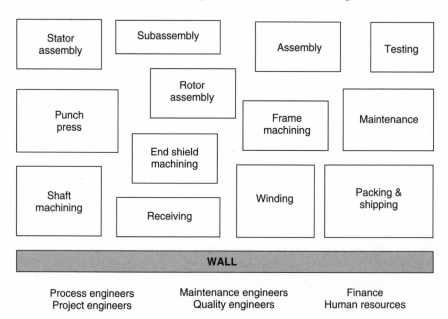

Notice that a wall separated the production floor from the offices of the salaried production support people. This was not just a *psychological* wall; it was actually a *physical* wall that imposed a formidable barrier to easy communication between the two populations. Had the teams attempted to function under this schemata, it would have taken them much longer to deal with everyday problems because the production support personnel would have been physically out of the loop. In addition, floor personnel were grouped by function rather than product line, making it harder to develop strong personal and working relationships with the others on the team.

THE REDESIGN

In the redesign, instead of separate departments, management created four different kinds of teams.

Production teams are made up mostly of employees with some supervisors. Each team is organized around a different product. Teams each have from 5 to 15 people.

Production business teams consist of from four to six people. These teams may include a quality engineer, materials specialist, process engineer, maintenance person, and one or two team support specialists.

A **project maintenance team** focuses on facilities maintenance: heating, air conditioning, hydraulic systems—equipment that is common across all teams throughout the plant.

A **technical support team** focuses on the manufacturing process. It includes the experienced, technically competent engineers who can manage projects, install major equipment, communicate with people at headquarters, and deal with vendors.

By executing a thoughtful and carefully planned work redesign, management literally and figuratively removed the wall that stood in the way of effective team functioning. This resulted in more cohesive teams as well as teams that can respond quickly to any situation that arises.

WHICH DECISIONS AND RESPONSIBILITIES SHOULD BE GIVEN TO TEAM MEMBERS?

Once the work has been redesigned, various responsibilities must be transferred to the teams. How quickly the team should assume these new responsibilities is for the manager to decide. In evaluating whether a task should fall within the team's control, the manager must first determine whether the team has the necessary skills, information, and authority to make the proper decisions. If so, the responsibility for that function can be marked for transfer. It is also important that the manager gain the necessary support from outside levels of authority.

Consider the manager of a shipping department who normally supplies delivery information to anyone calling his department. The manager has established a work group, and one function of the group is to provide shipping information to internal and external suppliers. But the manager can't simply reassign this task and walk off. Group members need to have access to delivery information, and that requires additional training in using the department's computers. Approval to make this happen must come from higher sources.

Once the list is made, the manager goes to the team to negotiate the new set of tasks. It is important that this negotiation result in a partnership that satisfies both manager and team members. Since one of the reasons for teams is to create work that is personally meaningful, the decision to assign a particular set of tasks must always take the employee's job satisfaction into consideration.

The following is a list of questions that will help in determining which decisions and responsibilities can be more effectively assigned to team members:

- For which decisions do teams often wait?

- Which decisions, if made at the team level, would speed the process?
- Which decisions, if made at the team level, would improve the quality of life of team members?
- Where are most decisions made about how the work is done?
- Which decisions, if made at the team level, would help create "whole jobs"?

In executing a work redesign, the best policy is to invite input and ideas from all groups and individuals who will be impacted. However, postponing the rollout until all the *i*'s are dotted and all the *t*'s are crossed is unwise. It is not necessary to spend endless weeks and months addressing everything down to the most minute detail. This strategy stops paying off at a certain point. Experience has shown that it is more important to get the teams on line while momentum and interest are high. Remember that the redesign is always subject to modification as the influence and knowledge of the teams develop.

4

⊚ MEASURING TEAM PROGRESS

In organizations we are very good at measuring activity. In fact, that is primarily what we do . . . there is never a satisfying end to this reductionism search, never an end point where we finally know everything about every one part of the system. [But] when we study the individual parts or try to understand the system through its quantities, we get lost in a world we can never fully measure nor appreciate.

Margaret J. Wheatly

Questions Addressed in This Chapter

- How have organizations traditionally used measures?
- Why do teams need to share in performance data?
- Who should select the measures?
- How do you choose which measures are most critical?
- What common traps should you avoid?
- What are the core measurements to get you started?

There is a simple way that members of our wilderness survival team— or anyone trying to get from here to there—can avoid drifting off course. All they have to do is carry with them two invaluable direction-finding aids: a map and a remarkable device called a global positioning system (GPS) receiver. The portable receiver communicates directly with the network of GPS satellites circling the globe to allow people to determine their coordinates down to 100 meters or less. No matter where people are located, with just a map and a GPS receiver, they can determine exactly how far they've come, where they are now, and in which direction they need to move next.

Unfortunately, many organizations do not properly go about making the measurements that tell their teams where they are and where they need to go. This is not to say these organizations don't attempt to develop useful data. It's just that many executives make the common mistake of (1) providing little guidance and direction for the team and (2) overloading their teams with too many measures. The data that emerge are often wide of the mark and unable to provide the teams with useful information.

HOW HAVE ORGANIZATIONS TRADITIONALLY USED MEASURES?

In the past, the practice was to run measures only when something wasn't right. For example, if business were falling, an organization would make an effort to track down and isolate the problem. Measures were synonymous with trouble, and many employees were quick to regard an unexpected performance appraisal as simply a prelude to being let go or, at the very least, as a way of being investigated for substandard results. Not surprising, even today *measurephobia* ranks right up with *computerphobia* as a major employee fear.

What measurements often *didn't* do was provide teams with useful data that could offer purpose and direction, and as a result, teams would find themselves flying blind.

"If you look at the teams that failed in the '80s and early '90s," observes one consultant, "a major reason that they didn't make it was that we didn't measure team output in relation to corporate strategy. The only measures we cared about had to do with team building. We only wanted to find out whether people were happier being on the team.

"Managers became overly solicitous of the team's feelings. They wanted fledgling teams to have a positive experience, and that made them gun shy about putting teams through anything as pejorative as a productivity measure. The fear was always that the employees might feel intimidated. Consequently, teams often ended up spinning their wheels, focusing neither on the customer nor on the business issue. It was team activity for its own sake and not for the sake of the business.

"For that reason, it was hard to justify the value of the teams to the business. We were only measuring team satisfaction but we weren't relating team performance to how the organization was performing as a whole."

WHY DO TEAMS NEED TO SHARE IN PERFORMANCE DATA?

Today, organizations are becoming more realistic about measures. As they come to regard teams as business partners, organizations are recognizing that team members have a right and responsibility to share in current performance data. More and more managers are beginning to understand that initiative, self-direction, and motivation are all linked to realistic expectations, and that these expectations can be fulfilled only if teams are able to maintain clear goals and objectives. Instead of measures being simply an adjunct to finger pointing, managers are saying, "Now that we see what's happening, what assistance can we provide these teams so their measures can reverse direction?"

This is leading to a new *quid pro quo*. Organizations are more willing to support the teams with useful data because management recognizes that sharing such information allows the teams to more effectively support the organization as a whole.

WHO SHOULD SELECT THE MEASURES?

Which measures are best left to the teams? Generally, these are the hard measures because team members are usually in the best position to understand the fine points of a process. One of the biggest mistakes that organizations make, however, is to leave *all* measures up to the teams.

"I read an article a while back in *The Harvard Business Review* that said that because teams are empowered, they should be allowed to set their own measures," says consultant Anne Farrell of The Farrell Group. "But how do they know what is critical to the business? Who has the big picture? Anyone can decide, 'Gee, this looks important. I think I'll work on this.' But until someone culls out the vital few issues from the compelling many, you'll end up with teams that are focusing on the wrong thing."

A case in point is this example from Federal Express.

FedEx has always spent enormous energy on measuring and improving on-time delivery. Over the years, the company had come to believe that punctuality was the primary customer concern. As competition increased, however, management began making substantial efforts to improve the quality of service, and in doing so, the people involved came up with some rather startling information.

Federal Express polled its customers and asked, "What dissatisfies you? Give it a 10 if it makes you mad enough to leave us; give it a 5 if it makes you mad but you'll still work with us; and give it a 1 if you could care less." Responses were then analyzed and ranked in order of importance. The company was shocked. "On-time delivery" was ranked at the very bottom of the scale, while "damaged packages" was ranked right at the top, with a rating of 10. Had this issue been left up to the teams, the company would have put itself at risk in a highly competitive market by not placing enough emphasis on its number-one customer concern. Measures of quality would have focused primarily on punctual delivery. By finding out what was really on the minds of customers, FedEx management was able to direct team efforts into areas that directly influenced the customer's perception of quality. Measurements of team performance could now be focused in areas that were the best predictors of customer satisfaction.

Teams that function deep within the organization—and that includes most teams—seldom have direct contact with the customer. This is why those at the top must provide guidance. If management wants to be able to make meaningful measurements, it must be able to identify those factors that are most critical to the business.

"Leaders often don't understand that it's their responsibility to provide focus and direction through analyzing what is critical to the business—what some people call *business planning* or *strategic planning*," says Dr. Farrell. "It is up to management to separate the vital few from the compelling many by understanding the needs of the customer, then to use this information to clearly establish a purpose and direction for the teams."

Determining performance parameters such as how many units the team should produce daily or how many phone calls are reasonable for the team to handle in a single work shift must be jointly determined by teams *and* by management. Why? Because in both cases, management has productivity guidelines that must be met, and if each team doesn't do its share, the organization will be unable meet its goals. Acting alone, the teams would not be likely to address the same set of criteria.

Let's see the role that management might play in determining measurements for the sales department of a large service organization.

The senior team has set out to identify the critical business issues as they relate to their customers, their competition, their industry, and their technology. Let us suppose that team members have determined that their key issue is the company's plummeting customer satisfaction.

As they've discovered, the reasons for the decline are several. Their pricing is way out of line. They are not using updated technology, and they can't get anyone to support them in sales. They also have tremendous issues in the order fulfillment process. They've discovered that their competitors' sales forces are much more strategic, trained, and honed in consultative selling, while their own sales force is tactical.

Now the critical strategic measures for the company have been identified. The CEO goes to the teams and says, "We're doing three things this year. We're improving sales force effectiveness. We're taking out waste and rework within these three areas. And we're improving the order fulfillment process. Instead of taking three weeks, we're going to get it down to one week to get an error-free order to our customers. That is it folks . . . that's where the emphasis will be this year!"

If you were a team member within that organization and you were involved in one of those areas, you now would understand what your assignment is. All of a sudden everyone on the teams has focus.

"Given our critical issues," the CEO says, "we want to measure cycle time for product development. It's way off, people. It's twice what it should be. We want to measure customer satisfaction in this area of how customers think our people really understand their business. Over here we are going to measure all the waste and rework that's going on."

Because the guidelines have been laid out, a team knows not only what it has to measure, but what the findings mean. When someone says to the team, "What have you done lately to prove you are worthwhile?" team members can point to this measure and say that they have improved cycle time, or they can point to the measure that shows increased customer satisfaction or the measure that indicates a more effective sales force. When someone says to them, "Show us what you have done to improve the return on investment," they may not be able to provide a definite number because the results of their efforts will not show up until later. But they can certainly tell you how they have improved the cycle time for training, development, or whatever issue has been determined as critical to the business.

Teams may also want to get feedback from their internal customers. In many plants, teams do not have ownership of the whole product or process. Therefore, some of the team's most critical measures may come from those to whom they hand off their work.

HOW DO YOU CHOOSE WHICH MEASURES ARE MOST CRITICAL?

Determining what measures are most critical to the organization always comes back to the same question: Will the data help to move the organization toward its mission or plan? Let's see how this might apply to a self-directed work team that has been asked to remove inefficiencies in its work process. The company is a manufacturer of circuit breakers.

The first step is to identify the top three or four critical requirements and establish measures for each of them.

The most obvious of these measures, since the team manufactures a product, is cycle time—*how long it takes to turn out product. If you were the manager, you'd begin by having the team track and trend cycle time and productivity time to develop a baseline. The team may find that it takes four people six hours to produce a certain piece of the circuit breaker. How does that stack up to other organizations? If you do a benchmark study by researching similar operations, you may discover that another organization is getting similar results with only two people in three hours. Reducing cycle time will therefore be a critical factor in making your product more competitive.*

Another of the "critical few" issues you'd want to consider would be "once-through yields." If you find the team has to run 20 percent of all components through the line three times before the components meet specifications, then your manufacturing costs have tripled for those items. This will have a direct effect on your bottom line.

How about customer satisfaction? *Are customers happy, or has the company been getting complaints? If excessive customer complaints have been received as indicated by warranty obligations or field maintenance staff, monitoring customer satisfaction should be high on your priority list as well. Ultimately, the information you collect may even lead to changes in manufacturing procedures or product design.*

The way you design your measures will be substantially influenced by what you're measuring. For example, if you find the team can typically produce a circuit board in two days, then you had better check that measure every two days. On the other hand, if you're measuring response time to customer complaints, then you want to measure that on a continuous basis, since concerns over customer satisfaction are ongoing.

To make sure that the teams are addressing the issues that are most critical to their overall purpose, they always need to come back to the basic questions: *Why do we exist? Why are we critical? What is our output?*

What do we do? The answers will lead to measurements that keep the teams aligned to the overall mission of the organization.

Evaluating Team Development

Another useful kind of feedback relates to how effectively the group operates as a team.

"Do you know what I first like to measure on a senior executive team?" asks Anne Farrell. "The first thing I want to know is cycle time for getting a decision made. It'll tell me how functional or dysfunctional the team is. I'll ask, 'How many times do you typically remake a decision?' Team members might answer, 'On the last decision we remade it three times before we finally took an action.' That tells me a lot about how efficient they are at organizing as a unit.

"I'll design measures to find out how well they communicate. I'll even measure integrity—the underlining rules for building trust. Integrity simply means, will the team members do what they say, and will they say what they do? If you don't trust each other, you're not going to work as a team. It's difficult to measure integrity directly, but I can pose questions that will give me a feel for the level of integrity that exists on the team. All these measures will be indicators of how healthy the team is and how efficient it is at operating as a decision-making body."

"On a work team, I'll want to know how the members are developing as a team," Farrell continues. "This means looking at issues that are critical to their performance. For example, communication. Let's suppose that a self-directed work team depends on Monday reports to ascertain certain production numbers from the previous week. I'd ask them, 'Do you receive your information to do your job in a timely fashion? Where do you rank on this one?'

"I'll also want to ask them, 'Do you receive timely feedback from your team members and team leaders about your performance?' And, of course, I'd want some measure of team satisfaction."

WHAT COMMON TRAPS SHOULD YOU AVOID?

An Obsession with Measures

Companies that move to teams often become obsessive about measurements. How are the teams doing? Are they progressing fast enough?

What is the teams' impact on the numbers? Management can become compulsive about amassing performance data, especially since those championing the team initiative may be putting their reputation and even their careers on the line.

This can be something of a trap. When you overload teams with too many measures, they can end up believing that their job is to measure. You can encourage team members to the point where they're tracking so much data that their regular work suffers. Team members may, on their own, become obsessive about measures. As they discover the benefits of working in a team environment, members may feel a need to prove that management's decision was a smart one. Left unattended, this desire for more and more performance data can get out of hand.

The way to avoid this is to provide focus and direction by helping the team select just those vital few measures that will provide the greatest impact on team performance. For example, the team may want to update production data from once a week to several times a day. This may be a wise decision if it helps the team more efficiently schedule its work. But all too often, obsessive data collection is a reaction to the multitude of charts and graphs papering the walls that remind the team that their performance is being watched.

> *One information services team spent a large percentage of its time deciding what kind of information it didn't have. Team members were constantly running to other departments to collect data. They started activity logs to be able to track in minute detail everything they did. They even generated their own computer programs to help monitor what they were doing. Over time, management became concerned that team members had become so wrapped up in collecting data on team performance that they were allowing their regular jobs to suffer. This was borne out by performance levels that were on a downward slide.*

In this instance, because the organization did not do the necessary up-front work of establishing focus and direction, the teams were left confused about what to measure. Remember, it remains up to management to identify the vital few measures from the compelling many.

Failure to Create Buy In

No matter who the employee or what organizational level you're addressing, virtually everyone wrestles to one degree or another with a common experience—fear: fear of not performing well, fear of not looking good, fear of losing one's job. All these are related by a common concern: losing control.

It is easy to forget that in collecting measures, people's performance is being held under a magnifying glass. If they are not told why the measures are being made, they are left to imagine the worst. "You have to create the right environment," says Farrell. "Without getting buy in from team members and without giving them a say in how those measures are built, you're increasing their fear level. In some cases this can lead to skewed data if team members feel threatened and end up being less than honest in their responses."

Data Are Collected But No Action Is Taken

Another mistake organizations make is failing to act on what is uncovered through data collection. Lack of corrective action sends the wrong message to the teams. It says that the organization and the teams are not really in partnership. It suggests that the measures have been taken simply to enable management to give thumbs up or down on team performance. When data are shared with the stated purpose of helping the teams function more effectively, however, teams are less likely to arrive at this conclusion.

Common Sense Takes a Back Seat

Common sense would suggest that if a team exists, it had better produce a meaningful output and know the quality of that output. It had better have an idea of its level of productivity. And it had better have a purpose that is critical to the entire organization. Alas, such is not always the case. Anne Farrell recalls a time when she was working as a manager at a large corporation.

> "I had 15 direct reports in my organization of about 100 people," Farrell remembers. "This was the first time I was actively managing this group— it was a product marketing training function—and I wanted to see what they did. So I took my 15 managers away on a retreat. This gave us a block of uninterrupted time when we could really explore our team performance in depth. We used a variety of quality tools.
>
> "I had everybody list on huge flip charts what their output was for their particular department or function. Then I asked them, 'Who is your customer for this output? What are your key customer requirements?

How do you score against those requirements? How many people do you have, and what is the cost per person?'

"We filled the room with all these flip charts. And guess what I found out? I had three teams that had virtually no customers for their work. I'd ask things like, 'Why do you create this report? What is it used for?' And the person would say, 'We've always created that report.' It turned out in some cases that there was simply no reason for a particular team to exist. It was misaligned to the goals of the organization. It may have represented a useful function at one time, but the organization had moved in a different direction, and what the team was now doing was not useful."

Measures Become Counterproductive

People often carry around traditional measures that are so deeply ingrained that they are difficult to shake—one of the most common being that "more is better." In many environments, more *is* better, but sometimes this perspective creates havoc. For example, measurements that encourage higher production can lead to unneeded inventory and tie up capital in a just-in-time environment.

Here's another example that defies the "more is better" rule. Let us suppose you're managing a sales team. Department policy says that bonuses are paid on orders rather than installed product. At the year's end you tell your sales force, "Either you hit this number in the fourth quarter or you don't get your bonus."

Now you have this salesperson with a mortgage to pay and two kids with braces. Will he hit those numbers? Of course he will. But he may end up flooding the channel with false orders or ones that he knows will fall through. Result? Customer satisfaction goes down, and orders already booked are lost. When you close your books on the quarter, you realize that not only don't you have the sales, you've actually chased some customers away.

As previously mentioned, measures may also become counterproductive if they are initiated only when a person, team, or business is in trouble. In such a climate, even the most benign measures will come to be regarded as a threat, and their presence will create anxiety in team members. The solution is to track data on a more consistent basis. Such consistency will help to quiet any lingering *angst* by demonstrating that measures are only a normal part of doing business.

A Few Other "Do's" and "Don'ts"

Several additional suggestions can have a significant impact on how effectively you use measures.

- *Always ask specifics.* Never ask something like, "Are you happy with your pay scale?" Without specifics, there will not be enough information to take appropriate action.

- *Don't ask about things that you are not prepared to act on.* For example, don't ask whether team members like their HMO when you have no intention to give them other options. Lack of action can only lead to ill will.

- *Don't ask about things that you don't control.* Your inability to act on the information you get back may be perceived as a rejection of the team's interests.

WHAT ARE THE CORE MEASURES TO GET YOU STARTED?

Of course, any number of measures can be appropriate to a team or organization. We have found, however, that the following types of information are basic to the successful functioning of any team.

1. Performance description. Where is the team in its stage of development? The assessment of the team's progress using the "forming-storming-norming" performance description can help you understand how the team is developing, as well as assist you in determining whether its output is appropriate to the team's stage of development.

2. Team personality identification tool. What kinds of personalities is the team composed of? Identifying the personalities on the team—how introverted or extroverted they are and their level of agreeableness, conscientiousness, emotional stability, and openness to experience—will help you to understand the styles of individual team members. It will also help you determine the balance of personalities that composes the most functional team and will give you a picture of the whole team's overall personality.

3. Team morale. Being able to evaluate team morale and compare team performance against normative data will help to indicate how team morale is impacting performance.

4. Production index. Where does it make the most business sense to put a team? Developing the production index will help you to understand what parts of the business the teams should focus on.

The tools to assist you in these four measures are listed in the Tools and Techniques section, beginning on page 207.

5

⑥ MATCHING YOUR STRATEGY TO THE ORGANIZATION'S LEVEL OF COMMITMENT

Managers don't need anyone to tell them that employee alienation exists. Terms such as blue collar blues and salaried dropouts are all too familiar. But are they willing to undertake the major innovations necessary for redesigning work organizations to deal effectively with the root cause of the alienation?

Richard Walton

Questions Addressed in This Chapter

- What are the different levels of management commitment to teams?
- In what ways should your team strategy be changed to match management's support of teams?

Executives often underestimate the amount of executive support a team rollout requires because they've already been through a quality initiative and assume that the process is similar. When they do become aware that the two rollouts are very different and that their previous experience may not be of much help, it can be something of a jolt.

A quality initiative usually evolves from a "center-out" approach. Management creates a compelling vision that radiates out to employees. Senior executives set the direction and tone to drive the initiative, and employees are expected to buy in to it. A quality initiative is leaner and more hierarchical than a team initiative and is backed by early strong executive commitment.

However, as Lyman Ketchum notes in his book *All Teams Are Not Created Equal,* a team initiative is a "periphery-in" approach in that teams are less likely to be driven by senior management. These teams are originally promoted by someone such as a director or manager in the organization who then pressures the executives to get on board.

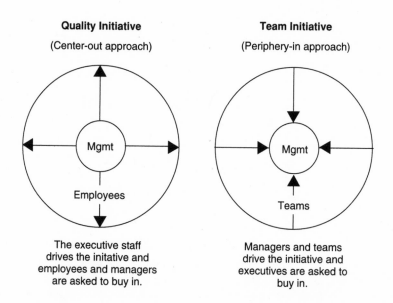

Quality Initiative

(Center-out approach)

Mgmt

Employees

The executive staff
drives the initative and
employees and managers
are asked to buy in.

Team Initiative

(Periphery-in approach)

Mgmt

Teams

Managers and teams
drive the initiative and
executives are asked to
buy in.

Don Emert, plant manager of Air Products and Chemicals, Inc., believes that "by trying to involve everyone in this process of change, the bottom up (periphery-in) approach allows you to increase your success rate and have a better organization. You have a greater chance of success because there's less resentment and a better opportunity to maximize results."

There is also a greater feeling of risk, however. Since the impetus originates with the teams, executives can feel pushed far beyond their comfort zone, and they can soon come to believe that they have lost control. Therefore, management may be reluctant or not forthcoming in supporting teams.

WHAT ARE THE DIFFERENT LEVELS OF MANAGEMENT COMMITMENT TO TEAMS?

When considering a transition to teams, the manager must step back and make a realistic appraisal of how much executive support he or she can expect.

Knowing where the organization is positioned on this scale will help the manager evaluate how difficult it will be to make the change and whether he or she has the tenacity to see it through. It also will help in determining what kind of a strategy should be employed.

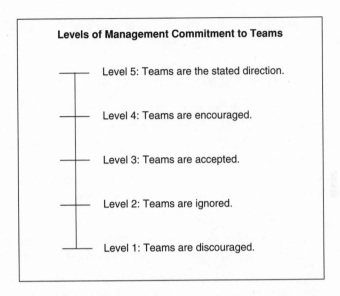

Level 5: Teams Are the Stated Direction

In organizations in which management is totally committed to teams, everyone from the CEO on down makes it clear that teams are the future of the organization—no ifs, ors, or buts. In this environment it's assumed that teams will be incorporated into any undertaking, and any system that doesn't support teams will be subject to change.

In such organizations, empowering others is pursued with a ruthless energy. Teams are an integral part of the vision, and this is reflected in countless ways, right down to the mission statement that's posted throughout every building.

> *At Herman Miller, a manufacturer of office furniture where commitment to teams is unequivocal, former president Max DePree established something of a reputation for his story-telling sessions that focused on team accomplishments. These sessions were a regular part of meetings and forums. DePree found that recounting stories of team successes was one of the best ways to help people retain the learning. At Herman Miller, nobody doubted the direction in which the company was headed.*

In this environment, advancement is closely tied to team success. For example, plant managers will not be promoted to a larger facility if their accomplishments are not team related, even though they may have posted good numbers. A high-participation approach is recognized as the only accepted methodology for accomplishing the organization's objectives.

Level 4: Teams Are Encouraged

Level 4 represents a high but somewhat less enthusiastic commitment to teams. Executives think that teams are a better idea, but—and it's a big *but*—they are not sold 100 percent that teams are the best way, so they don't push them as the primary way of working. Nevertheless, management makes available a variety organizational resources to support any site that wants to move to teams. Here are some of the common ways that this level of management support is manifested:

- Internal people are assigned to provide training for employees or are asked to hire an organizational development consultant to do it.
- People are educated on the benefits of teams, and examples of teams that are doing well are highlighted. For example, NCR stages regular internal conferences highlighting what work teams have done and are doing at various locations.
- Networking events are held to share the accomplishments of teams at particular sites. At these conferences, team members have an opportunity to give personal accounts of their work team experiences.
- The organization's internal magazine features what various team have accomplished.
- Internal resource people are made available to work with any branches or divisions that show an interest in moving to teams. This is a strategy followed by Air Products. In addition, Air Products invests time and resources in work redesign and in bringing in strong internal consultants to help guide the organization in the work redesign program.

Level 3: Teams Are Accepted

With this kind of lukewarm reception, teams are regarded as one possible option. Whatever you do, you can do it with teams or not; there are no pats on the back or penalties either way. Management in this kind of organization usually likes the idea of having people in teams and is willing to release some funds for training. You'll recognize this environment by signs such as these:

- You clearly have to have good numbers if you want the team environment to continue.
- Management is less willing to change policies, practices, and systems to encourage teams.
- If a site informs an executive that it's changing to teams, the executive won't bother to make a personal visit because he or she is not totally convinced that teams are the best solution. On the other hand, the executive won't immediately pull the plug if there are initial problems.
- Because teams are not integral to the stated direction of the organization, managers don't get their hands slapped if the teams don't work out, but the teams' success doesn't particularly help their careers either.
- There's encouragement to stay with the teams, but at the same time, there is pressure to contain them so the team concept doesn't migrate to other locations.

Level 2: Teams Are Ignored

At this level of commitment, teams find themselves tolerated but not much else. Like children whose parents are always involved in other activities and have little time for them, these teams don't earn any attention or interest from management. In this kind of environment, teams can expect the following response:

- No additional resources will be allocated to teams. If the funds aren't already in the budget, forget it.
- If the plant manager leaves, teams can't expect to be sustained when a replacement shows up.
- Management is inclined to close its eyes to what's going on.
- Because the people who initiate the teams are far removed from long-range corporate planning and have established teams only in response to local situations, teams are cut off from the vision and mission of the organization. Thus isolated, they lack clear direction and a knowledge of corporate goals.

Level 1: Teams Are Discouraged

What factors create an antiteam atmosphere? What is going on when the team appears stuck or when no one seems to be growing and learning?

When teams are not supported, it is often because the facility has previously experimented with them and found them too uncontrolled, too difficult to manage, and not really worth the effort. Here are some of the ways in which a lack of team support shows up:

- The organization has had a low level of success with *any* organizational change. Consequently, when the opportunity for teams arises, both management and employees are riddled with cynicism and apprehension and are discouraged from doing anything constructive.

- The emphasis is on doing it "the old tried and true way." The company credo is "Keep your eye on the ball" and "Don't let things get out of hand." Consistency is paramount. There is no tolerance for variation, either within the organization or from site to site, and management seems happy only when everyone is moving in lock step. This mindset is not consistent with teams. Teams provide people ample leeway to work out their own procedures and approaches for the way they run their operation, something that a nonsupportive management will not tolerate.

- There is a tough adversarial relationship with the union.

- Leaders are suspicious of change and are prone to back stabbing.

- There is an overall low level of trust throughout all areas of the organization.

- Previous change efforts have failed.

- People attempting to initiate a change are penalized and seen as "rocking the boat."

Not surprising, setting up teams in such a nonsupportive environment is usually an exercise in futility. Without someone high up to champion the cause, there is little chance that teams of any sort will succeed.

To determine whether your team is stuck, see Diagnosing a Stuck Team—on page 275.

HOW CAN TEAM STRATEGY BE MATCHED TO MANAGEMENT'S SUPPORT OF TEAMS?

How much effort will the executive have to invest to ensure the teams' success? Here are some of the considerations that will have to be addressed, depending on how much support can be counted on from upper management.

1. *Low level of support.* You may have to consider whether teams offer an appropriate strategy because one thing is for sure: You won't be able to do it alone. You can't mandate participation. You must be able to find a champion somewhere in the higher echelons of the organization who believes in teams and who will support this kind of change. If you don't, when you eventually leave this site, you risk having the team fail, creating yet another layer of cynicism within the organization.

2. *Medium level of support.* You can probably go ahead with teams, but you'll have to build in ways to monitor the transition first-hand. This is because it's difficult to rely on your direct reports to give you the information you need, since people may say the right things but not do them, or not do them consistently. To compensate, you'll have to conduct some of the training yourself and personally demonstrate your commitment.

3. *High level of support.* Your job will be to keep the momentum going by acknowledging the changes that people are making. Some of your tasks will be these:

- Promote and encourage the leadership at all levels and continue removing roadblocks that impede the teams' progress.
- Show how quickly you're willing make changes to support the teams by making occasional on-the-spot decisions in front of the group.
- Learn which people are resistant and where additional customer data are needed.
- Continue to protect the teams from layers of the organization that are hostile or resistant.
- Continually ask yourself how you're doing and what other things you might do to make the change more successful.
- Consider showcasing your more successful teams by opening them up to site visits.
- Share the successes of teams with other parts of the organization.

How successfully and skillfully you lead will ultimately be reflected in the performance of the teams. Max DePree observes that good leadership can best be seen among those who follow. Are they reaching their potential? Are they learning and serving? Do they achieve the required results? Do they change with grace? Do they manage conflict efficiently? If all of these are happening, you can assume that you've adopted the proper strategy for your organization's level of support.

DEALING WITH THE UNEXPECTED

6

⑥ WHAT TO DO WHEN PROBLEMS CONTINUE TO SURFACE

We landed within four miles of our destination point on the moon—only because we made mid-course corrections after we launched the space shuttle.

Neil Armstrong

Questions Addressed in This Chapter

- What are the 12 most common problems that teams face?
- How do you know when you're straying off course?
- How can you evaluate your team environment's strengths and weaknesses?
- Why should you expect the unexpected?

In an earlier chapter, we noted that workers new to teams share similar challenges with any group learning to function in an unfamiliar world—for example, a group embarking on a wilderness survival course. Let's continue with this analogy.

Your team has been in the wilderness for several days. The environment is becoming more familiar, and people are starting to understand what is required of them. But there is infighting among the team members. The trek is running behind schedule, and some jobs aren't getting done. Various members keep running to you for answers rather than relying on their own resources. That night you find yourself stumbling around a campsite that's improperly organized. The team seems to be at loose ends, but you're not sure what's happening or what to do.

This is not unlike the way a team manager feels as the weeks roll on and problems continue to surface. The team keeps running into snags, but you just can't put your finger on where the problems lie. Perhaps you're discovering that the teams are spending too much time trying to be a team and are not meeting production goals. Or perhaps people are confused about why they're a team and, as a result, are showing up late to team meetings or not at all. You may be hearing about discord within the team or chronic complaints about the team leader.

Although you thought you were approaching the rollout correctly, nothing you try now seems to have any effect. In general, when teams resist efforts to get them back on course, it's because there is some part of the team environment that is not being well served. This is the point at which you need to stop and reexamine how the environment has been set up.

WHAT ARE THE 12 MOST COMMON PROBLEMS THAT TEAMS FACE?

Although teams have their own distinct personalities and styles, they share many common problems. This is true whether you're looking at a work team, cross-functional team, or any other kind of team. Many of these problems show up only as the days and weeks go by and team members develop experience in working together. If the manager can anticipate the difficulties that are likely to arise, there is a better chance the teams will stay healthy and functioning. The following sections discuss some of the most common problems to watch for and ways to address them.

Problem 1: Painting Over the Same Old Body

The central reason that the team is not functioning properly may have at its core an all-too-common problem. It is a team in name only. Car buffs from the late '60s might recall the fiberglass Volkswagen bodies advertised in the back of auto magazines. These kits allowed a person to transform a homely little beetle into a sexy looking sports car—a throaty-voiced hot rod that could seemingly blow the doors off of a Porsche 911—Except it couldn't. True, it might make more *noise* than the Porsche when the engine was gunned at the stop light, but when the signal turned green, the Porsche would be halfway down the block before you ever got out of first gear.

Simply changing the outward appearance of a group or department to make it look and sound like a team doesn't necessarily mean that it *is* a team, although this is a common strategy in many organizations. To really effect a transformation, you have to give the group a new "engine"—in this case, you need to restructure it to redistribute responsibility, empower team members, and increase participation and satisfaction. Without such an engine, changing the work environment will produce only cosmetic results. It is unlikely that real, significant change will follow.

For an idea of how appearances can deceive, look at this actual case history from the trust department of a large U.S. bank. The bank was searching for a way to increase production and resolve job dissatisfaction among the corps of assistant underwriters.

There were two kinds of associates in the trust department. The licensed associates were responsible for setting the initial investment strategy and direction. The assistants were responsible for executing this strategy by searching out the placements; that is, they had to identify the best areas in which to invest the funds according to the guidelines established by the licensed associates. Once the business was booked, the licensed associates then signed off on the final documents.

Although both groups were fully accredited MBAs, substantial inequities existed in job responsibility. Many assistants felt like little more than lackies. They had no leeway to question the initial investment strategy, even though they might happen on information they believed would substantially benefit the trust department's customer. Consequently, they could not exercise their own initiative or make recommendations. Finally, a substantial disparity in earning power favored the licensed associates, even though the assistants did most of the work.

To resolve these nagging problems, the vice president of the trust department was instructed to switch to a team environment. All associates, as well as the bank president, attended a big kick-off luncheon that formalized the program. The vice president made considerable fuss about the new compensation system that qualified anyone on the team for team bonuses. Base pay scales were also adjusted to make them more equitable. Supervisors were now called team leaders, and all the associates were organized into teams.

Four months later, little had changed. Assistants continued to gripe. The modest increase in production didn't even cover the payback for the new compensation plan. A puzzled senior management called in a teams consultant to investigate the situation and make recommendations.

The consultant quickly identified a familiar pattern, one that occurs all too often in a so-called team environment. Although the trust department had applied a new coat of "paint," it still operated in the same old way. Because the vice president of the trust section did not have a strong background in institutional trusts, he resisted assigning additional responsibilities to the assistants. Instead, he preferred to maintain several layers of management that could check on the performance of team members.

From the point of view of the assistants, nothing had changed. True, there was an opportunity to earn more money, but there was no real motivation to improve the process. That's because team members still did not feel empowered. The assistants still felt like functionaries without the ability to make a significant contribution. They wanted the job satisfaction that comes from an increased sense of responsibility, but what they got were "team leaders" who, beneath the new title, were still supervisors with the same levels of approval and authority.

The consultant concluded that until the vice president was committed to creating a team environment that offered assistants new levels of empowerment, the prevailing discontent and low performance would continue.

This example is also a good illustration of how a work *team* differs from a work *group*. In a work *group*—which is what the bank vice president had actually created—the focus is on each person's individual contribution to a particular segment of the process. People interact to share information or to help one another, but there is no group purpose or goal for which each person accepts mutual accountability.

A work *team*, on the other hand, requires a common set of values as well as common measures and goals. Individual contributions are important but are always considered within the context of the team objective, and the team shares common metrics, purpose, and vision. Everything is in a delicate balance, and all decisions and actions must be weighed in terms of how they impact the equilibrium of the team's work process and social relations. "The leader," said Mary Parker Follett, a prophet of management in the 1920s, "must understand the situation, must see it as a whole, must see the interrelation of all the parts. He must do more than this. He must see the evolving situation, the developing situation. His wisdom, his judgment, is used not on a situation that is stationary, but on one that is changing all the time."

Problem 2: Excessive Meeting Requirements

How often do teams need to meet? How much time should a team spend in meetings? What kinds of issues should the team be dealing with? Because teams call for a high degree of individual involvement, a common trap is to believe that all team members have to be involved in every last aspect of the decision-making process. Sometimes this think-ing can get out of hand. Consider this runaway situation that evolved at a steel plant on the east coast.

Not long after the steel company switched over to work teams, it began experiencing a significant drop in productivity, so much so that manage-ment actually began thinking of closing the facility. A consultant was called to see if the problems could be identified. She started her investi-gation by asking the work teams to track each member's meeting time to see if they could come up with an average figure.

The findings were shocking. The company discovered that on average, team members were spending over 90 percent *of their total work time tied up in meetings.*

"How could this be?" managers asked.

The company's interpretation of empowerment created the problem. Corporate belief was that everyone needed to be involved in all signifi-cant decisions. This was accomplished by requiring work team members to also participate on problem-solving teams, project teams, and every other kind of team that seemed relevant. Consequently, people ended up on multiple committees and task forces.

Problems also arose with the meetings themselves. Team members spent considerable time talking about superfluous issues. In one meeting, for example, a team discussion went on and on regarding inequities in how the plant manager was compensated. In another, the teams ate up nearly the entire meeting talking about the smoking policy, parking lot considerations, hygiene matters, ways to reposition tables that were too far apart and trash cans that were too far away, whether to change the uniforms from polyester to cotton, and how to fix the cracks in the bath-rooms so people couldn't see in.

The consultant first worked with the teams to give them guidelines for determining who needed to participate in a particular meeting, depend-ing on the topic being discussed. Not all members needed to be at all meetings.

The company reduced unnecessary team participation in another sig-nificant way. Instead of asking everyone to sit in on so many different team meetings, managers appointed representatives from each team to attend relevant meetings and report back. For example, the member who attended the safety team meeting would bring back safety information and share it with his or her own team. In this way, any good idea would be passed around to all team members. People also received training in how to keep meetings on track by establishing a clear purpose, a desired objective, and a manageable agenda.

When a high-performance team holds a meeting, it usually limits topics to two general categories. A topic either pertains to day-to-day team decisions, such as scheduling, feedback from customers, or production problems, or it concerns current business issues or issues relating to team development and how effectively members are working together. Keeping subjects focused on relevant issues prevents the team from spending unnecessary hours discussing topics of little importance to the customer or to efficient team functioning. If team members are experiencing frustration or complaining about a lack of time to do the work, one area to examine may be meetings and their dynamics.

Problem 3: Lack of Empowerment

Imagine what it would be like if someone presented you with a high-performance automobile but rationed your gasoline to 5 gallons a month and installed a governor that kept you from going above 45 miles per hour. This is analogous to how some organizations set up their teams. Organizations make a space for the teams to form and operate, but they don't support them with the commitment and resources that allow them to run full force.

Most managers seem to keep a tighter rein than most teams are comfortable with. In the study conducted by Zenger Miller mentioned previously, fully 61 percent of team members reported a lack of authority to make decisions. They saw themselves as ready to take on more responsibility and perceived the organization as standing in the way. The following example is typical of the kinds of scenarios that develop.

> *In a fast-food restaurant chain, the decision was made to go to self-directed teams and give each store manager multiple stores. Although the managers readily handed off scheduling and daily store openings and closings, they were extremely hesitant, even after the first full year, to allow the team any input into the work process itself. As far as they were concerned, processes and store layout had been standardized by corporate and were not to be tampered with. The team saw clear opportunities for improvement and even offered some estimates of improved productivity and reduced waste, but management was unswayed. There was, after all, a "right" way to do things.*
>
> *The team's reaction became a mixture of cynicism and disappointment, and eventually rumor began to spread that management wasn't really serious about teams and that teams were merely some sort of manipulative ploy. Only after a severe loss of momentum did management recant and listen to the teams' "case for action."*

A curious finding in the Zenger Miller team study was how luke-warm most executives are about the presence of teams. According to the survey's respondents, almost three-quarters (71 percent) of executives offer only passive support of team initiatives, and in those organizations with passive executive support, only 49 percent are experiencing satisfactory progress. Conversely, in companies where executives actively support the team initiative, 84 percent reported satisfactory progress or the surpassing of goals.

As far as managers are concerned, most (80 percent) do believe in teams, and in companies with supportive managers, 67 percent reported satisfactory team progress. When managers do not believe in the team effort, satisfactory progress levels drop to a mere 27 percent.

Why are so many managers reluctant to share responsibility or provide the support that the teams need? There are several reasons for this.

1. *Fear that the job won't be done correctly.* "If I'm in charge," thinks the manager, "there's a better chance the job will be handled right. After all, I've been in this situation hundreds of times before. Why should I waste company time having other people try to figure it out when I have the answer? I'd rather have the people out there getting the work done."

That might be true, especially in the early days of the team. After all, who has had more experience in decision making than the manager? There also may be a concern that other people will not perform to expectation and therefore reflect badly on the manager. Furthermore, managers often derive a deeply felt satisfaction from making decisions and giving directives. They feel grounded. Their self-esteem goes up a notch as they see their impact on the organization. No wonder that kind of experience is hard to relinquish.

"What makes it doubly difficult," observes Don Emert of Air Products and Chemicals, Inc., "is that these front-line people have gotten to where they are by doing exactly we wanted them to do—supervising and being the old-style leader. Now we're telling them that this was right for the time, but today we expect something different."

2. *Fear that the teams are moving too quickly.* As team members discover how meaningful and satisfying their work has become, they are likely to become hungry for additional responsibility. But managers often retain accountability for the bottom line, and if they observe the teams spending too much time and energy in meetings, they may believe the teams are trying to do too much. In fact, if the manager thinks the teams are moving too fast, he or she may hold back the resources they require and inadvertently curtail the teams' energy and motivation at a time when it is most needed. When teams falter, it is frequently because they are not given the resources and authority to move ahead.

3. *Fear that the teams will negatively impact other parts of the organization.* Managers in service environments are often leery of assigning particular responsibilities to teams because of the way this may impact not just the team but other parts of the organization as well. A good example is the typical mortgage company. When mortgage companies move to teams, they often assign the teams such responsibilities as taking in applications, verifying employment, doing credit checks and credit reports, reviewing real estate appraisals, reviewing taxation guidelines, and interfacing with the customer. Two of the biggest bottlenecks, processing applications and placing funds, are seldom assigned as team tasks.

Actually, it would make good sense if teams could take over these functions as well. Cycle times would be reduced, and the company could be more responsive to customer needs. That would help give the company a competitive edge. But managers are often reluctant to assign these tasks to teams. Suppose team members approve a mortgage for a poor risk or their lack of experience causes funds to be invested unwisely. Managers see themselves as check points and are unwilling to put themselves or the company at risk. Their concern often discourages them from seeking viable alternatives.

Bottlenecks are likely to occur wherever there is little empowerment. A good way to recognize these bottlenecks is to ask the teams: "What decisions do you wait for?" Those decisions may be good candidates to transfer to the teams. You also want to distribute enough authority to the teams so that many people, rather than a select few, have the power to move the process along.

> *One loan company that addressed this problem creatively is able to give clients a conditional response within 24 hours because they allow their teams to do much of the internal auditing themselves and to make a preliminary recommendation. From the bank's point of view, it hasn't given out a penny yet; however, there's a perception from the client's point of view that the company is a very responsive organization because the client has gotten tentative approval and doesn't have to put off looking for a home while the loan is being processed. Meanwhile the auditors have 24 hours to respond with their final approval.*

When there is concern over assigning too much authority, it is useful to remember that the situation does not have to be perceived in an all-or-nothing context. As the preceding example demonstrates, task descriptions are arbitrary and can be broken up and reassigned. Responsibilities can be more precisely matched to capabilities. By staying flexible and addressing the situation creatively, managers can empower the teams without sacrificing their own peace of mind.

4. *Blind belief in old answers.* Another way managers limit the teams' responsibilities is to force them to follow some ancient "time-tested" formula that explains what the customer wants. But if the teams have no way to determine customer needs directly, it is difficult for them to provide what is necessary, and those nagging problems will persist. On the other hand, if you can give teams a chance to see how changes in their behavior or process impact customer satisfaction, improvements are more likely to occur.

> *When a customer began experiencing problems with its products, production teams from a textile manufacturer began visiting the customer site to catalog precisely what was happening. Problem-solving activities focused on "what element of our product or product packaging is creating the problem and how do we solve it?" Working closely with the customer, team members set up internal real-time measures of the difficulties customers were experiencing and fed them directly back to the team. In turn, members of customer organizations sat in on team meetings to offer critical information and provide a customer perspective.*

A supportive manager open to new ideas can be a team's friend. If team members are citing lack of resources and authority, the root of the problem may lie with a manager who needs support and training as much as the team does.

Some Team Members May Reject Empowerment

At the team level there may be members who don't want the pressure and responsibility of decision making. Most workers have grown up in organizations where hierarchies are the norm. They are accustomed to having someone else define boundaries and shoulder the burden of responsibility. If there is an absence of excitement, there is also a comfort in knowing that the buck doesn't stop with them but with someone higher up, and that at the end of the day, they can leave the job and all its concerns and worries behind.

What of such people? Is it worth trying to fit them into the team environment? If they are competent and want to work with the team, then give them a try. A small percentage of people will not make it, however. Their attitudes will always clash with the prevailing team thinking. It is best to identify these people early, allow them to return to a more traditional corporate environment, and replace them with others who are stimulated by the challenges presented by teams. Given the opportunity, there are almost always enough individuals who are willing to step outside their comfort zone for a chance at a job that offers higher personal rewards.

The Team Personality Tool on page 256 can help you to recognize early on who may have difficulty in a team environment.

How Much Authority Should You Give the Team?

The degree to which a team should be empowered is answered only through experience. Answers to certain useful questions, however, can serve as guidelines:

1. *How prepared is the team for the responsibilities you're giving it?* To assess whether the team is prepared for more responsibility, you need to conduct a thoughtful assessment of its skill, authority, and information level. You can accomplish this by showing team members what their responsibility entails, walking them through the process, observing them perform these responsibilities, and then letting them try things on their own. At this time you may want to add more checks until the team demonstrates consistency in its ability to perform the new responsibilities.

2. *Are you making the team responsible for the right things?* One company assigned revenue responsibilities to the team but failed to make them responsible for profits as well. Consequently, the teams ended up making a number of unwise decisions because they never had to experience the impact of their decisions on the bottom line.

3. *Are you making an active effort to get the support you need?* To quote Don Emert of Air Products and Chemicals, Inc., "You will run into obstacles along the way, and you need to deal with them head on. A lot of times when you think you know the answer, it would be a whole lot easier to go out and resolve these issues yourself, but you can't do that. You need to let the people in the plant and in the field have enough time to come along in the learning process. You have to be patient."

Problem 4: Failure to Link Skills to Responsibilities

In the early stages of the team, people will need new technical skills to get up to speed. They will have to learn how to operate the computer system, run machinery, perform particular operations, and master certain business skills. As the teams mature and their sphere of activities expands, members will need to acquire team communication skills to assist them in decision making, conducting presentations, leading effective meetings, and so on.

Some organizations invest a tremendous amount in up-front training for team members. Unfortunately, members who are saturated with training often walk away more confused than enlightened. Not only do they fail to develop a true understanding of what the new skills are about, they also have no real clue as to where or when to apply these skills. It is never a good idea to overdose people with skills that are not relevant to their current activities. It is more effective to provide skills on a just-in-time basis as teams take on additional responsibilities. If team members seem confused or overwhelmed, one cause may be the training plan. A more innovative, focused approach may be needed, like the plan that follows.

> At the Enfield, Connecticut, division of DEC, the teams themselves determined when additional training was needed by conducting their own training needs gap analysis. Whenever production goals were not being met, the teams looked at the skill level of each team member involved. The training department made available written skill surveys that covered every important operation, and it prepared additional surveys at the request of team members. These surveys were stored in the computer system. When problems arose with a particular operation, every member of the team completed a skills survey using one of the computers located on the shop floor.
>
> The computer then scored the results, collated the information, ranked the team's training needs in priority order, and delivered a needs gap analysis. This allowed the team to identify its training priorities and the additional skills it had to acquire. Not surprising, team members developed tremendous ownership of the training because they continually identified their own needs and pursued the mastery of new skills with a high degree of energy and motivation.

Problem 5: Lack of Management Training

Max DePree, of Herman Miller, observed that "leadership is much more an art, a belief, a condition of the heart, than a set of things to do.

The visible signs of artful leadership are expressed, ultimately, in its practice."

DePree's words are really put to the test when it comes to managing multiple teams. It is usually obvious when team members need skill development, but what is often ignored are the skill needs of executives and managers. Most executives find a team environment very different from the command and control environment they grew up in. They are less accustomed to listening to the needs and requests of team members than they are to barking out orders and directions. Therefore, it is sometimes difficult for team members to gain their attention.

> *The design team at Westinghouse Norden questioned the lack of executive support. Some Westinghouse executives had little understanding of the team culture, and for a full year they resisted every overture to engage in training to get themselves up to speed. Either they didn't have time, didn't think it was necessary, couldn't decide who should attend, or couldn't agree on where to have it.*
>
> *The design team, to its credit, wouldn't give up. It met repeatedly with executives to share information about how the team was moving ahead. It also invited executives to review the team meeting minutes whenever members had identified difficulties they were facing. Finally, several executives were persuaded to attend team meetings and were able to hear firsthand how disappointed members were with the lack of executive support. The situation finally came to a head when the company brought in a new operations manager who saw no value to the teams and started to reverse the progress that had been made. Because the executives had by this time experienced some of the team's successes, they realized they did not want to forgo the benefits of these efforts and at that time consented to further training.*

This is, of course, doing it the hard way. To help the teams move forward, it is more productive to identify training needs at the beginning so that managers and executives can be given the skills they lack and better facilitate the team process.

Alan Cheney of Air Products and Chemicals, Inc., notes that in traditional organizations "managers are rewarded for blowing off change." Thus it is not surprising that in these organizations, the efforts at change are usually unsuccessful. On the other hand, encouraging managers to acquire new skills communicates a different message—that the transition to teams is something to be sustained. Furthermore, giving managers new skills also helps them become more confident in dealing with changing systems and cultures. Additional training may cover such practices as negotiating team boundaries, improving team decision making, and handling disruptive behavior. In other words, when you look at training, don't limit your examination only to the needs of the team members.

Problem 6: Lack of Belief in the Team Process

For a certain percentage of the population, functioning in a team environment is akin to walking over hot coals. These people simply do not believe in the effectiveness of teams, and their every action supports their self-fulfilling prophesy that teams don't work. In fact, a national study by the Work in America Institute shows that between 1 and 2 percent of the population will never make the transition to teams.

John Saunders, director of Operations at Binney and Smith, can speak to this issue in even more dramatic terms. In the two years that Saunders has been working with teams at Binney and Smith, he has had to move out half of his direct management staff members because they were not willing to support the team concept.

How do you change someone's beliefs? Do you challenge the person head-on? Probably not. People's beliefs evolve over time through personal experience, and consequently it is nearly impossible to change them by words alone. What you *can* do is offer skeptics a clear vision and an unequivocal demonstration of how to support the teams and then encourage them to stand back, trust the process, and observe the results. If your actions are well taken, the teams will respond with higher levels of performance, and you will win over the skeptics through the time-tested rule that "seeing is believing."

It's important to remember that managers may genuinely have the best interests of the business at heart but simply believe that the team's performance cannot rise above the capabilities of its weakest member. They have no experience with, nor understanding of, team synergy.

How, then, do you map out an effective strategy for your next team rollout? If you suspect that scepticism exists and that you won't have support to move ahead quickly, you'll want to consider a more conservative and elongated rollout strategy. Here are some ways to approach this.

1. *Carefully pick and choose the areas in which you roll out the teams.* It is best not to select an area for the rollout where the majority of people lack a fundamental belief in teams. You're only increasing the chance for failure. Look for areas of the organization where success is more likely to happen. When the first organizations introduced their team initiatives, they did not have many true believers, so management chipped away at the resistance by including in its pilot teams those executives and team leaders they knew would back the team concept. When these efforts succeeded, others began to feel more confident.

2. *Whenever possible, don't mandate; wait for volunteers.* In the past, the practice has been to mandate participation on teams. This is supported by the findings of the Zenger Miller teams survey, which indicates that 57 percent of all team members report having no choice about their inclusion. The study also indicates that 41 percent of the team members *are* participating of their own free will and that on these teams, *overall success is significantly higher than on teams where participation is mandated.* If someone doesn't want to be on a team, don't force the issue. To do so makes it that much more difficult to get the team up and running. Be willing to temporize until you have more supporters than disbelievers.

3. *Trust in the power of the grapevine.* Once the initial teams are established, the grapevine becomes highly effective in carrying information about team dynamics and processes. Success is contagious. People talk in cafeterias and hallways. They share their team experiences, both good and bad. Of course, there are frustrations. But there's also an infectious excitement. People will talk about their successes, increased job satisfaction, and the heady experience of self-determination,. Those who have not been believers may slowly become receptive. Once such people have made the shift from disbelief to simply holding reservations, they will be more open to participating on a team or having their area included in the next phase of the team rollout.

4. *Select pilot areas in which people can observe and become familiar with the team process.* Encourage skeptics and disbelievers to sit in on team meetings, review results, and experience how problems are handled. Giving them a vicarious team experience will gradually draw them into the fold. But beware. Pilot strategies can also be slow and may show fewer dramatic changes.

5. *Tune in to the organization; sense the pace of change that it can accept.* We often use strong leadership as an excuse for pushing through change at too rapid a pace. It is useful to treat the organization the way you would treat a single individual. You just can't order a person to think a certain way. You have to provide an opportunity to broaden his or her experience. You have to introduce ideas at a pace that the individual can assimilate and accept. You have to be patient until someone's thinking comes around and he or she can be more receptive to what you have to say. As any salesperson can tell you, there is a time to make the sale, and there's a time to wait because the customer is not yet convinced.

> *Steve Terni, president of Carter Mining, recalls two people on his team who were highly skeptical of the team process. One was head of security, the other head of engineering. Terni knew he had to listen carefully to their concerns because they were raising issues and speaking for constituents within the organization who were not familiar to him. By being receptive and not dismissing their concerns out of hand, he began to see how he could avoid pitfalls and more easily introduce all participants to the team culture. He also recognized that if he ignored their concerns and tried to ramrod his ideas through, he was going to experience the precise problems these executives were warning him about—but on a much larger scale.*

Never discount disbelievers out of hand. There is a tendency to want to dismiss their perspective and push them aside, but if you learn to listen to the skeptics and work with them, you can move the team initiative forward at a rate that both the organization and its people can accept.

6. *Continue to communicate the success that teams are having.* As the doubters see the good results pile up, their resistance will begin to melt, so don't hide the successes. Take every opportunity to share what is working. You can do this at meetings and by posting results in public areas where they are most likely to be read.

Problem 7: Lack of Communication Among Teams

In *De-engineering the Corporation*, Meg Wheatley points out that "we have the capacity within ourselves to create order as needed, if conditions are present. Those conditions, quite briefly, are that people need to bump up against one another, to have access to many more relationships than we usually plan for, to work in an information-rich environment, and to truly understand why they are working together and what they are trying to accomplish."

Managers are often skilled in setting up team meetings and other informal communications between members, but they give little thought to ways that would make it easy for *teams* to pass information to one another. As a result, each team is stuck with having to reinvent the same wheels. The remedy is to increase the opportunities for intrateam dialogue.

In *The Fifth Discipline*, Peter Senge differentiates between two types of team communication: skillful discussion and dialogue. The intention of *skillful discussion* is to come to some sort of closure so you can make a focused decision, reach agreement, or identify a priority. The intention of *dialogue* is simply exploration, discovery, and insight. There is no purpose to the dialogue other than to bring people together to get the creative juices flowing.

Dialogue Is the Key Ingredient in a Creative Stew

Because dialogue is something people take for granted—it happens at the water fountain as well as in meeting rooms—organizations often fail to assign it much value or to set aside specific times and places to encourage this kind of interaction. An organization's most innovative thinking, however, is likely to emerge from the creative stew of a stimulating dialogue. Senge strongly believes that an organization needs to have as many dialogues going on as possible, because the more you have, the more opportunity there is for learning and for sharing information at a team member level.

Most managers are quick to recognize the benefits of intrateam dialogue—the stimulating back and forth that happens whenever team members get together to talk over business, yet they seldom think of structuring the team environment to create opportunities for teams to talk to other teams. One notable exception is Canada Life.

When Canada Life set up its information services planning teams (which plan applications for various software programs and hardware), the company formally structured the team meetings so there is always a person from another team sitting in. In fact, the representative from the other team acts as the meeting facilitator.

This allows a tremendous amount of cross-fertilization to take place. Visiting facilitators are able to share with the teams any new ideas their own teams have developed. Facilitators, in turn, take the information learned at the meeting back to their home teams where the process is repeated. In this way, any worthwhile ideas eventually make the rounds to all teams at Canada Life.

Previously, team members were having a hard time understanding the need to share information. But once team members started attending other team meetings, they could recognize that applications extended beyond the limited areas in which they worked.

Many executives are schooled to believe that communication has to move through formal channels. Consequently, they often ignore the benefits of impromptu dialogue. When people start crossing team boundaries through dialogue and discussion, however, they create a fluid, flexible learning environment in which teams become an important source of innovation and productivity. This kind of communication also addresses the alienation that team members may feel when only a few teams are up and running. It is useful to let team members know that they are not battling these issues and concerns all alone but that there are others out there who are actively supporting them.

Problem 8: Unclear Communication of Team Purpose

If you showed up at work each day without a clear purpose or an understanding of how your work affected the customer, wouldn't you find it difficult to be inspired?

Unfortunately, teams are often established without such direction or purpose. Perhaps someone jumped on the team bandwagon because "everybody's doing it." Or perhaps this champion had a misguided belief that mandating a team structure would automatically make people more effective.

Here's the truth. *For teams to sustain a high level of performance, they must be linked to very clear business objectives and, specifically, to the needs of the external customer.* When they are, team members can determine what work needs to be done and decide which roles are necessary to carry out those tasks. They can also evaluate the impact of their work on the customer. This, in turn, allows team members to determine what new skill sets and additional roles the team may need.

This common sense approach is all too rare. A more typical scenario is this: An executive remembers the way things were done in a previous organization. He digs out the old role descriptions from a bottom file drawer and passes them to current team members under the assumption that "what worked there will work here."

He also arrives at another false conclusion. He assumes that because these role descriptions led to success, they had something intrinsically "right" about them. He forgets that these role descriptions were a solution to a particular problem in a particular environment. He forgets that not all customers or situations are alike, that all solutions are not interchangeable.

Lack of purpose puts the team at risk, especially when there is a change of leadership at the top.

At Carter Mining the teams had been running for about 18 months and by and large were showing good results. But good performance notwithstanding, many team members were unclear about their purpose. When the new president came in, he found the teams still in transition. The team environment seemed too loosely managed and too different from what he had previously experienced. The problems he encountered were unfamiliar, which meant he had no clear sense of how to help the teams grow. What he did *know was how to help individuals establish clear accountability and be better individual contributors. Therefore, one of his first acts was to abandon the team philosophy, eliminate the teams, and take the organization back to something with which he was familiar.*

An incoming executive may have little understanding of team culture and may believe that good management means tight controls. Without familiar touchstones, the new leader's anxiety mounts. From that moment on, the team's days are numbered. Therefore, when new leadership takes over, one of the team's best insurance policies is to have previously established a clear purpose and objective.

Teams can be coached in ways to win over an incoming executive. For example, team members can track their own productivity data. Nothing convinces an executive as much as good numbers, and having them on hand will place the team in a stronger position. Teams can also take the initiative by educating the executive. In formal presentations, team members can detail how they function, what kinds of results they've produced, and what they need from management to further their objectives.

In turn, the incoming executive can be encouraged to get out and talk directly to team members. Nothing is more reassuring to an executive than discovering that team members are skilled businesspeople with tremendous commitment and loyalty to the organization. The executive can also talk with customers to get direct feedback on team performance.

Problem 9: Lack of Alignment with Corporate Direction and Policies

If an organization has adopted a pocket strategy or a separate section strategy, teams will initially exist only in a few parts of the organization. This means that systems, policies, and procedures will still be aligned with a traditional, hierarchical organization. There may also be little pressure to generate the commitment, energy, or resources necessary to transform the organization into a team-based system.

For example, many organizations have skill-based pay systems that benefit team members while they are being called upon to learn new jobs. Once the new abilities have been mastered, however, the opportunities for financial betterment can suddenly disappear. This can be deflating when employees realize that their discretionary efforts will have no monetary rewards. The point can be painfully driven home as they see others in the organization continue to receive financial recognition for their hard work.

> *When Allied Signal awarded CEO Lawrence A. Bossidy a six-year, $47 million pay package in June 1994, the* Philadelphia Enquirer *reported that the increase was primarily due to gains made by quality teams at the Claymont, Delaware, plant. Workers at the chemical plant shaved operating costs by 8 percent, but while the CEO reaped substantial financial rewards, workers groused that fancy TVs and camcorders were not adequate acknowledgment for what they had been able to accomplish.*

Once the team initiative is up and running, the organization often pays little attention to what will continue to keep the teams motivated. When team accomplishments are directly linked to specific business objectives, however, the organization is more likely to change its systems and policies to those that will better sustain the teams. That's because it can see how the teams' successes are helping to meet business goals. If teams seem to have reached an impasse and ceased to progress, a close look at the organization's systems and policies may be in order.

Tie the Team Rollout into the Business Plan

One way that management can help ensure the success of teams—and discourage the organization from abandoning them when the going gets tough—is to incorporate the team initiative into the organization's business plan. This is what two-thirds (69 percent) of the companies responding to the Zenger Miller study did, and 67 percent of them reported satisfactory progress.

Embedding the teams in the fabric of the organization means that they are no longer an afterthought or sidebar. It means that everyone, not just the top 10 percent, looks to the business plan to meet objectives. It encourages all channels to stay open so that everyone is able to contribute. This is the true power of teams. By contrast, only 35 percent of respondents in the study reported satisfactory progress when initiatives were not reflected in formal business plans.

A team environment is also more likely to flourish if it is closely tied to the organization's quality initiative. In fact, it is enlightening to see how the success of teams falls away as the team initiative stands more and more alone. Satisfactory progress was reported in

- 64 percent of programs in which team and quality initiatives were integrated.
- 59 percent of programs in which team and quality initiatives were coordinated but separate.
- 30 percent of programs in which team and quality initiatives were completely separate.

In a garden, the seeds you plant are more likely to flourish if the soil is nourished. Teams also must be nourished by the corporate culture and supported by healthy forces present within the corporate environment. When that happens, a synergy develops that can sustain teams during the trying days after the launch.

Problem 10: Managerial Sabotage

Almost any homeowner has at least one story about a problem that failed to show up until it became a *problem*. Termites, dry rot, cracks in the foundation, fraying electrical wires—all these undermine the integrity of the home yet may not announce themselves until a wall suddenly sags or an outlet sparks as you plug in the hair dryer. "Invisible" threats are hardest to defend against because they cannot be seen until the damage is well under way. This applies to team environments as well.

Executives usually find that team members are eager for new opportunities to participate. Unfortunately, the same enthusiasm is often not apparent among middle and front-line managers and supervisors or those in nonsupervisory positions such as technical support, planning, and control. These individuals often feel they have something to lose if the team succeeds, and their resistance may continue over an extended time.

Sometimes resistance arises because too much is happening at once. Jim Lawler of Union Camp recalls a failed attempt to install teams at his previous company, Blue Cross/Blue Shield of Virginia. The company had just undergone a merger and had transferred major parts of its business to Roanoke. "They shuffled people and had to retrain them," Lawler remembers. "Then right after that, they tried to start up a pilot with team concepts, so you had people struggling with their new role and at the same time struggling with self-management."

His team rollout at Union Camp also went through some difficult times but for other reasons. "I don't know if it was resistance as much as it was not understanding what it took to get performance out of the organization," says Lawler. "Getting organized into teams was difficult, and people's expectations were often out of line."

Sabotage Can Be Hard to Spot

Managers who are threatened by the team can find subtle ways to sabotage it. Often this takes the form of passive-aggressive behavior. Either the manager withholds necessary information or does not offer the team a process that's needed to solve a problem or make a decision. This kind of sabotage, which can be directed toward anything from selecting the proper technology to making hiring decisions, is not easy to identify. Here's an example.

> One of the manager's traditional roles involves hiring and orienting new employees. Because many managers are reluctant to hand over this responsibility, more than one manager has been tempted to prove that teams cannot carry out the job as well. This can be done in a very subtle way.
>
> For example, the manager may know specific things about hiring and orientations that aren't in the HR manual. There may be seasonal attrition rates and burn-out periods that can affect the makeup of the team. There may also be nettlesome logistical problems such as how to get the person hooked up to the voice mail or E-mail systems. If none of this has been written up for the team, and if the manager withholds this information, the team will naturally appear more inefficient at performing the same activities.

Another scenario is to allow a situation to deteriorate to the point of near failure (where no actual harm is done and no significant cost is incurred) and then to rush in and save the team with information to which the manager alone is privy. This way the manager is able to make a point without having to suffer the team's total failure, which would reflect poorly on that manager.

Another type of passive sabotage occurs when the manager refuses to assist team members who are undergoing personal difficulties.

> When a team member has a personal problem, the employee may feel reluctant to share it with the team. It's often easier to confide in the

manager. A manager who wants to be supportive can present the employee's plight to team members in a way that gains the team's support. The manager can coach team members in how to redistribute the work, make key support people available, and arrange for facilitators to be more accessible. In a variety of ways, the manager can help the team avoid being penalized while simultaneously drawing away hostility from the troubled team member—all this without taking over for the team. On the other hand, if the manager wants to make a case against team autonomy, he or she can simply withhold active support and watch the problem escalate and then step in and execute a dramatic 11th-hour rescue.

It is precisely when people start to dig in and resist that managers and teams could use a little help. The teams need someone who can champion their cause at higher levels, and the managers need someone who can provide moral support and offer a more positive spin on any problems that are occurring. Meeting the needs of both teams and managers begins with looking for problems beyond the teams themselves. It requires recognizing that managers may need help, too.

What Can Be Done to Discourage Sabotage?

One positive step the executive can take is to move managers around to different teams so that everyone starts off fresh. Another step is to cascade more decision-making authority to the middle managers. This means inviting them to participate in such activities as developing strategic plans, setting goals and measurements, determining new technology for the workforce, and meeting with customers. By broadening their decision-making opportunities, the executive allows middle managers to extend their sphere of influence into other areas. This way the team transition becomes a winning change for them as well.

Jim Lawler of Union Camp offers this suggestion. "Once design is complete, I think you have to implement teams gradually so that people can handle it, and you must get the managers to buy in by explaining why teams are necessary. People have to be able to see for themselves why you want teams to happen and how they will positively impact the business. They have to have personal reasons for being involved."

Problem 11: Lack of Continuing Management Support

Organizations are most likely to support teams in the early days of the launch, but as time passes and skills are mastered, this support has a tendency to fade away. This is unfortunate because the needs of the teams change but don't disappear.

Some executives do go out of their way to remain acutely aware of the teams' continuing needs. When Harvey Golub, now the president of American Express, headed the company's financial services division, his goal was to spend one day a month manning the customer service phones to hear firsthand the issues and frustrations that team members had to deal with. As he better understood these problems, he was able to provide the teams with appropriate support.

Executives may not want to go to such lengths, but at the very least, they should take time to walk the floor and talk to team members. Is the work providing a greater sense of dignity and satisfaction? Is the company giving teams the backing they need? Is there something lacking that could make team members' jobs more rewarding? Executives need to regularly take the pulse of the team to check on its state of health.

For example, executives may discover that teams don't have access to relevant information. Without primary access, team members may not understand how to interpret the data they do have and, therefore, may be unable to request information in the form they need.

How can you make certain that support for the teams will not slip quietly away? One approach is to create a steering committee comprising executives actively involved in the team transition. This committee is charged with collecting firsthand information on how the teams are faring. Based on its findings, the committee updates management on what the teams need and simultaneously serves as ombudsman for team members, providing strong organizational support and protection and acting as referee on any controversial issues.

Executive Myopia

Sometimes it is what the executive cannot clearly see or understand that is the real factor in holding back teams from functioning effectively. Here are some ways executive shortsightedness can throw a damper on team performance.

• *Executives have a proprietary interest in maintaining a particular process.* This situation often occurs in a technical environment where an executive has moved up the ladder because of recognized know-how in a specialty. This recognition may discourage the executive from looking at practical ideas proposed by less technically accomplished team members. Such executives may feel compelled to maintain a particular process as well as the exact sequence in which the process is carried out.

- *The executive adopts a "father-knows-best" attitude.* This kind of attitude is exemplified by the information services (IS) manager who prevents user groups from selecting the hardware and software they want because they don't have the "proper" IS training even though the teams are closer to the application and have a better appreciation of how such resources will be applied.

- *Policies are kept overly rigid.* Redefining and improving the work process can be inhibited by corporate policy. Here's an example.

> *Team members in the final assembly area of a helicopter manufacturer wanted to change the order in which certain components were installed. According to written procedures, doors had to be installed before windows. The teams discovered that it was much faster to install the windows first, however, because they could shim the doors to make everything fit properly. The same adjustments could not be made by shimming the windows if they were installed last. Unfortunately, the teams could not get executive approval to have the revised procedures written into policy.*

- *Teams are given authority without having sufficient information and understanding to make sound business decisions.* Sometimes team members are allowed to make decisions for which they are ill prepared.

> *At GenCorp, a manufacturer of specialty car parts for the auto industry, a team in the quality department saw an opportunity to speed up quality testing for a product by reducing bake time. To the team, the product still appeared to be able to meet the same test characteristics. Weaknesses in the integrity of the product undetected by the shorter bake time did not show up, however, until after several years of use. This situation could have been averted if the executive had had a more realistic appreciation of the team's abilities and knowledge.*

- *The work has not been redefined to fit the team structure.* All too often, teams are introduced with the understanding that the work processes will remain the same even though it is the process itself that is causing problems.

> *At one company, customers complained that they had to keep giving the same information to one company employee after another. The problem lay in how the collection function was structured. As a debt became more and more delinquent, it moved progressively from a department handling Level 1 debts (30 days overdue) up the line to the department handling Level 5 debts (six months overdue). Consequently, a customer whose payment continued to be late had to tell the same story over and over*

again as his or her file was passed along to the next level. This was particularly annoying to people who had a legitimate reason for the late debt. A more efficient and customer-friendly approach would have been to have personnel divide up the files alphabetically so the same people could follow a late payment through all the various states of aging.

• *The executive introduces teams where they are not appropriate.* Dr. Sue Freedman, principal of Knowledge Work Associates, says that you should look at three things when designing teams: (1) key work processes, (2) key deliberations, and (3) task interdependencies. You don't want to organize a work team when members do not depend on each other to get the job done, although people may team to improve processes or develop skills. Without shared objectives and the opportunity to assume responsibility for making the process work, there is little benefit for workers to be working on a team.

HOW DO YOU KNOW WHEN YOU'RE STRAYING OFF COURSE?

How do you know when things aren't working and changes need to be made? By what criteria do you judge the development of a team? What do you look for? The mosaic you create as you review your answers to the following questions will help create a clearer picture of the strengths and weaknesses of your team environment.

1. How are decisions being made?
2. How often and how quickly is information shared with the teams?
3. What is the expected longevity?
4. How much daily supervision is required?
5. What is the scope of tasks assigned?
6. How much investment is being made in teams?
7. How are team leaders using their roles?
8. What is the level of team commitment?
9. What is the level of trust within the team?
10. How clear is the team's purpose?
11. What are the communication patterns?
12. What are the levels of involvement and responsibility assigned to the team? Is responsibility shared equally or unequally? When is it shared?

13. Do teams have a good process orientation? Are they just beginning to understand the process, or are they a mature team actively identifying ways to continually improve it?

14. What are the major challenges the team is facing?

15. What kind of performance can you expect from the team?

16. What kind of training is needed? What skills are required?

17. What is the breadth of positions and responsibilities?

18. Is the team accountable for defining the problem? Making recommendations? Implementing its recommendations within the current scope of work?

19. Who makes performance evaluations and compensations? And who determines what they will be?

20. When problems arise (as they are sure to), are people beginning to say, "This is a bad *experience*," instead of making a blanket condemnation of teams?

21. Are the teams coming to management with solutions as opposed to problems?

22. Are the team members merely stakeholders or are they team players?

23. Are problems being solved more quickly?

24. Are the teams measuring their progress? Are these teams using hard data versus relying on gut feelings?

25. Has there been a measurable shift in consciousness? Are people beginning to recognize that their skills may have to change and that their work activity might have to be combined with other resources within the system to get the job done?

Managing successful teams take vigilance. As Dick Kamischke of Herman Miller notes, "We have to learn how to maintain the team environment and not be slow in making decisions. We need to learn how to organize our data and know what to do with it and how to keep the team informed. We need to build into the teams the ability to self-reflect, to address such questions as 'what just happened and what did we learn from it?'"

WHY SHOULD YOU EXPECT THE UNEXPECTED?

In a famous science fiction story by Ray Bradbury called "A Sound of Thunder," an adventurer, Eckels, slips back through time to the days of the dinosaurs. Before he begins his journey, Eckels is cautioned against disturbing any aspect of the prehistoric environment but while fleeing through a primeval forest, he inadvertently crushes a butterfly. On returning from his time trip, he discovers that the impact of this event has been magnified endless times. Through the cumulative effect of millions of small interlocking events, the killing of a prehistoric butterfly has transformed the outcome of an important election, and the wrong candidate has gotten into office.

As the story reminds us, seemingly insignificant events can have a big impact. Change the accounting procedures and you impact the financial system. Modify just-in-time manufacturing, and you'll see the implications in planning and control. Changes to a team environment are often felt where you least expect them because you're managing both the technology *and* the social system, and many processes are transforming at once. For this reason, even though you may have executed careful planning and gained the executive commitment you need, the transition will never seem to unfold as you expect.

Anticipating the unexpected is part of the team experience. The willingness to look for roadblocks and causes on many levels is critical. When team progress turns into team confusion, the transition plan itself may have to be revised to solve the problem.

7

⑥ STABILIZING THE PLATFORM

Until executives understand the two fundamental choices of organizational design (bureaucratic or democratic) and their profoundly differing effects, they will continue to select quick fixes that retain the bureaucratic design.

Fred Emery, 1995

Questions Addressed in This Chapter

- What are the characteristics of a team culture?
- How important is CEO support?
- How does a team culture sustain the teams during difficult times?

Your wilderness survival team has been out on the course for several days now, and, by gosh, people seem to be getting the hang of it. They're showing more independence and initiative, and it looks like they're adapting to the rugged surroundings. Now that they're functioning like a more cohesive group, would you be willing to lead them on a two-month trek through the Peruvian jungle?

Probably not. At least not yet.

To build an enduring team culture that will give team members support if more challenging problems arise—as they are sure to do the longer the team stays together—fundamental changes have to take place in how the team thinks and perceives. This does not happen overnight, nor is it likely to happen unless you create the psychological and social foundation that encourages its development.

People often think they're a team-based organization simply because they've introduced teams into a few areas of their operation. They may even point to team meetings and other outward trappings associated with work teams. But is it an *empowered* culture, or is it simply a traditional culture with teams? A true team culture is defined by some very specific characteristics that give it its unique power and creativity.

WHAT ARE THE CHARACTERISTICS OF A TEAM CULTURE?

A Compelling Vision

Because a team culture is more fluid and flexible, everything seems to happen in quick time. The speed at which things can change makes it difficult to feel on top of all the decisions and team issues. Often these cultures have few rules, guidelines, and policies.

How, then, *do* team members manage to keep on target?

The answer is to have a compelling vision that can guide individuals in both familiar and unfamiliar situations, a vision that will motivate them by engaging their hearts and minds, a vision that serves as a criterion for decisions. You can see how such a vision operates in a small start-up operation where people share a strong set of values. When people come together to build market share, little discussion is needed about who will do what. Everyone understands his or her job. People simply contribute whatever skills they have. This same principle can also apply to a larger organization.

> At a rehabilitation center the CEO kept asking department heads over and over again, "What is your vision for responding to customers?" He asked this question repeatedly for 18 months. Some department heads grew frustrated and angry with the incessant questioning. "Why does he keep asking us this?" they complained. "Why doesn't he actually take an action and do something?"
>
> Finally, at the Christmas party, he asked a different question: "How do you feel about your vision, now that you've been thinking about it for 18 months?" People were shocked. They realized that simply defining their vision had already had an influence on the way they spent their time, on how they worked with clients, and on how they made decisions. People began talking excitedly about how motivated they felt and how many changes they had made. When they thought about it, they recognized that in being asked to define their vision, they had automatically, without conscious effort, created a central focus for their activities.
>
> The executive knew from experience that only after people had a vision could he motivate them to move forward. He also knew from

experience that had he tried to act prematurely, his actions would have been met with resistance and his efforts would have been largely in vain.

Strong teams are always built on a compelling vision. Like the north star, this vision serves as an aid to navigation. Whenever teams get lost and are not sure where to turn next, a compelling vision will help them make choices that support the organization's business objectives.

A Belief in the Unique Power of Teams

A team initiative is more likely to succeed if executives and managers can foster not just a vision but also a deep-seated belief in the power and synergy of teams. This belief is especially important to sustain momentum during the hectic weeks and months after the launch, when everything seems to be in a perennial state of chaos.

Brenda Overton, plant manager of an air separation plant for Air Products and Chemicals, Inc., believes that everyone in her organization has something to give and that teams allow people to give their best. She says she's never doubted this, regardless of the time and expense it has taken for the teams to develop. She is totally convinced that if you make it possible for people to give their best, the company can achieve the results it needs.

Overton describes a team culture as one in which "everybody feels they can solve anything they have to. They can say whatever they want within reason without people becoming upset or irate. The question is always, 'How can I help you?' There is no longer any finger pointing, because we all share the same goal. If we do well as a unit, it's because we need every single person, so if someone is having a problem, the team is quick to support them."

Ed Luttenberg, manager of Manufacturing Services at Air Products and Chemicals, Inc., observes that it can take a while for people to believe in the team process. "We grow up with the belief that somebody will always be there to take care of us," he says. "But once people discover that nobody will rush in to take care of them, they begin rising to the occasion. They start looking for ways to take on responsibility for planning work processes and transforming the workplace." Luttenberg's personal philosophy is to empower teams by maintaining a hands-off policy. If there's something that isn't working for them, he says, then let *them* change it.

Both Overton and Luttenberg have seen what empowered teams can do and are true believers, but until more managers have had similar firsthand experience, it is important to have someone at the top who can be the standard bearer—someone who believes in the power of teams, is committed to the team initiative, and is determined to make it work.

Open Communications

In traditional organizations, information goes from executive to middle manager to supervisor and ultimately to the individual. In a team environment, the information path is messier. Information flows up, down, and sideways; it can come at you from any and all directions. You're as likely to hear significant news in the parking lot as you are during a team meeting or at your workstation. The grapevine is valued as much as the corporate briefing—often more so.

One consultant calls this "bungee information management" because the information seems to bound from one place to the next. People are open and responsive, and there's no perception that "this is my information and that's yours." You bump into someone in a hallway, share something you know, hear new information, move on, pass that along, and so on. This is different from the hierarchical organization where information is segmented by corporate level or by need to know.

Consultant Sue Easton offers her own version of the bungee metaphor: "You and I are attached with a bungee cord around our wrists," she says. "Either one of us can pull and tug and send a message, but neither one of us is structurally connected with the other in rigid ways, so we can move freely."

Of course, information is also shared in a traditional environment. It's just that in a team culture, people are *looking* to pass along what they know, so they remain tuned to what's going on. Information is seen as a valuable commodity. There is a responsibility to pick up whatever one can find out and to share what is known with others—not simply office gossip but also information about the organization, its customers and markets, and anything else that might impact its welfare. Thus, an unofficial sign that the team is coalescing is seen in the way team members communicate.

Dick Kamischke at Herman Miller observes that when you walk through the cafeteria, you're less likely to overhear talk about basketball than to hear people sharing the latest technology or customer information. People use the break time to stay tuned in. He considers this one of the most dramatic differences that have taken place at his company. Seeing information as an important commodity is one of the marks of a mature team environment. It is not a structural change but a fundamental change that implies that a shift in ownership of the workplace has taken hold.

Human Resources Manager Jill Heiden recalls that when teams were introduced at ABB Power T&D Company, "We began holding open employee meetings where everything was explained. People became very involved, and we'd get lots of questions. We also had an I-Team (integrated team), which consisted of people from different areas of the plant—nonexempt, exempt, management. They would go to all areas of the plant to talk and get ideas."

There are several other distinctions that characterize the more open communications of a team environment:

It's Okay to Challenge

Dr. Sue Freedman, principal at Knowledge Work Associates, observes that often in traditional organizations, the only acceptable questions are those that clarify, whereas quite the opposite is true in a team environment. Not only are people invited to ask clarifying questions but also they are encouraged to ask *challenging* questions that put pressure on a decision or an idea. You're actually less valued as a team member if you don't ask why because failure to question suggests you're just going along with everyone else. You're seen as not making an effort to think independently and be responsible.

Ideas Are Readily Shared

In traditional organizations, if you come up with a good idea, you earn points and recognition—just as long as everyone knows it was *your* idea. Obviously, if new ideas are regarded as currency, there is little motivation to give them away. By contrast, in a communication-rich team environment, people give away ideas all the time. That's because ideas are plentiful. What earns recognition is not the idea per se but figuring out what to do with it, working it through, and making it productive. The Not Invented Here syndrome so common to organizations seems to dissolve as teams build and network their ideas.

In a team culture people are also more likely to volunteer ideas that relate to matters outside their immediate work area. Jill Heiden recalls a person out in the manufacturing area who came up with a money-saving suggestion for one of the company's instruction manuals.

"The piece was printed in two colors. This person questioned whether that second color was really necessary. It really wasn't, so we reduced the piece to one color. His suggestion is continuing to save us big dollars because we print thousands of those brochures each year."

Everyone Is Customer-Focused

In traditional organizations the job of listening to the customer generally falls to a few people in marketing, but in a team environment, customer awareness becomes everyone's job. One way that Baxter Health Care brings customers and teams together is by selecting team members to conduct plant tours. This gives team members a chance to chat openly with customers about product performance issues. High-performance teams may even talk candidly with customers about problems they're having. Customers not only appreciate the opportunity to share in this knowledge but also often walk away in awe of the overall level of awareness that team members have about their company and market.

A High Level of Trust

In a transition to teams, no issue has been more thoroughly researched and discussed—nor has earned less executive attention—than trust. Why does this ingredient, which is so important in the alchemy of teams, so frequently slip through the cracks?

Part of the answer is that trust is one thing executives have little direct control over. They can set up new systems. They can rearrange the physical layout. They can design schedules and programs and incentives. But trust? There's no way to create it directly. They can plant the seeds. They can water and feed them. But there is no guarantee that anything will grow.

Team members need time to trust in the organization. Building confidence in the system develops slowly, like fine wine. You can only create the circumstances in which trust is likely to flourish; then you must stand back and wait. Unfortunately, because trust is not something that executives are able to bring about quickly, they find it easy to overlook its importance.

Executives are usually under short-term pressure to get things done and achieve results. Since building trust takes time, the process is often seen at cross-purposes with the situation at hand. Also, many executives are more comfortable in an authoritarian role. They would prefer to issue a directive, have people act on it, and see the results—very clean, very efficient. Consequently, they grow impatient about investing the time and consistent action needed to develop trust. They, themselves, do not trust the process.

Building a Reason to Trust

We still live in a culture of Lone Rangers and individual heroes. Books and magazines and the broadcast media still peddle the belief that success is measured by one's latest promotion. People may buy into the idea that teams are good for the organization, but many find it hard to believe that teams are actually good for *them.*

Look at it from the worker's point of view. The organization initiates teams, and over time, positive results start showing up. There is greater efficiency, higher customer satisfaction, and, most particularly, reduced costs. Managers are happy, executives are pleased, and senior management looks good to the stockholders because stock prices have climbed. But what benefits accrue to the team members?

Are salaries higher? Have individual benefits increased? Not likely. If teams succeed in lowering costs, few managers will immediately raise them again by increasing overhead.

Can employees move more quickly up the corporate ladder? No, they cannot, because there are fewer rungs to climb.

At this point, cynicism is likely to arise. Employees entered into the team environment trusting there would be something in it for them. Although higher job satisfaction is certainly a benefit, in a status-oriented world it can be quickly invalidated by a feeling that one is "stuck" or pushed to the side.

Executives can't mete out such traditional rewards as higher rank and privileges. These options are no longer available. To gain the trust of team members, they need to take a more personal approach. They need to prove that *they* are trustworthy. They need to model the behavior themselves if they want others to follow.

Gaining the Trust of Team Members

There are several effective ways to build commitment and bring people on board. One clear way is to decrease the gulf that normally exists between executive and employee. This can be done in part by renouncing the obvious status symbols that set the executives apart from those lower in the organization.

Probably the easiest way to level the playing field, statuswise, is to do away with such perks as reserved parking spaces, time clocks, and executive travel upgrades. Removing dress codes and moving executives out of mahogany row are also effective ways to obliterate distinctions between boss and employee.

> *A manufacturing facility in Bloomington, Illinois, showed unusual imagination in how it resolved the question of executive offices. Management simply turned the offices along mahogany row into team meeting rooms. As for the executives, they ended up in open cubicles or sharing offices with others. Some executives were undoubtedly not comfortable with the change, but the transformation didn't go unnoticed by the teams. It became clear that the executives were working hard to earn the trust of employees and to demonstrate that their own commitment to the organization was more important than status.*

A similar approach was followed at the greenfield site of another company.

> *The plant comprised a large open area with executive offices around the perimeter. After the facility converted to teams, people found they had no place to assemble if they needed to discuss personal or private issues. Once again, the executive offices were sacrificed. The executives were moved out and the offices made available to anyone who needed privacy. Today, any person or group that needs to talk confidentially can retreat to one of these offices to have a closed-door conversation. This same plant also requires executives to wear the same work uniforms as people on the floor.*

A number of other strategies will help you communicate to team members that you are worthy of trust, that you are concerned for their well-being, and that you are serious about giving them more responsibility. Here are a few of the more obvious strategies:

1. *Provide people with the information they need.* Holding back information may give you a greater sense of control, but people will be aware that they do not have your total trust and confidence. Sharing information creates the opposite effect.

2. *Share the reasons for a decision.* Don't just tell team members what's been decided. Bring them into the circle. Give people the background so they fully understand *why* a particular decision was made. If possible, make your communication personal, preferably one on one. Respecting people's intelligence and judgment goes a long way toward gaining their trust. If you keep saying "that's what's been decided," people will feel that you are acting in an authoritarian role and that their buy in counts for little.

3. *Allow team members to work on meaty, results-oriented issues.* Do you find yourself thinking things like, "The customer is mad. I better deal with it myself"? If you discourage team members from handling such situations, you are inhibiting them from developing their own personal resources. In this case, team members will learn by talking directly to the customer, doing their own analysis, and, if necessary, initiating their own process and schedule changes to solve the problem.

4. *Don't make important resources off bounds.* Team members won't understand why you're not giving them access to materials that help them do their job.

5. *Don't insist on knowing all the team secrets.* Allow the team to keep some knowledge proprietary, especially information relating to personnel issues. If you insist on having constant updates on *all* interpersonal conflicts, even though the team tells you that "we're working it through," you will reflect a lack of confidence in the team's ability to deal with important issues.

6. *Don't allow rules and policies to outweigh suggestions.* Managers can be insatiable in their need to set up procedures. A common example is the manager who publishes a list of *dos* and *don'ts* relating to team participation, such as how many teams an individual is allowed to participate on and when he or she can participate. A more responsible approach is to trust that team members are adults who are capable of meeting expectations, and that if they find themselves being asked to participate on too many teams, they'll know when to say no. A team environment with a minimum of rules, procedures, and review forms sends a strong message to team members that they are trusted and respected.

7. *Don't constantly rush in to "save" the teams.* Supporting a team is like raising a child. You need to expect mistakes. Often, in a misguided effort to build the team's self-confidence, the manager shields it from things that haven't worked out, but this plays to people's weakness. You need to provide team members with an opportunity to experience the consequences of their actions, which means restraining yourself every time you feel like jumping in and "saving" them. People learn through success *and* failure.

This need to save the teams can also stem from the manager's own insecurities. In relinquishing direct control over the team, the manager may discover that he or she is not quite as needed as was previously the case. This can be a sobering and frightening revelation. In extreme cases, managers may even find ways to sabotage the team effort, just to prove that team members cannot function without their assistance. Remaining on the sidelines as you coach may push you far outside your comfort zone, but if you don't allow the team to work through its own issues, team members won't be able to experience any significant degree of personal growth.

8. *Empower the teams to make decisions.* Research indicates that this is the most important signal management can send to indicate that the teams have the confidence and the support of management. Peer reviews may be an option for team members to make decisions on other team members' performance.

The Peer Review Tool may be found on page 280.

Freely Shared Business Information

Getting teams on solid ground calls for making sure that information is available to precisely those people who can most benefit from it. It also calls for sharing the significance or implications of the data and interpreting it for those who are learning to do so for themselves. The following are examples:

- An insurance company actuary may have to spend time discussing the logarithm of risk management with the claims processing team.

- An engineer might have to explain to the process improvement team why a facet of the process can't be changed.

- A controller may need to spell out to the team why a specific detail is essential in tracking expenditures.

- A medical resident may be needed to explain to a process improvement team of nurses and technicians why certain protocols and procedures must be followed in a specific sequence.

In all these examples, it is easy for the expert to forget how long it took him or her to master the material. Patience can wear thin, yet patience usually pays big dividends when team members begin to make more informed and intelligent decisions. When the teams are educated, they end up as partners in the business, and their decisions are more likely to reflect the organization's business goals.

Many Opportunities for Participation

Teams feel more empowered when they can have a say in how the organization conducts its business. Consultant and author Marvin Weisbord has developed a way for the organization not only to tap the creativity of the entire organization but also to give people a greater sense of participation.

Wisebord's concept of "search conferences" is to bring together large groups for the express purpose of exploring ideas. The executive may cringe at the logistics of bringing tens or even hundreds of people together. However, getting people involved this way allows the organization not only to tap into the collective wisdom of employees but also to seed the organization with enthusiastic individuals who will champion the results that management is trying to achieve.

When one of the Baby Bells found itself losing an inordinate number of customers, management felt compelled to broaden its thinking about how to address the problem. To do this, the company took a novel approach. It brought together 800 employees at an off-site location for a day-long problem-solving seminar.

Managers had previously come up with suggestions for how they might address their situation. These were written on large sheets and posted around the walls of the meeting room. The room itself was organized into 80 tables with 10 people at each. Those at each table were asked to discuss the customers they had lost or had not succeeded in signing up and to use any of the posted solutions as a jumping off place to brainstorm ways in which the outcome could have been reversed.

Prearranged seating ensured that people wouldn't feel inhibited in what they said. Those who normally worked together or who were related by direct lines of authority sat at different tables. Instructions directed people to introduce themselves by name and area only without giving titles or job functions.

Before the discussions began, five individuals provided the group with added material: (1) a Wall Street analyst presented a picture of the company from the point of view of the financial community, (2) a former customer spoke about why he chose to go with another carrier, (3) a current customer shared why she had chosen to remain with the carrier, (4) a potential customer explained why he chose not to sign on with the carrier, and (5) a telephone executive talked about changes taking place within the industry.

The group then spent the rest of the day brainstorming solutions. These were written on flip charts located at each table and later posted on the wall.

Several days later a second group of 500 employees came in to pick up where the first group left off. Using the ideas developed by the first group, they were asked to provide input that would help the company develop a new set of values and create clearly defined mission and vision statements. This group worked on its part of the process for two full days. At the end of the workshop, company executives used the collected information to develop official mission and vision statements and a common set of values.

The logistics required in carrying out this approach were clearly an enormous challenge for the company, and the sheer volume of information that still has to be processed and evaluated remains daunting. But apart from what is ultimately learned, one thing has already been accomplished. The 1,300 employees involved in the process have returned to their jobs with a different awareness and attitude about the company, its problems, and its potential. They take pride in knowing that they helped set a new course for the organization, and their renewed attitude and involvement have been shared with all of the company's 9,000 employees. No finite number of memos and articles could have motivated people to the same degree nor created such a strong sense of 9,000 people working together for a common goal.

Innovative ideas like this become cornerstones of fast-cycle redesign and real-time strategic change. Both undertakings call for a reduction in resistance and miscommunication and for an increase in buy-in, and both are based on the premise that all minds have to participate in the organizational change effort.

HOW IMPORTANT IS CEO SUPPORT?

A final element needed in a developing team culture is a chief executive officer who gives whole-hearted support to the team environment. The attitude of the CEO does make a difference to team members, and 29 percent of respondents in the Zenger Miller study had very specific requests of the CEO:

• *Give us direction.* More than one in four respondents saw a need for their CEO to develop and communicate a fundamental focus for the organization as a whole and to drive the plan down through the ranks. They also looked to the CEO to help resolve "turf wars" and assist them in overcoming resistance from senior and middle management.

• *Relinquish control and empower people.* Almost one in five respondents brought up such issues as "trust your employees. They're not the enemy." Others requested, "Spend more time with workers on the shop floor and less time in your office." Still others said, "Come down out of your tower and work once in a while with your people."

• *Walk the talk.* Team members are quick to note when executives' actions are not consistent with their words; in fact, 17 percent of respondents noticed a credibility gap between top leaders and the workforce. Over and over, respondents asked their CEOs to prove their commitment with action. One respondent asked the CEO to "look in the mirror." Another advised that "commitment is shown by doing, not by saying." "Walk the talk" and "stay the course" were the most common comments. "Ninety-five percent of American managers today say the right thing. Five percent actually do it. That's got to change," writes John Huey in a 1994 *Fortune* magazine article, "The New Post-Heroic Leadership."

• *Invest in quality people — train.* Seven percent of respondents specifically requested that CEOs invest in employee training. Operating in new ways requires additional skills. Interestingly, many of the respondents in this category specified executives and middle management as the groups most in need of training.

• *Focus on the customer.* Six percent of respondents felt compelled to admonish their bosses to "talk to the customers" and "make decisions with the customer in mind, not only the shareholders."

The CEO may think that he or she is comfortably sequestered in an ivory tower away from prying eyes, but the CEO can be as conspicuous by not being visible as by putting in an appearance.

HOW DOES TEAM CULTURE SUSTAIN TEAMS DURING DIFFICULT TIMES?

As you can see, creating a stable platform capable of sustaining teams over the long haul, and especially during the difficult times, requires planning and introspection. A team environment is more than just a reassembled organizational chart. Transforming a group of individuals—whether front-line workers or a group of executives—into a true team calls for the emergence of a team culture—one that supports a compelling vision, a belief in teams, open communication, a high level of trust, and the backing of senior management. Teams must also have access to the kind of information that allows them to make informed decisions, and there must be many opportunities for participation. None of this happens quickly, which is why virtually all teams are fated to go through a "storming" phase before they can coalesce into efficiently running units.

8

⑥ MANAGING STRESS

If you have a job without any stress, you don't really have a job.

Malcolm Forbes

Questions Addressed in This Chapter

- What stresses are associated with a new environment?
- What stresses are introduced with added responsibility?
- How does top management support impact stress level?
- How can the manager keep employee stress within bounds?

There is a saying that there are only two certainties in life: death and taxes. To these we can add the stresses that occur whenever people are placed in an unfamiliar environment. Whether it's suburbanites undergoing wilderness training or a group of workers, managers, or executives moving to teams, each will have to learn to function and survive in unfamiliar territory.

People tend to regard all stress as negative. This is a common misconception. A certain amount of stress will act as a motivator to get people moving. Stress can also add energy to what you're doing, as any professional actor can tell you. Without that edge, the actor is likely to give a lackluster performance.

When stress builds beyond a certain point, however, it can inhibit and degrade performance. Therefore, it is a good idea to develop an ability to recognize those factors that increase stress among team members and to develop in advance a strategy for how you plan to manage stress after teams are introduced.

There are several kinds of stresses that team members are likely to experience. The first relates to the workplace itself, and the second is associated with the assumption of added responsibility.

STRESS IS ASSOCIATED WITH A NEW ENVIRONMENT

The team culture serves up unique pressures, presenting opportunities for misunderstanding and discord that are not as likely to show up as in a traditional work environment. Some of the special opportunities for stress include the following:

- Employees must rely on other team members in situations where they would normally act alone.
- Lines of authority are blurry because roles are redefined as the team moves along.
- People work toward multiple goals.
- It's harder to measure success because it takes place gradually and in small steps.
- Many people, rather than just a few, have to buy in and support the team solutions for the project to be implemented or the process changed.

Cross-functional teams also impose additional stress as team members struggle with having to please multiple managers and finding time to participate in team activities while maintaining a regular work schedule.

STRESS IS ASSOCIATED WITH ADDED RESPONSIBILITY

As anyone who has functioned in a executive or managerial position can tell you, stress comes with the territory. Developing competitive strategies, meeting the numbers, and dealing with other managerial concerns involve complex issues that often are not easily resolved. Managers frequently have to wait to see how a situation develops, and, consequently, they learn to live with a continuing level of uncertainty.

Team members, on the other hand, are generally unaccustomed to the chronic stress that comes with managerial responsibilities. In a traditional environment, a worker may be stressed about an upcoming performance review, technical issue, corporate downsizing, or unhappy supervisor or co-worker. Once the situation is resolved, however, the stress usually goes away.

When team members find themselves feeling jointly responsible for the well-being of the organization, it is not so easy to just turn off one's concerns and go home. Moving to teams redistributes managerial-type stress as team members are called upon to address higher-level problems such as the following:

- What can the team do to help turn around the organization's slipping return on investment?
- How can the team reduce departmental expenses?
- Should temporary workers be hired to help with the work flow? What would each new person cost? How many workers can the department afford? Can the team come up with alternatives that might work even better?

Team members now have a stake in the company's earnings, market position, customer satisfaction, long-term projections, and the like, and if the picture does not look rosy, it's their concern as well as management's.

What—Me Run the Meeting?

In a team environment anyone may be called upon to run meetings, interact more frequently with fellow team members, provide input to someone else's performance review, and communicate with other layers of the organization. This can push people far outside their comfort zone as they take on unfamiliar roles.

The manager can help employees with the transition by helping them to understand that discomfort arises naturally from broadening their role and becoming involved with the welfare of the entire organization. In fact, the idea of a stress-free team may be one of the classic oxymorons of organizational life. A more realistic strategy for the manager is not to attempt to eliminate all stress, a futile objective at best, but to help people learn how to manage the stress that comes with higher levels of responsibility.

HOW DOES TOP MANAGEMENT SUPPORT IMPACT STRESS LEVEL

When management support is forthcoming, teams will sense that their fortunes are built on bedrock rather than quicksand, and they'll have a clearer sense of where they're going and why. When support is vague or nonexistent, however, teams will quickly feel like they're living in no-man's land, and stress levels will rise. The situation is not unlike the land surveyor in Franz Kafka's classic novel, *The Castle*, who tries time and again to have his position confirmed by higher authority but to no avail. The protagonist's limbo-like existence leaves him riddled with *angst*.

Similarly, team members look upstairs for their direction and confirmation. If senior management is ambiguous, team members often find themselves immersed in their own *angst*, having to fill a role, Kafka like, for which they are not supported and often ill prepared.

The Zenger Miller 1994 survey, "Team Members Speak Out," confirms that lack of support from senior management is often a major contributing cause of employee dissatisfaction with teams. Respondents were asked to what extent they felt their top management was actively committed to their team's effort. Respondents had to rate the commitment of their top management on a scale from 0 (not at all committed) to 3 (very committed). The overall mean of management commitment was only 2.21, which indicates that typically top management is only a little more than moderately committed.

How is this lack of commitment shown? Respondents whose management was either not at all committed, slightly committed, or moderately committed were asked which factors indicated a lack of commitment to their teams' efforts. Note that each factor contributes another layer of stress to the team environment. Here's a summary of the findings:

Lack of decision-making authority	60.6%
No reward/low reward	56.7
Inadequate resources	52.9
Managers who do not participate on teams	49.6
Lack of trust	47.3
No recognition	46.3
Lack of coaching	38.5
Inadequate time for team meetings	33.3
Inadequate training	28.7

Why does top management often hold itself back from totally supporting teams, especially since many managers and executives go to considerable trouble to establish a team environment? Is it lack of interest or a control issue? Is it a fear that moving to teams pushes the manager into unknown areas and creates a level of insecurity not easily tolerated? Depending on the situation, it may be one or all of these factors.

One thing is certain: decision-making authority is a heady elixir. The more authority one has, the more one may fight to hold onto it.

This observation could explain why managers at smaller work sites are more likely to resist sharing authority. They have more to lose. The Zenger Miller study indicates that at smaller sites where the authority is likely to be centralized at the top, 47 percent of respondents say their managers are unwilling to share decision-making authority. At larger sites where managers have less authority to begin with, the figure drops to 25 percent.

To gauge team member morale, see Evaluating Team Morale on page 264.

HOW CAN THE MANAGER KEEP EMPLOYEE STRESS WITHIN BOUNDS?

Although it is unlikely that team members will ever function within a stress-free team environment, those who lead and manage teams can do several things to keep stress levels within tolerable limits.

Reduce Situations in Which People Feel Overwhelmed

Stress is most destructive when people have to deal with factors that seem beyond their control. For example, if a team leader wants to share leadership duties with team members, he or she can't simply dump new responsibilities on members and walk away. If your plan is to hand over jobs like budgeting and scheduling, team members may require additional training as well as continued coaching over a period of weeks or months. You'll also need a way to assess their performance so you'll know when particular individuals are ready to assume additional responsibilities.

Be Willing to Negotiate Responsibilities

Sometimes team members may openly object that they don't yet have the necessary skills or experience. They may feel they need more preparation. Therefore, it is important that the team leader be willing to consider delaying the hand-off until a more appropriate time. This can be accomplished by sitting down with team members and negotiating the transfer of new responsibilities that the team may not be ready to accept.

Make Stress Reduction Part of the Infrastructure

Some companies find ways to deal with stress-related problems before they happen. For example, at a paper company one member in each team is cast in an employee assistance role. This individual is charged with keeping an eye out for co-workers who appear stressed. If someone does seem chronically pressured, the team member will call the individual aside, inform the person of the Employee Assistance Program, and provide advice on how to initiate the process to get the proper assistance.

Create a Safe Environment without Blame

Teams have a natural predisposition to avoid blaming. A strong sign that a team spirit has taken hold is when there is a low incidence of finger pointing at team meetings. Ozzie Hager, team leader for Training, Organizational Development, and Employee Relations at Air Transport Systems of Honeywell, notices that in team meetings people don't think to blame an individual if things don't work right. "If something isn't going well," says Hager, "everyone assumes accountability for resolving the problem at hand. Team members ask, 'How can we use team resources to get out of the situation we're currently facing and move the company ahead?'"

Provide Time for Structured Team Building

Another way to lower stress to tolerable levels is through structured team-building sessions. Such meetings allow people to voice personal problems and give and receive feedback. The facilitator might open the meeting by raising the question, "How are we doing?" Once the question is asked, individual team members are allowed to take over the discussion. Other compelling questions the team facilitator might pose include these:

- What's going well? What's not?

- What makes it easy for us to work as a team? What gets in the way?
- What kinds of personal differences are showing up, and how are we resolving them?
- What long-term vision do people have for the team?
- What would enable us to work more effectively together?
- Have there been opportunities for innovation that we've failed to act on?
- What's changed since we've become a team?

Once the major problems have been identified, the team may hold a structured problem-solving session. This session can be facilitated by the team leader or someone from human resources. If the issues are particularly sticky, the team may want to call in the services of an outside consultant.

For help in evaluating an outside consultant, refer to Team Leader/ Facilitator Evaluation on page 284.

It is a good idea to hold team-building sessions at least once a year, though some organizations schedule them quarterly or even monthly if the environment has turned into a pressure cooker. During these sessions you also may want to make use of the Team Morale Tool, which is especially useful when teams are experiencing a high level of stress.

The Team Morale Tool can be found on page 264.

Give Teams a Sense of Purpose

People can easily be duped into thinking they are a team simply because they follow the prescribed *form* of team procedures and activities. There is undue emphasis on team etiquette, and a big to-do is made about staying within ground rules. In and of themselves, these concerns are reasonable, but when the discussion does not sail into deeper waters, the team is really just a team in form, not in function.

When a team has no compelling business goals, the focus of activities remains superficial. Too often, teams are formed because it's "the thing to do" or because the manager has bought into the prevailing popularity of teams in order to gain recognition. This is the kind of quicksand that quickly promotes insecurity. For team members to feel that their work has purpose and meaning and that they have ownership of their work, the goals of the organization must matter.

A team with clear business goals operates more confidently. Team meetings are not focused on the thin veneer of organizational protocol but address more substantive, underlying issues. Topics relate to company performance, such as "what did we do wrong last week?" and "how can we prevent it from happening again?" People speculate on different scenarios. Discussions are reflective, the learning richer.

Similarly, members don't walk around encased in their own team's cocoon and worrying about their own little piece of the pie. By creating the entire organization as "their" environment, team members become more willing to venture into areas that previously would have had a self-imposed "no trespassing" sign.

At Baxter Health Care, a Mannbord, Oklahoma, manufacturer of hospital equipment, teams are given monthly goals that address products, quality, cost reduction, and customer satisfaction. These goals are posted on a blackboard in each team's production area, at a location visible to anyone walking by. Any problems, goofs, failures to meet quotas, or other performance data are also displayed.

One day a team member walking through another production area saw on a blackboard a problem that his own team had just experienced. The problem related to a process that etched marks on hypodermic needles. The marks, which guide the doctor on how deep to insert the needle, had been etched at the wrong location, and the team considered the batch ruined.

The passer-by knew this was not so. His own team had figured out a process to remove the marks so the needles could be re-etched. He stopped, chatted with members of the other team, and described the process. The team listened enthusiastically and, shortly after, tried his procedure with complete success, saving the company a tidy sum.

In a nonteam environment, this employee might have read the situation on the white board, thought, "Gee, tough luck," and moved on. After all, why should he go out of his way? There wasn't anything in it for him. Taking initiative happens only when team members have a clear sense of purpose and ownership, when they feel supported, and when the stress of walking into the unknown is counterbalanced by the excitement of being able to make a difference.

9

⊚   **KEEPING TEAM**
           MEMBERS MOTIVATED

*What the leadership in a business does will always have a far greater
effect than anything it says. You're already leading by example—you need
only make certain that your example is a good one, the one you want to
emulate throughout your business.*

Paul Levesque

Questions Addressed in This Chapter

- Why should managers keep alert to the team's special needs?
- How can status symbols demotivate a team?
- What are some commonly available motivational tools?
- How do you know if you have a self-motivating team culture?

It would be ideal if the work experience, by itself, were always sufficient to inspire a high level of performance. But people's concerns are
more complex. They have families and schedules and babysitters and
VCRs that go on the fritz. They worry about economic security. They're
sensitive to how others see them—not just their fellow workers but also
others within the organization. If a company does not support team
members in personal ways, even the best work team environment will
produce apathetic or disgruntled workers.

Consequently, after the novelty of the launch has worn off, after a
flatter organization has taken hold, and after the numbers have started to
improve, team members will inevitably raise the question—"What's in it
for me?" They may not say it out loud. They may not even think it con-
sciously, but the question will be reflected in how they perform their
work.

The way the company responds will be tied to where the teams are in the development process. In the early stages, the company can respond by offering team members the opportunity to achieve a broader set of skills and greater job security. Later, when the teams have started taking on additional responsibilities, the response is likely to be some kind of personal "attaboys" and acknowledgments of the contributions the team has made. When the team has started to show bottom-line results and improved customer satisfaction, the "what's in it for me" can be more tied to the compensation system.

There are, however, various other ways in which the manager can encourage people to rise to greater heights.

ADDRESSING THE TEAM'S SPECIAL NEEDS

To keep teams motivated, a good manager or team leader stays alert to the particular needs of the team, looking, probing, and listening to worker concerns. Often this kind of trolling lands only a few small fish, but sometimes paying attention can net the big one.

> *A team manager at a health care organization in the Midwest was faced with a chronically high absentee rate. It had always been the manager's practice to pay attention to worker concerns, and over time he felt he had identified a major cause of the absentee problem. Many of the single mothers needed additional time at home. If there were important family matters to attend to and not enough time to do it, people often called in sick. As the team became more efficient, the manager proposed a schedule change. Instead of people working five 8-hour days, he changed the schedule so people would work four 10-hour days. This allowed the single mothers to spend a whole weekday at home.*
>
> *Because of the manager's sensitivity to the personal needs of his team, the team's performance exceeded its goals, and absenteeism dropped substantially. All this happened because the manager went out of his way to look, listen, and acknowledge that certain parts of his team had special considerations that needed to be addressed.*

REMOVING STATUS SYMBOLS

Among the many ways in which the manager can make the team environment more motivating for team members, one of the most effective is to remove the usual work-related status symbols. Perks like fancy offices and special rights and privileges no longer bestow rank and title to the privileged. With everyone functioning on a level playing field, team members are more likely to feel like partners than employees and are more motivated to stay alert to new ways the work can be improved. Even so, status symbols have a way of creeping in, and when they do, the team leader needs to be aware of how they might be undercutting team morale.

A team leader at a midwestern company sensed there was an unspoken chasm between team members and the managerial staff, but he couldn't pinpoint exactly where the problem lay. To find out, he went out on the floor and did some probing and listening. It didn't take long to identify the issue—a difference in dress code. Team members were required to wear jump suits while the managerial staff wore coats and ties. This disparity in dress created an obvious difference in status. The problem was easily resolved by doing away with coats and ties so that everyone wore essentially the same kind of clothes. Giving everyone the same profile made it easier for team members to communicate with members of the managerial staff when problems arose.

A similar situation arose in another organization. Team members complained they were feeling like "second-class citizens." Again, some sleuthing by the team leader quickly identified the problem.

Team members were required to enter the facility through a door that was accessed by an unpaved path. In inclement weather, the path turned muddy, requiring workers to clean their shoes before entering the building. The team manager, on the other hand, entered through a door reached by a paved path. The solution was apparent: pave the second path. Once done, the complaining stopped instantly.

It may be hard to imagine that something as "inconsequential" as muddy shoes can have such an impact on team attitude. Yet, organizations that have been at this awhile can attest to the seemingly insignificant issues that affect team members. This is why it is important for the team leader to remain sensitive and approach each situation with an open mind. Responding promptly to areas of team concern builds morale by demonstrating a commitment to listen and take action.

OTHER COMMONLY AVAILABLE
MOTIVATIONAL TOOLS

For all the benefits of teams, workers in a team environment will always be at a certain disadvantage. In a typical management structure, people progress up the corporate ladder. A line worker moves to supervisor or foreperson. A manager transfers to a larger plant or perhaps becomes vice president of operations. Position is status, and status is a visible sign of achievement.

Because of the flatter organizational structure, team members don't have such opportunities. There aren't many ways to move up. Consequently, you need to provide opportunities for people to advance by broadening and deepening their knowledge and experience, and you need to know how to reward them in a personal way when they perform up to and beyond expectation.

Not everyone responds to the same kinds of rewards. Some are primarily motivated by their own sense of purpose and direction. This worker will feel more acknowledged by a personal "attaboy" from the team leader. Additional acknowledgments might take the form of access to a special library of resources or an opportunity to become a trainer for others on the team—an effective, low-key way to highlight the person's talents.

Other team members might be motivated by some type of public fanfare. This could be a mention in the company newsletter or having the person's picture displayed on the departmental bulletin board. Special windbreakers are sometimes given away to those acknowledged as having contributed the most to the team. Earning a jacket can become a person's motivating goal, rather like receiving a varsity letter. To get a better idea of which type of rewards would most befit a team member, you should have each team member complete the Team Personality Tool on page 256.

Other effective motivational tools include the following:

Supplier Field Trips

Field trips give team members a fresh perspective by offering a change of scenery at the company's expense. Because the team member is often accorded VIP treatment when he or she shows up at the supplier's site, a field trip can also be a great status builder. Field trips provide employees with an opportunity to talk person-to-person with the supplier about any material problems—and perhaps even have a say on which raw materials the organization will work with. Exercising this kind of responsibility makes the field trip a great motivational tool.

Privileges

Who gets to represent the team at the next management seminar? Or even more important, who gets to conduct the VIP tours? If you choose a team member to conduct a tour when visitors come to the organization, that person will perceive your assignment as a powerful vote of confidence. The recognition the team member receives from co-workers won't hurt either.

Continuing Education

If team members excel, they can end up being selected for special workshops and seminars. This will give them an opportunity to broaden their skills and to make their work more interesting. Qualifying for special training may bring team members up to speed on new processes or equipment and turn them into experts who teach new skills to others on the team.

Challenging Work

An opportunity to do work that is interesting or that offers unusual variety can also motivate people to higher performance.

Giving the Team Firsthand Information

One of the most effective ways to motivate people is to give them the sense that they matter to the organization. Managers can do this by making sure that team members find out *firsthand* about breaking news inside and outside the organization. Did sales rise dramatically? Is there a merger in the offing? Is there a shift in the world market? Most employees only learn such news as it drifts through the grapevine or is printed the company newsletter. This carries with it an implied message:"You're not important enough to be personally briefed."

Because teams are encouraged—even expected—to become involved in the welfare of the *entire* organization, it is only fitting that they be accorded the same recognition as management whenever there's important news to share. This can be arranged though regularly scheduled briefings by the team manager or by higher officials, such as the plant manager or division vice president.

Traditional managers frequently chafe at the idea of giving away knowledge that used to be their own private domain. But sharing information doesn't have to be equated with losing stature. Being the person who gives away the news also positions the manager in a favorable light.

Controlling the Urge to Overcontrol

You know the decisions that have to be made. You've given the team everything it needs, but people aren't taking action. Or they're not going about it in the right way, at least from your perspective. Where does the problem lie? It's easy to point the finger at the teams. But sometimes that's not where the problem really resides.

One CEO recalls a time in the late 1980s when his group of executives was actively exploring how to institute teams that were not so vulnerable to individual managerial styles.

> *"I remember sitting in one group of six people we called a PDS [Performance Development System] and discussing the idea that if we could just get managers to focus on developing the teams rather than controlling them, we could resolve this problem. Interestingly, our group was led by one of the most controlling executives in our organization. We sat on this team for 18 months and tried to understand how to evoke developmental juices in our managers. We tried all kinds of tactics to discourage them from being so controlling, and none of them worked. We met every other Tuesday for a year and a half, and as we got into this, we finally realized what the problem was. The problem was us—the executives. We were the biggest control problem we had."*

Unfortunately, in the enthusiasm to get the job done, it is easy to lose sight of what works. It may even feel impossible to sit there and bite your tongue. But if you want to empower team members, you have to allow them to arrive at their own understanding in their own way and in their own time.

Supporting and Encouraging Innovation

Team members will also feel that there's "something in it for them" if they have the opportunity to innovate. In the traditional organization, innovation is often a risky issue because employees never know whose toes they'll be stepping on if they come up with a new and perhaps better way to do something. The thrust is on performing a job the way it's defined. Consequently, people are less likely to go the extra mile. They are motivated to play by the rules and are quick to define what they will and will not do.

In a team environment, however, especially when the manager actively acknowledges and rewards those who come up with good ideas, people are encouraged to play an active role in improving the organization. As team members find themselves empowered, ideas often bubble up in the daily give-and-take of team interaction. The process is spontaneous and unself-conscious.

> *MHI Group buys funeral homes in Florida and Colorado and runs them with self-directed work teams. Instead of maintaining a funeral director at each funeral home, the teams manage operations while a cadre of funeral directors rotates from one funeral home to the next. Greg Ferris, director of Personnel Development at MHI Group, observes that because the teams are empowered, they not only find ways to innovate, they even take on the job of figuring out how to finance the innovations, and have set up informal networks to help channel the new ideas through MHI.*

Encouraging Self-Disclosure

People are usually willing to pull harder when it's in support of those they care about. Consequently, if a manager can create a climate of trust in which team members create a more open and personal relationship with fellow workers, the result is likely to be a more effective team.

Members of such teams are often willing to share themselves in ways that would be unheard of in a less familial setting. The person leading the team can facilitate this atmosphere by trusting the others with his or her candid thoughts. In doing so, the leader makes it safe for other team members to be vulnerable in front of the group. They learn that they can speak up, share what they feel, and not be stepped on. The leader can also encourage self-disclosure by actively welcoming people's negative concerns.

> *One plant manager had to address 35 people about a change in the pay system. The manager knew that what he had to say would not be well received; pay levels were fixed, and nothing currently could be done about it. He felt it important that people not walk around stewing with negativity, so he set up a situation that allowed people to air their feelings in a group setting.*
>
> *He began the meeting by saying, "Let's make a list of the pros and cons of the new program and look at what each of these means to us as a group." The group immediately came up with a long list of cons. The manager encouraged everyone to talk about the cons and, in doing so, made it safe for people to vent their anger and negativity about the pay system in that environment.*

Finally, he said, "Okay, now let's look at a few of the pros," and he
threw out a couple. The group picked up the cue and started looking at
some of the positive aspects of the changes. Eventually people began say-
ing things like, "Well, maybe we can look at it another way." Once the
group was able to air its feelings, the manager was able to work with that
information and help everyone see the advantages of the new structure.

Typically, people feel most at risk when they openly disagree with management, so rather than speak out in the team meeting when they have a complaint, they often wait to air their feelings in a safer, less conspicuous venue—the cafeteria, the bathroom, or the hallway. This reserve can make it difficult for a team leader who is trying to promote trust, candor, and honesty.

In encouraging self-disclosure, the leader or facilitator should be discouraged from making out-of-hand decisions about how candid a team "should" be and instead should remain sensitive to where the team is in its development. Here are some ways to do that:

1. *Allow disclosure to unfold gradually.* Teams often go through a honeymoon phase where people feel that "we're all one big team." People are encouraged to be totally candid and share anything they want until it dawns on them that not everyone on the team is comfortable with such openness. When that happens, people can end up disillusioned and confused about what is appropriate behavior. Therefore, it's important that disclosure not be carried to a point where team members start having negative experiences.

For example, it's probably not good to encourage someone to be a forerunner into deep levels of disclosure before the team is ready. It's better to begin with a low level of personal disclosure and increase this only as the team as a whole becomes comfortable with it and is willing to accept it. The leader has a responsibility to team members to help them feel safe, and he or she does this by getting the group to metaphorically hold hands as they dip together into the disclosure pool.

2. *Encourage the airing of negative concerns.* To encourage people to reveal things that are bothering them, you might prompt them to begin talking about what part of the job they don't do well or don't like. This will often help team members to build support for one another. For example, as team members find out that a particular person has tremendous apprehension about public speaking or running a meeting, they will often allow that individual to pass up those tasks in favor of other things he or she is more comfortable with. This attitude goes a long way toward building an underlying feeling of acceptance and trust.

3. *Realize that some cultures invite disclosure; some don't.* Appropriate levels of disclosure also depend on the culture. In a high-tech environment, people may be reluctant to admit that there's something they don't do well. In a scientific community with its engineers and physicists, admitting you don't know something is often considered paramount to laziness. People assume that if you don't know something, you will automatically take the initiative to learn about it. On the other hand, in service environments, admitting you don't know doesn't automatically imply that you aren't doing your job well. It simply means that certain information is not currently available to you.

Not Succumbing to "Team Leader's Disease"

In a team culture, people are eager to learn," says Jim Lawler of Union Camp. "They're quick to welcome training and see the immediate application. That's a lot different than a traditional culture, where you have to prove to people how the training relates to their job and why they should bother with it."

There is, however, a down side to this heightened receptivity. Because people's personal receptors are unusually sensitive in a team environment, leaders need to remain alert to the implied messages they may be giving off. This goes for *everyone*—from the executive on down.

If you've ever had your small daughter shake her finger in reprimand at you, then you know how quickly others can read your unspoken messages. Though she might not be talking yet, she's still managed to pick up your attitude. What you feel about her has clearly come across, and now she's reflecting it back to you.

> *Teri Zurfluh, performance development consultant with Union Camp, notes that team leaders are often unaware of the tremendous impact they have on the team and of how their personal style is mimicked unconsciously by team members. For example, if the team leader is prone to complain, point a finger, and assign blame, team members are often likely to pick this up. They will catch what Zurfluh calls "team leader's disease."*
>
> *Consequently, team leaders must stay alert to the subtle impressions they make and must become sensitive to and aware of their direct and indirect effect on the team. They need to constantly remember that they are role models, that if they don't find teams a positive and energizing experience, team members aren't likely to either.*

Finding Ways to Enlist Management Support

Team activities impinge on so many facets of the organization that the potential for conflict always exists. Despite this problem, teams often show a hardiness for survival that testifies to the level of synergy that arises when like-minded individuals work together. Yet, even a team's demonstrated success is no guarantee that it will gain senior management's continuing support, and without such support, the team's ability to sustain itself becomes depleted.

The national sales organization of a large retailer established sales teams to more effectively respond to customer needs. Although the teams were beginning to show results, sales for the organization over the first two years didn't grow as expected, and expenses seemed high in comparison to what the teams were achieving. Nevertheless, the teams showed unusual energy in taking on new responsibilities and looked for creative ways to accomplish their objectives.

Among other things, teams wanted the freedom to choose how to use support personnel and requested the option of getting outside help if contractors could do the job better than staffers. They also pushed for better access to information and an opportunity to manage their own expenses.

Management was reluctant. Without greater up-front results, managers didn't want to empower the teams to this degree. They were cautious about making any significant changes and only wanted teams that were "slightly empowered." This made it difficult for the teams to move ahead.

Team members claimed that if they could be given budgets and an opportunity to manage their own expenses, they could keep costs under control. However, the accounts payable department, which managed expenses on a regional level, was not able to break down the accounting so expenses could be managed on a team level. In addition, management felt that hiring any outside personnel, even if they could do the job more effectively, meant paying twice for services already available on staff.

Another stumbling block had to do with information access. Teams needed access to information as well as new hardware and software, but Information Services was not willing to change its systems quickly enough to provide what the teams were looking for.

Resistance also came from regional managers who resented the teams' autonomy and were reluctant to hand over any control. This situation was exacerbated when a new vice president placed at the head of the sales organization was not favorable to the team environment. The teams, in turn, responded by withholding their own information and maintained an attitude that essentially said, "Why bother telling them anything? They won't give us what we need anyway."

Management continued to resist giving up control, claiming that the teams were too hard to manage. In retrospect, however, it appeared that the team culture was simply too different from the rest of the organization and that team members wanted more than the organization was willing to give. In light of all these difficulties, the teams found the going too difficult, and at the end of two years they were disbanded.

As this example illustrates, the difficulties and frustrations in trying to function as a team without the backing of management usually catches up with the team. There are simply too many potholes and hazards, and over time, the team's motivation simply wanes. Therefore, it is important to continually stay alert to ways in which management support can be brought on board.

HOW DO YOU KNOW WHETHER YOU HAVE A SELF-MOTIVATING TEAM CULTURE?

If you find that your teams are full of doubters and unbelievers, you might want to check to make sure you've not duped yourself into believing that you've created teams by simply whitewashing the old authoritarian structure. Here is list of questions that will serve as a reality check on whether or not you have created a viable team culture.

1. *Do team members actually enjoy being on the team?* This is one of the easiest ways to determine whether you've created a functioning team. People enjoy being on a team because the work is more satisfying and because they see an opportunity to make an impact. If you see an increase in people's willingness to assume responsibility, if they show initiative, and if they look beyond the immediate goal and consider the consequences of team activities, then you know that a team mentality has taken hold.

2. *Are people seeking out opportunities to share information, or do they interact with one another only when forced to do so at scheduled team meetings?* You'll know there's a team mentality in place when people look beyond their narrow jobs and find reasons to jointly seek out information, offer suggestions to improve a work process, or discuss the impact of changes and ideas on the direction of the organization. Over lunch and during breaks, people will talk less about babies and ball scores and more about business concerns.

3. *Are people finding new opportunities to work together?*
People are usually quick to see the advantages of working on cross-
functional issues as a team. True team members seek out opportunities
to work on common goals and projects because they *share* common
objectives and have built mutually supportive relationships with other
members of their team.

4. *Are new processes and procedures getting up to speed more
quickly?* Everything happens faster when people collaborate. For example, at a cereal manufacturer, engineers previously communicated with
line personnel only by written directive. Once a team mentality set in,
engineers brought new lines up to speed by actually working shoulder to
shoulder with line personnel out on the floor. As a result, cycle time for
getting product lines up and running was reduced from six months to
just two weeks. If key measures are not being achieved more efficiently,
then maybe your "team" is a team in name only.

5. *Are people relating to the team leader as if he or she were the
team manager?* The kind of interaction team members have with the
team leader is another dead giveaway. Are relationships between team
members and the team leader cautious and formal? Are people turning
to the team leader as their major source of information? If so, chances
are the leader is perceived as a manager, in which case the old authoritarian structure may still rule.

Here's a simple rule of thumb. A team leader looks *toward* the
team. He or she is a fellow worker, a coach—perceived as accessible
and responsive to the needs and questions of individual members. The
team manager, on the other hand, is constantly looking *outward*. Rather
than being caught up in team activities, the manager is focused on the
organization as a whole and alert to additional resources that can be
brought back to the team. The team manager functions more as an external resource.

6. *Are teams using customer data to make decisions?* If not, perhaps the teams are depending on top management to make decisions and
are not getting customer reactions firsthand. It's only when teams directly access customer data that they are able to understand the power and
pain of what the customer is actually experiencing.

7. *Is the team progressively being handed greater responsibility?*
Team leaders who retain unvoiced fears about giving the team more
responsibility—and who limit its authority and power—are really functioning as authoritarian-style managers. They may convince themselves
that this is not so, but team members will certainly see them that way. If

your intention is to build an effective team environment, having team leaders who hang onto the responsibility will be counterproductive and eventually will move the teams back to square one.

Team members are not just followers, observed management guru Mary Parker Follett. They are people who significantly impact the performance and direction of the organization. Follett, a professor of management theory whose ideas were well in advance of her colleague and contemporary Frederick W. Taylor, noted that, "What I see happening in some places is that the members of the group are not so much following a leader as helping him in control of a situation."

That sense of collaboration can indeed be a heady experience for many who have previously seen themselves simply as cogs in the machinery. Though collaboration can serve to motivate some to greater heights, it can also create its share of Doubting Thomases, who are reluctant to give up familiar rewards without finding something else to take their place.

It is up to the manager to stay sensitive and alert to where the teams are in their development and to the special needs that may arise. Motivation comes in many forms. A perceptive manager can work wonders by finding innovative ways to keep the team members on board.

10

⑥ IS YOUR COMPENSATION PLAN WORKING FOR OR AGAINST YOU?

[A plant-wide productivity bonus] would be an appropriate development in many respects: equity would be served by further sharing the fruits of this productive human system; the total plant would be drawn together as it never has before; individuals who are topping out in pay scheme would have another way to affect their income. In the most general sense, a plant-wide bonus could provide the work system with a timely "second wind."

Richard Walton

Questions Addressed in This Chapter

- What are the characteristics of a dysfunctional compensation system?
- When should a reward system be introduced?
- What form should compensation take?
- How can you be sure your compensation system works effectively with teams?

There is a story about two men who are laboring in a quarry under a hot summer sun. A stranger strolls by and stops to watch, and after a while, impressed with their effort, he asks, "What are you doing?" The first worker straightens up, wipes his brow with his arm, and says, "I'm cutting granite blocks." Then the other worker stands up and wipes the sweat from his brow and says, "I'm helping to build a cathedral."

If there's one single thing that distinguishes a team member from an ordinary worker, it's a sense of vision. What makes the vision so compelling is that it touches on every aspect of team activities. Nothing is exempt, including the compensation plan.

"When the compensation plan is directly linked to the mission and the vision of the company," says San Francisco consultant Patricia Haddock, "it allows you to say to an employee, 'This is the mission of the company. This is the mission of your division. Here's how the compensation plan supports that.' Creating this connection lets employees know how and why they will be rewarded.

"Without this understanding," says Haddock, "Their reaction to taking on additional responsibilities would more likely be, 'Why should I do this? What's in it for me?'"

Unfortunately, many organizations do not bother to bring their compensation plans in line with the purpose and direction of the teams, and as a result, compensation does not end up supporting team activities and may even end up being counterproductive.

Today it is becoming increasingly crucial to reward teamwork. According to a 1995 article in *The Wall Street Journal,* two-thirds of major U.S. companies assign some workers to self-managed teams, up from 28 percent in 1987. The article noted that "many of these employers are revamping their pay systems, especially for their self-managed teams, because hierarchical pay plans centered on individuals no longer make much sense for them."

"Many firms we know are trying to get away from annual reviews and pay adjustments and the like," observes Dr. Michael Schuster of Competitive Human Resources Strategies, "but reality is that the bulk of the people in the United States get a pay increase every year. It may be small, it may even be in a lump sum, but they get something."

"We're at a point now," says Huey Greene of Baxter Health Care, "where if we give the teams a fixed goal and if they reach those goals, they need to be rewarded. After all, as a company we reap the benefits, so we've made a commitment to the teams that by the end of the year we'll have a program in place, and if they hit their goals and the plant hits its goal, we'll share in some type of incentive pay."

Some organizations even offer team members incentives for special achievements. When teams were introduced at Textron Inc.'s Defense Systems subsidiary, employees could earn an additional bonus, as much as 10 percent of their base salaries, for special achievements such as devising an important patent or taking what was considered an intelligent though unsuccessful risk.

"When people start asking the question, 'What do I get for what I do?'" says Schuster, "the organization is compelled to listen. Decision makers are forced by their own sense of fairness and logic to acknowledge that through the team process, people are taking on more responsibility and making a bigger contribution to the organization. If people are doing more, then that needs to be factored into the compensation analysis.

"This is not to say that a reward-system is a 'must-have.' We see companies with very successful team processes with rewards, and we see companies with very successful team processes that do not include rewards. What you learn is that this is a company-specific issue where certain factors drive you toward having rewards and other factors drive you in the opposite direction."

Just instituting rewards does not guarantee that they will be productive or even appropriate. How, when, and where they are introduced will have a bearing on their effectiveness. When rewards do not deliver anticipated gains, it is often because some aspect of the compensation program has not been designed to accommodate the unique characteristics of a team environment.

WHAT ARE THE CHARACTERISTICS OF A DYSFUNCTIONAL COMPENSATION SYSTEM?
The Wrong Behavior Is Rewarded

"Organizations really have to work hard at not having compensation be dysfunctional," notes Schuster. "Once you settle on the amount, then you're into the question of what form it should take. You want a compensation system that reinforces the team process. However, what often happens is that management provides a reward structure that benefits individuals at the expense of the team.

"Maybe a half dozen times a year I get a call from a general manager who tells me he has a team-based organization, but the worst team in his organization is his own staff. So I sit down and do one-on-one discussions with the staff members. You know what I often find out? Their reward system is based on a zero-sum gain. Zero-sum gain is a fixed pie. Anything you get comes at my expense, and anything I get comes at your expense. So if I'm in a reward structure where our boss has a fixed sum of money, and if the average is five and you get seven, that means I can only get three. So no wonder his team isn't working. People may want to be good citizens, but not at their own expense. In this kind of a situation, it makes better sense to measure the performance of the staff rather than of individuals on the staff."

This raises an interesting question. If a compensation system is not accomplishing its stated purpose, why isn't it promptly replaced with a system that does? The answer is partly rooted in human nature. We tend to be victims of our past history—whatever we did before is what we will continue to do. That's especially true of compensation plans. At an established site that is transitioning to teams, just the sheer time required to change the compensation system is such that people often try to get by without doing it. The volume of details can be overwhelming.

"If you were looking for fun things to do next year," says Schuster, "one of the very last things that you would consider getting involved with is revamping your organization's compensation system."

Poor Internal Communications

An organization has a variety of tools with which it can disseminate details of the compensation plan. Management can hold general meetings or personal briefings. It can publish flyers and brochures. It can even invest a few dollars more and produce an entire video covering compensation issues. Patricia Haddock observes that from her experience the number-one problem is the lack of communication or miscommunication about the compensation program. Organizations simply don't make the necessary effort, or what they do is executed improperly.

Employees Don't Understand Why Bonuses Are or Are Not Forthcoming

Because everything is so interconnected in a team culture, it is easy for team members to draw false conclusions. Therefore, it behooves executives to stay aware of the impact that seemingly unrelated changes in the compensation program can have on team performance.

Consider what happens when management simply implements a bonus without communicating the reasons for it. Not only is the bonus unrelated to anything the teams have done but also they have no understanding of what they have to do to get it again. This is the worst form of reward because management is simply giving out gifts. The incentives are not tied to performance in any way.

The converse is also true. Let us say that even though people are taking on more responsibility, the business dictates that there can be only a very limited financial incentive or perhaps none at all. If management fails to properly communicate why expected bonuses are not forthcoming, team members can be quick to assume that the organization has taken advantage of them. This can easily create a simmering resentment and act as a disincentive to team performance.

A company made the decision to introduce self-managed work teams and took steps to implement the rollout. At the same time management was just concluding negotiations of a labor agreement that was designed to cut pay by 15 percent. Because these two decisions were not coordinated and no effort was made to explain the reason for the salary drop, the team rollout got off to a very poor start.

Differences in compensation programs may also need to be explained to the teams. For example, because of the ways business is conducted, the compensation program for a company's retail division might of necessity be very different from that of the system division.

"All the more reason," says Haddock, "for including compensation as part of the strategic plan."

Teams Are Being Oversold

"I've had communications go out from major companies explaining massive changes in the benefits and compensation programs," states Haddock. "The message put out in these communications is that these changes are great; this is a real enhancement. But when we've sampled the teams in focus groups, we've found a less than favorable attitude. People say, 'Don't tell us that it's good. Let *us* make that judgement ourselves. Just give us the facts.' People are more likely to buy in if they're not oversold."

In Haddock's opinion, candor and honesty are critical. "Employees know when you're being honest with them. For example, some companies don't want to admit that they're not in the top 5 percent of the compensation ranking. But employees know when you're hiding something and when you're not. In a more participative type management, even if employees are not involved in the decision-making process, at least they're being told the rationale for what's happening." Haddock notes that if you're in an organization that typically has not been forthright with employees, employees are going to meet anything with suspicion. But if you're in a company that has always been open, you're not going to see that problem.

"Employees also tend to be a little myopic in that they often fail to look at the whole benefit package," Haddock adds. "They need to take a more holistic view of compensation. One thing that employees do appreciate is an annual compensation statement that summarizes all of their compensation and benefits. They may only be getting $35,000 a year in salary, but they may also be receiving another $15,000 in benefits. The annual compensation statement is a good way for a company to get a lot of bang for its buck by showing employees exactly how much compensation they *are* getting."

Management Makes the Wrong Assumptions

"Many people think they're compensation experts," says Michael Schuster. "They know how *they'd* like to be paid, so they assume that everybody would like to be paid the same way. The process tends not to be fact-based or analytical, so the whole thing gets off on the wrong track because everybody is clouding the issue with his or her own ideas."

Focus Groups Are Useful
One of the best ways to learn what employees would really prefer is to sample their opinion in focus groups.

"I don't think there is any other kind of two-way communication that's more valuable than a focus group if it's conducted properly," says Haddock. "You get extremely valuable information."

Schuster concurs. "We oftentimes try to get employee input about how often a bonus should be paid. There are some companies that would like to pay it once a year, whereas their employees might prefer something more frequent. This means that if you do give bonuses on an annual basis, they may not be as effective as they might otherwise be."

Questions that provide useful information include the following:

- How do you feel about your compensation today?
- Do you feel that your compensation is fair for the work you do?
- Do you have any ideas on what the ideal way would be to pay people in this organization?
- If you had your choice between a plantwide, gain-sharing approach or one based on small groups or teams, which one would you prefer?

"Sometimes," says Schuster, "employees come up with recommendations or concerns that the managers have not factored into their own analysis." For example, many managers show a preference for team-based bonuses, whereas employees will often shy away from that.

They'd much prefer a facilitywide bonus because they're not sure that management is capable of administering the team-based bonus fairly. Employees know that it can be difficult to measure the performance of particular teams, especially in support areas. Team-based bonuses find greater employee acceptance in those industries where information is more quantifiable.

Why don't companies use more focus groups? Haddock observes that many companies conduct frequent internal employee opinion surveys, but they don't do as many focus groups as they might, especially around compensation. The fear is that most employees think they're underpaid. So unless the company has a strong justification for its compensation schedule, conducting the focus groups puts it in the position of having to explain the compensation plan to employees, and often it doesn't want to have to do that.

Another finding, says Haddock, is that employees tend to think that their company's compensation package is lower than the industry average. Even if it isn't, companies are often reluctant to publicize that fact to their employees. That's because doing so would require them to actually show numbers and industry specifics that many companies believe employees wouldn't understand.

Not Enough Teams Are Up and Running

"We get calls from people," reports Schuster, "where someone says, 'We're in the process of implementing a team-based organization, and we know we need to address rewards. What should we do?' So we go out there and find that they've just recently implemented their first team and they've got 22 to go. We'll tell them it's a little bit premature to put the rewards in. Here's how we explain it to them.

"Let's say that you install the reward system but you have only one team. All of a sudden team members are rewarded, but 90 percent of the organization still isn't on teams, so team members can't really see the impact of their efforts. What's happened is that you've devalued the reward, because they've received it even though their efforts have produced no discernible improvements.

"To consider rewards, you want to be far enough along in the team rollout so that teams have the capability of actually making improvements. To do this, you need to have more people involved on teams. You don't want to have one person rowing while everyone else is riding in the boat, so to speak.

"However, even if your immediate plans are to have only one team up and running, that team needs to be in place for a long enough period to be able to link compensation with something that it actually accomplishes."

There Aren't Enough Mechanisms in Place to Create Improvements

The team is installed. The bonus plan is in place. But strangely, there are still no improvements. What could be wrong?

Organizations need to look at whether they have sufficient mechanisms in place—cooperative labor-management relations, work redesign, and so forth—to create gain. Teams are only one of the vehicles for making improvements. If you have just a single way to increase performance, you're not giving your employees much leeway. You need sufficient mechanisms in place so that if you put in a bonus program, the employees will have a variety of ways to address the problem. This gives them a better opportunity to create gain and ultimately receive a payout.

Failure to Meet Employee Expectations

In some organizations it is very difficult to get people to take on more responsibility without some kind of added financial recognition. In other organizations, employees are motivated to make such changes without added incentives. This disparity can be explained by variations in the organizational culture and the different employee expectations that they engender.

The organizational culture is shaped by several factors:

• *The organization's own history.* If this is a location that has historically offered incentives, people's behavior will have been molded in a monetary environment, and they will expect monetary rewards to be closely tied to performance and responsibility.

• *Current levels of compensation.* If this is a workforce that is not highly paid, additional compensation will be of foremost concern. The reverse is also true. Employees who are already well paid are more likely to be more motivated by other kinds of rewards, such as the opportunity to exercise greater control over their work environment.

• *The overall values in the community.* Is this a community in which the cultural mores dictate that "you never give somethin' for nothin'" or where the cut of one's clothes and the make of one's car play an inordinately important role? In an area where dollars speak more loudly, the pressure to increase earnings will make itself felt, and people will expect some kind of financial rewards.

• *The nature of the local labor market.* How well paid are employees at other organizations in the community? If employees are being paid either higher or lower than the going rate, that will also have a bearing on the importance of additional compensation.

If team performance is not up to par, it may be because expectations around compensation are not being met. In a traditional organization, if an employee starts taking on additional responsibility, he can go to his manager or the human resources department and ask to have his job reevaluated. His added efforts may logically entitle him to a pay increase.

In a team environment, the *whole organization* is changing its job, so it is not unreasonable for the team to expect financial incentives as it takes on added responsibilities. If members do not believe that they are receiving a wage that is at parity with their efforts, they may end up subtly adjusting their efforts so that their compensation and performance on the job fall more into balance.

Employees Have Not Had an Opportunity to Offer Their Input

"If management comes up with a newfangled compensation idea that hasn't received input from the employees," says Schuster, "it's going to be received with greater skepticism than if employees had an opportunity to contribute their ideas early on.

"Let's say you have a facility of 300 people and you ask for employee input on a new reward system. When it comes time to implement the new concept and the sceptics ask, 'Who came up with this?' you can turn around and say, 'Well, gee, we had employees involved in the design.' In these situations the sceptic is more likely to say, 'Oh, I didn't realize that. I guess it's a better deal than I thought.'" Inviting employees to contribute their ideas lends credibility to a new compensation program and makes it easier for team members to sell the concept to their peers.

Management Doesn't Understand the Rationale for a Particular Compensation System

In determining compensation, top management usually makes the final decision, getting its information from internal and external experts and from its own past experiences. Unfortunately, executives often don't spend enough time in trying to understand the context in which the compensation system must be regarded, and they end up imposing their own context based on their own experience and prejudice. This is why compensation systems are often not clearly thought through.

"I had a call from a company we had worked with four or five years ago," recalls Schuster. "At that time we had recommended that they move away from individual incentives because they were destructive for both the team process and the quality process, although at the same time we had also worked out a way to protect people's earnings.

"Well, the new president who came in was quick to tell us that [what we did four years ago] was the dumbest thing that anybody could do and that it was costing them a lot of extra money. This person had no history of the problem and had developed no realistic context of how the issues had to be addressed. He had no idea why compensation was changed in the first place and how difficult it had been to make that change. He made assumptions that simply weren't true. All he knew was how *he* would like to be paid."

WHEN SHOULD A REWARD SYSTEM BE INTRODUCED?

In designing an appropriate compensation plan, most firms look at multiple factors: (1) what's going on in the labor market both nationally and locally, (2) how able the business is to compete, and (3) what will be satisfactory to employees. Usually, none of these is a controlling factor, although the business's ability to compete generally swings more weight.

"Our preference is to stage rewards subsequent to the setting up of teams," says Schuster. "First we get the team processes in, get the teams up and running, and get the process down so it's working without too many bugs. Then sometime between 6 to 24 months into the process we begin to look at rewards."

But this is not a universal timetable. In some instances organizations have found it necessary to initiate a new reward structure or bonus plan at a much earlier stage in the process. Here are two examples.

Let's say management looks at next year's pay decision and determines there will be no money available for pay increases. To keep employees' motivation from flagging, a performance-based pay plan is installed. But what measures will the organization take to bring about increased performance? One answer is to install teams. In this instance, the compensation plan precedes team performance.

In other cases a team-based organization finds itself in a tight competitive environment in which there is a severe limit to raising wages and salaries at the annual review. Management knows that not doing anything will have an adverse effect on team performance, so it decides to introduce a group bonus or a gain-sharing plan as a motivational tool.

Whether compensation will be used primarily as a reinforcer or as a motivator ultimately relates back to the organization's history, employee expectations, and especially the organization's unique culture and character.

WHAT FORM SHOULD COMPENSATION TAKE?

According to Schuster, four different compensation strategies can be effectively employed in a team environment: pay for knowledge or skill-based pay, gain-sharing, team bonuses, and merit plans. Let's quickly look at the advantages and disadvantages of each.

Pay for Knowledge or Skill-Based Pay

This system rewards employees for the amount of skills and knowledge they possess. Its *advantages* are that employees are motivated to learn more to be compensated at a higher level and the organization ends up with a better skilled and more flexible workforce. *Disadvantages* are that employees are compensated for skills whether or not these skills are used. Compensation costs are generally higher for the employer, and additional costs are entailed for potentially expensive assessment, training, and certification administrative procedure.

Gain-Sharing

Cash bonuses to team members are tied to improvements in productivity, quality, and overall business performance. *Advantages* include rewarding all employees when the organization improves performance. Employees are motivated through common goals. All employees receive the same bonus. *Disadvantages* are that employees who do not deserve it are compensated and the same performance might have been achieved without gain-sharing. Also, the performance measures are not always within the control or influence of employees.

Team Bonuses

Bonuses allow teams to be measured and rewarded for their performance against a set of team objectives. *Advantages* to team bonuses are (1) they provide an opportunity to recognize only those teams that have made improvements; (2) they help build stronger teams, and (3) they need to be paid only when performance is achieved. *Disadvantages* are that there's no way to measure the performance of support teams and bonus measurements may be inequitable across teams. Management may find it difficult to isolate the contribution of a single team. Cross-team efforts may suffer, and team bonuses may place too much emphasis on rewards.

Merit Pay

This scheme compensates employees for their individual performance based on a set of criteria. *Advantages* include rewarding only those individuals who deserve it and motivating employees to perform better. *Disadvantages* are that employees are forced to compete against one another for a fixed pool of money. Also, team members are often uncomfortable in evaluating one another and generally do not want to assume this responsibility, while managers are less effective at evaluating individual performance.

Organizations may also introduce mixed compensation plans combining some or all of these schemes. Gone are the days when management selects one plan and stays with it forever. Today, as organizations become more sophisticated in measuring team performance, it's more likely that mixed plans will be effective and that compensation plans will change to accommodate the evolving needs of the team environment.

HOW CAN YOU BE SURE THAT YOUR COMPENSATION SYSTEM WORKS EFFECTIVELY WITH TEAMS?

Compensation is a complex subject and has been treated in extensive detail in many books and articles. Consequently, the intention in this chapter has not been to present a comprehensive review of compensation issues but to highlight some of the problems that arise because of the unique character of a team environment.

In summary, here are some of the important issues to consider in developing a compensation plan that works effectively with teams.

1. Make sure that your bonus system is rewarding the right behavior.
2. Don't leave teams in the dark. Maintain good communication with them regarding any significant aspects or changes in the compensation plan. Don't oversell a program. Be direct; be honest; be forthright. Give teams enough room to buy into the plan.
3. Avoid making assumptions about what teams want. Get employee input, research the situation; use focus groups whenever possible.
4. Coordinate bonuses with team activities. Make certain that teams will be able to see the effects of their efforts before you install rewards.
5. Facilitate buy in by allowing employees to contribute their thoughts and ideas to the compensation program.
6. Make sure you're taking employee expectations into account.
7. Be certain that you understand the rationale for a particular compensation system. Don't just make decisions based on your own personal preferences.
8. Make sure you have enough mechanisms in place to create the desired gains.

Having a strong compensation plan is no guarantee that it will work effectively. Compensation can be both a great motivator and a great reinforcer of desired performance. But, like most other aspects of teams, to be effective, it must be looked at within the full dimension of the team culture.

11

⑥ KEEPING CROSS-FUNCTIONAL TEAMS ON TRACK

Hierarchy is one means of achieving integration, but it is not the only means; and hierarchy destroys flexibility and almost guarantees that knowledge will not be aligned with authority.

William Passmore

Questions Addressed in This Chapter

- What causes cross-functional teams to falter?
- What are tactics that work?
- How can having a compelling purpose resolve team difficulties?
- Why is building trust critical?
- How can functional managers be supported?
- How can internal problems be arbitrated?
- How can managing process improvement be formally structured?

If you bring together leaders from different sectors of the community to work up a city budget, you quickly learn how tough it can be to reach agreement. Each person brings the values, allegiances, interests, responsibilities, and accountabilities of a particular group, and each feels compelled to take a position loyal to those he or she represents.

Homeowners want additional funding for safer streets and more services. City workers want assurances of continued benefits and a living wage, and city managers are concerned about available revenues. Those representing special interest groups such as hotels, hospitals, and the homeless all push hard for their particular needs. Any conflicts existing among these groups are likely to show up in the meeting room because the meeting is simply a microcosm of the larger community. In such a pressure cooker it's not unusual for emotions to flair and for people to be drawn into adversarial positions.

WHAT CAUSES CROSS-FUNCTIONAL TEAMS TO FALTER?

Cross-functional team members are often pulled in two directions. On one hand, they feel compelled to maintain a strong allegiance to their home team; on the other, they are asked to cooperate with members of their cross-functional team to solve problems that cross functional boundaries.

Cross-functional teams are able to draw on a wider base of skills and knowledge to address problems and work processes that cross many functional boundaries. Each person brings firsthand experience that others don't have, and the synergy that results can produce highly imaginative solutions. Difficulties arise, however, when a decision to support one group appears to require the individual to compromise his or her commitment to another group.

> *In 1987, Boeing advised the Commercial Aviation Division of Honeywell that to be a supplier, it had to install quality circle teams. Honeywell responded. Most of the teams that Honeywell developed were functional quality circle teams, but in 1991, the company realized that to support the work it was doing on the Boeing 777, it would need concurrent engineering teams as well. These were cross-functional teams that drew from personnel in various departments such as quality, engineering, procurement, and design.*
>
> *Honeywell soon faced a sticky problem. The more the members of these cross-functional teams worked together, the stronger their allegiance grew to their own functional concerns. This situation led to conflict, animosity, and resistance during team meetings. Not only did people feel compelled to defend their functions but team members actually saw other team members as being disloyal and untrustworthy if they didn't energetically defend the interests of their own functional areas or teams.*

Unfortunately, many organizations cobble together these teams without preparation, without an infrastructure to support them and without a compelling vision or mission. The seeds of failure and discord are planted even before the team gets rolling, and hundreds of personnel hours are wasted in fruitless activity.

Cross-functional teams are given a separate chapter in this book because the team problems that arise are often unique to this particular team environment. When a cross-functional team is rife with conflict and the team manager is ready to call it quits, it is generally because of one or more of these conditions are prevailing:

- The team reflects the problems that are inherent in the hierarchy of the organization and that make accord difficult.
- Turf battles are not clearly resolved.
- Team members don't trust the team process.
- There is no compelling purpose or objective.
- The organization has established no supporting infrastructure.
- The team doubts the implementation of its efforts.

This chapter will look at strategies for addressing the various issues that are inherent to cross-functional teams.

WHAT ARE TACTICS THAT WORK?

In the article "Work Teams Boost Productivity," J. Schinder notes that when self-directed teams are given responsibility for all functions, the impact on the organization can be very clear and dramatic. Management has to do more than just transfer responsibilities; however, it also must support the teams in ways that draw forth the teams' full powers. Let's look at what form this support might take.

TACTIC 1: IDENTIFY A COMPELLING PURPOSE

Cross-functional teams are frequently formed without being given a shared purpose or mission, that is, one that everyone buys into. With no clear purpose to engage their passions and minds, members can easily believe that it's not worth the effort to work through team issues. They know the organizational barriers are awesome, and they doubt their ability to have any significant impact. This is borne out by the frustrations that team members quickly encounter. Because the teams are cross-functional, they are a microcosm of the larger organization, and the dysfunctions of the organizational hierarchy are likely to be played out on the team level.

It is the exceptional team member who is willing to go back and face his boss with news that he didn't stick up for his department. Consequently, members may find themselves locked into rigid positions and forced to reject out of hand key suggestions that could further the team's interests. When this happens, team members can end up feeling like rats in a cage—running hard on their exercise wheels but getting nowhere fast.

Many Members, One Purpose

Most cross-functional teams meet only once a week, and in the intervening time, people are absorbed by the requirements of their regular duties. The time involved with the team is only a fraction of the time spent with their own functions. If the team's purpose does not affect the members personally, it's going to be difficult to get them to remain enthusiastic during the 37 or so hours a week when they are not meeting together.

The way to approach this problem is not to become embroiled in internecine skirmishings but to define a *common purpose*. The team's purpose must be external to the functional group. It must be seen as of concern of the whole company or organization, and there must be a compelling reason to resolve it. The purpose must be something that all team members really care about and can get behind.

> *Think about the city budget example that began this chapter. If you take the same conflicted civic groups and organize them into an ad hoc action team during a natural disaster such as a flood or earthquake, suddenly individual differences are put aside. People who just one day before may have been at each other's throats are now working together as a team to solve a common problem. Efficiency goes up, communication barriers fall, and the level of trust rises as people focus on shared concerns.*

This same principle is true for organizations. People need a common purpose. Although winning the Malcolm Baldridge Award, launching a Boeing 777, or curing cancer can encourage people to work in harmony, the most compelling purpose is often simply that of meeting customer expectations. Having a larger purpose shifts the team's focus from internal conflicts and places it on a goal in which all parties have a stake. This is exactly the approach that the Commercial Aviation Division of Honeywell followed in resolving the problem described earlier of how to encourage cross-functional team members to cooperate with one another.

> *Honeywell discovered that the way to resolve the issue of conflicting loyalty was to give the teams a new focus—the customer. Instead of placing total emphasis on coming up with the best design or the least expensive*

part, management asked, "What is the goal of the customer? How are we going to give customers what they want?" This became the new rallying point. The shift in focus encouraged team members to let go of their allegiances and to work cooperatively with one another.

Here are some other examples of customer needs that call for a cooperative effort:

The competition has gained a large piece of our professional equipment repairs due to lower costs and faster turnaround.

We have been mandated by management to merge these two warehouse operations.

Six patients have died in the last quarter due in part to missing or late lab reports.

In all these cases, team members are unified by the need to resolve an issue that crosses functional boundaries.

TACTIC 2: BUILD A FOUNDATION OF TRUST

A team environment calls for collaboration and sharing information. When other people's motives are suspect or when one feels constantly at risk, there is a natural impulse to pull back, much to the detriment of the team's overall performance. What creates this lack of trust?

Pressure from the Home Team

When team members have interests they feel compelled to protect, it is often because they have been encouraged by their departmental manager to define their responsibilities in a functional way. It's not uncommon for a manager to say to an employee, "Remember now, whenever there's an issue, don't be afraid to stand up for our group. Make sure you represent us well." Managers who burden their employees this way reinforce functional allegiances and discourage people from working collaboratively with other cross-functional team members. Over time, those on the team begin to cast each other in adversarial relationships.

To reverse this mindset, managers of cross-functional teams must start by defining and clarifying the purpose of the team and must do what they can to encourage buy in from all parties. Then, instead of looking at what department each team member comes from, they must encourage people to ask what distinctive resources each can offer. "Who are we as a group? What are our individual strengths?" Once team members have inventoried the resources they bring to the table as a group, they can better understand how to build the synergy of the team.

Turf Battles

Trust may also break down over turf responsibilities because in crossing functions, boundaries are often left unclear. Fuzzy boundaries lead to confusion and resentment when people perceive others as treading on their territory. As a result, people argue, bicker, and maneuver for position as they look to protect their interests.

> *A cross-functional sales and service account team was set up to improve the way order taking and the selling and delivery of services were carried out. The team included not only local and national sales managers but also tactical and strategic service representatives. The cross-functional team assignments left considerable gray area as to who was responsible for what.*
>
> *For example, local sales managers became involved not just with sales to local outlets, but also with the national strategy for the account. They also became involved in how to position and price service interventions. These areas had previously been the sole responsibility of the various other managers on the team, and the changing involvement led to competition, jealousy, and conflict.*

Interpersonal Problems

Trust can be broken down easily when team members are inept at supporting one another on a personal level. Subtle put-downs, open competition, intolerance of others' ideas, and personal criticism cause people to adopt a defensive posture that makes cooperation difficult.

How can a team build a supportive climate in which people are more willing to put themselves at risk? Here are five basic principles that are the cornerstone of any infrastructure.

Five Basic Principles That Lead to Trust

As a team manager or leader, you are in an excellent position to model behavior that fosters trust. In particular, following these basic principles in your dealings with team members will help to empower the individual and create a climate in which team members are willing to be mutually supportive.

Basic Principle 1: Focus on the Process, Issue, Behavior, or Problem, Not on the Person

Cross-functional teams call for considerable risk taking: the environment is new; the problems are unfamiliar; team members are being asked to venture into uncharted territory; and consequences are often unforeseen. Furthermore, team members usually spend only a short time together each week, so it can be difficult to develop the easy familiarity they have with their own departmental co-workers.

The team environment itself adds unique pressures, presenting opportunities for misunderstanding and discord that are not as likely to show up in a traditional work environment. Some of the special opportunities for stress include the following:

- Employees must rely on other team members in situations in which they would normally act alone.

- Lines of authority are blurry because roles are redefined as the team moves along.

- People work toward multiple goals.

- It's more difficult to measure success because it takes place gradually and in small steps.

- Many people, rather than just a few, have to buy in and support the team's solutions for the project to be implemented or the process changed.

People can easily get caught up in the fear of looking bad as they tackle problems foreign to them. During vulnerable moments, criticism can be deflating if it is not properly presented and it can easily strike a blow to self-esteem. Usually, it's not the criticism *per se* that does the damage; it's that the criticism has been made personal.

People are much more likely to be receptive to negative feedback if it is kept objective; that is, if it's directed at the issue, process, behavior, or problem but not at them directly. If team members discover they will not be judged, they are encouraged to take more chances, volunteer for new projects, and speak out whenever they feel the need. If something doesn't work out as planned, they learn there is no penalty. The situation simply becomes a team issue, something to be studied and corrected. The best indicator that team members are beginning to feel safe within the group is the absence of finger pointing and defensiveness. Instead, people stay clear and objective about the problems at hand.

Basic Principle 2: Maintain the Self-Confidence and Self-Esteem of Others

Self-confidence and self-esteem emerge when team members are willing to do more than they thought they could, when they operate outside their comfort zone, take chances, and discover that they have resources they didn't know they possessed. A manager or team leader can help promote this feeling by shaping people's experiences in a positive way.

One way to do this is by acknowledging the difficulty of certain tasks and recognizing people when they are successful. Ideally, we would all be the best reinforcers of our own behavior. Some people have this measure of independence. They are the best arbiters of their own performance and can operate with little reinforcement from others. More typical are the people who shape their self-perception in part by how others see them. Even the most stalwart individual can get a boost when others acknowledge his or her accomplishments.

The biggest killer of self-esteem and self-confidence is failure or, more specifically, what is *perceived* as failure. People can be quick to judge themselves when things don't work out as planned. In such cases, you can help keep the situation objective and emotionally neutral by acknowledging the person's effort and casting the negative results as simply useful feedback for the individual.

Another way to build the team's self-esteem is to share what was formerly management-only information. This is especially true in times of change. When the team realizes that information is not limited to the usual communication channels of newsletters, official briefings, and scuttlebutt, members will be inclined to walk a little straighter, especially if they are invited to add their voice in higher-level decision making. You also need to allow the team to implement changes, not just make recommendations.

Finally, those who lead can help to build self-esteem in team members by not positioning themselves above the team but by inviting the members to collaborate on setting ground rules, deciding guidelines, developing daily communication procedures, and the like. This fosters the feeling that everyone is empowered to make a personal contribution.

Basic Principle 3: Maintain Constructive Relationships

For the team to function effectively *as* a team, individual members must be willing to reach out and trust one another. There is less likelihood of this happening on a cross-functional team because people's involvement with their own functions usually limits the time they can spend together.

In addition, many members may be used to communicating only through managers and supervisors and may be unfamiliar with how to construct effective working relationships.

As a leader there are things you can do to promote strong intra-team relationships. For example, there may be a team member who volunteers to take on specific responsibilities for the team and is then unable to fulfill them. Perhaps he or she even fails to attend some meetings because of an undue work load outside the team. Whatever the reason, relationships are often at risk over broken commitments.

If other team members are becoming disgruntled, you can find out whether the individual needs assistance and, if there are difficulties, try to help resolve them. At the very least, you can share the problem with other team members and enlist their support. Some people are not very good at being their own advocates. You can help them keep communication channels open.

The diversity of opinion present on a cross-functional team can also cause a person to ask, "Why do I have to work with these people, anyway. I just don't see the purpose." You can help the team see that this diversity is precisely its main strength and that encouraging diversity rather than resisting it can lead to better ideas and solutions.

Basic Principle 4: Take Initiative to Make Things Better

Think how good you feel when your mechanic does a few extra maintenance checks on your car even though you hadn't been experiencing any noticeable squeaks or thumps. You feel that the mechanic is really looking out for you. People who do their jobs conscientiously are constantly looking for ways to make things better. Their philosophy can be summed up in a novel twist to an old adage: "If it ain't broke, it still may need fixin.'"

Every job can be improved, if only in small ways. If each person believes that others are constantly looking for ways to improve and support the team, people will build a belief that members are taking care of one another. They'll believe that people are not just going through the motions and doing what they have to do, but that they've made the team's success a priority. Their actions say they are *personally* involved.

Such involved individuals will often go out of their way to tackle the grungy jobs, like getting process definitions put into the computer program. Or they might give up some of their own power to begin the necessary changes to the process. Acknowledging people who take those extra steps is a good way to reinforce such behavior and make it a priority.

Basic Principle 5: Lead by Example

Keshavan Nair, author of *A Higher Standard of Leadership: Lessons from the Life of Ghandi,* observes that "we lose respect for our leaders if we do not approve of their conduct—public or private. Leaders who do not command our respect reduce the legitimacy of their leadership and lose our trust."

How true. "Do as I say, not as I do" doesn't work in raising children, and it's no more effective in leading or managing a team. In fact, one can point to this attitude as one of the leading reasons that organizational changes fail.

Like it or not, managers and leaders at all organizational levels set the tone for the team. Team members will take their cues for what's important and how to behave based upon what others do, especially others in more senior positions. If you show by your actions that you're committed to the team, team members will be motivated to match your commitment. If you treat people fairly and with understanding, if you focus on team performance without judging, team members will be encouraged to follow your lead. If you trust them by admitting your mistakes, even if you risk looking bad, they'll be more likely to do that with one another. If you trust the team with information and allow members leeway in making decisions, they'll be more inclined not to squirrel away important information but to share what they know with other team members. Similarly, if you do a first-rate job in building trusting relationships, you'll see the results in team members who feel it's okay to be loyal to the team.

All this takes time. Depending on people's nature and what's going on within the team or organization, some people may need a while to come around, but ultimately persistence pays off. Teaching by role modeling is not the easiest way to lead—you have to be genuine and willing to step outside your comfort zone—but it is always effective.

TACTIC 3: GET THE FUNCTIONAL MANAGERS ON BOARD

Often overlooked in the chemistry of a successful cross-functional team is the indirect role that functional managers play. Their attitude toward team members will have an impact on the team's overall performance. If each team member's boss feels good about the team and openly supports an employee's participation, you'll have a more enthusiastic and empowered team member. However, if you keep these managers in the dark, if they feel that they've given up control, and/or if they resent the time lost by an employee's participation, you're going to feel those effects instead.

For this reason, it's a good idea to get managers to buy into the purpose and direction of the cross-functional team before you get started. This is more likely to happen if they understand that a cross-functional team is a stepchild of the hierarchy and that, being a stepchild, it is fragile and needs their support.

Encourage Employees to Work with Their Managers on Cross-Functional Commitments

Releasing an employee to work on a cross-functional team may help provide solutions for the organization as a whole, but it will not necessarily have immediate payoffs for the individual's own department. Consequently, managers can easily resent having to give up hours or days of employee time without anything coming back.

If a manager is unwilling to buy in, the employee may want to negotiate the amount of time allotted for cross-functional activities. The manager may not cover all the time asked for, but by being reassured that the employee's work won't suffer, the manager may end up covering some of the time the employee spent on cross-functional work. The employee can then choose to donate personal time to cover the balance.

Give Functional Managers a Sense of Control

When cross-functional teams are being set up, managers often believe that control is slipping through their fingers, that employees are being recruited right out from under them. This can be a real concern because decisions emerging from the cross-functional team may have a direct impact on how managers run their departments.

Executives putting together a cross-functional team are well advised to meet personally with each manager and allow the manager to choose who will be on the team. Having some control gives managers a greater sense of participation than when their people are drafted without their say. During the meeting, managers have an opportunity to express their concerns and apprehensions. They may have issues about the team. Even if they have little control over which of their people will participate, at least they feel they've had a chance to be heard.

If you pay attention to the functional managers, get their buy-in to the issue, and allow them to shape the scope and boundaries, the issues previously discussed are less likely to haunt the team and restrict its impact.

Help the Functional Manager Deal with Resentment

One of the by-products of teams is that they breed jealousy and resentment. People who aren't chosen can end up critical of those who are. If you were to put these feelings into words, they might sound something like this:

> *"Great for you. You were chosen for the team, so you get the new training. You get the new technology. You even get to go on a site visit or two while I'm stuck in this cubicle. Not only that, I'm sitting here unable to finish my project assignment because you went traipsing off to do your team thing without giving me your part of the project."*

The functional manager who thinks that he or she has to personally square John's participation on the team with the other employees may be acting in an overly paternalistic way. This posture may be appropriate for new teams, but with more mature teams, it can be inhibiting. In these cases, it is more appropriate for John himself to clarify his expectations and responsibilities to the team. After all, he knows his own motivations better than anyone. Perhaps he has interests and skills the others don't recognize that better qualify him. By allowing team members a larger degree of independence, the manager is fostering a mindset that supports a team culture.

Encourage Team Members to Report to their Functional Manager Only What Is Necessary

Bosses can be pretty controlling in their effort to learn what's going on with the cross-functional team—and with good reason. Decisions made by the team often have an impact on the functional manager's job. Consequently, concerned bosses may expect a report from their employees after each meeting.

They'll want to know who's getting along with whom. How is the group functioning? What's standing in the way of the group getting better? They'll want to hear all the dirt. Sometimes, the more dirt the team member gives up about the team, the more the boss feels the team member is continuing to be loyal to the department or to the function. Cross-functional teams are much more productive, however, if important issues can be kept inside the team. This can put the employee in something of a bind. What *do* employees do when they are starting to trust the team but still have to answer to their own functional areas?

Teams often build in a communication plan covering how and what each member will tell his or her department or team. Don't expect these guidelines to be followed religiously. The information that team members pass along will be also be regulated by the kind of relationship they have with their boss as well as their fears, personality, and ideas about how protective they feel they have to be.

A useful guideline is to encourage team members to report back only when they need help or clarification but not to feel bound to give status updates while they're still testing the water with their ideas and working out loyalty issues. After team members experience some progress with the team, the amount of information they share will become less an issue. They'll begin to feel proud of their team experiences and will automatically be more willing to protect the team.

In general, rather than offering specific direction, managers are better off simply sharing observations about what is likely to happen if certain things are done or not done. It should be left to team members to figure out what their course of action will be.

Encourage Functional Managers to Let Employees Determine Their Own Multiteam Participation

In a mature team environment, employees often end up on more than one cross-functional team. Most managers keep tabs on this by having some sort of chart that says, "Mary is on this team, John is on that one, and Harry is on this one." This allows the manager to confirm that Mary isn't on more teams than she can handle. If the manager is concerned about how Mary manages her time, the manager may restrict the time she spends on cross-functional activities.

Functional managers are often quick to hit the panic button when people in their departments ask to participate on multiple teams, especially when managers believe they are losing too much employee time o r feel that they're operating with too small a staff. "How can we meet our goals if I have people working a fifth of their time outside the department?" the manager questions, "Sure, I care about the company goals. Sure I care about solving this customer's problem. But I have fewer employee hours to work with, and I'm still held accountable for my department."

In reality, Mary may be perfectly able to be on more than one team and still handle all her functional tasks successfully. The manager doesn't realize this, however, so Mary gets pulled back. When this happens, the organization is likely to say, "Okay, we won't take any more people from Mary's level. We'll take them from the manager's level because the manager seems able to balance this job better." This creates other problems because the manager doesn't know the ins and outs as well as the employee who is actually doing the work.

It is generally more effective if the manager passes the responsibility back to the employee. He's treating Mary as an adult by letting her decide whether she has the time to be on a team and then allowing her to negotiate her degree of involvement with the cross-functional team itself. Given this freedom, Mary is more encouraged to act in a responsible way.

TACTIC 4: PROVIDE A WAY TO ARBITRATE INTERNAL PROBLEMS

Suppose the team has no compelling purpose. Suppose the team doesn't have a clear vision to rally behind, or, as is often the case, it doesn't have a clear understanding of the customer's needs. In this case you have to give team members enough information to link their activities to organizational goals. You also need to give them an outlet for working through their issues by setting up an infrastructure to resolve internal problems and set out new roles and responsibilities.

> Consider a cross-functional team in the regional office of an elevator company. The salespeople want to sell a custom elevator because the model differentiates their company from the competitors. The custom elevator is also higher priced, so they get a higher commission and an impressive local reference in their sales territory.
>
> On the other hand, the service people aren't eager for custom elevators to be sold, because (1) they have to deal with the plant to make sure that the specifications are right (they often aren't) and (2) they're expected to install the elevator in the same time frame as a standard elevator (they usually can't). Because any added installation time is not built into the overall price of the elevator, the service people do not end up looking as good. Also, because a custom elevator is harder to maintain, there are more callbacks that can reflect badly on service. Consequently, the service representatives are less likely to support the sales activities and to meet the commitments made by the salespeople

Many organizations bring a team together without realizing that it needs basic survival skills and someplace to turn when it gets into trouble. In situations like this one, either the team itself must find a way to arbitrate or an internal arbitrator will be needed to help resolve the impasse. This arbitrator could take the form of a cross-functional team made up of managers who can consider the issues from a broader perspective. There might also be facilitators who have an understanding of both areas and who are able to work out win-win solutions.

TACTIC 5: FOLLOW AN ORGANIZED APPROACH

There are various ways to build cross-functional teams that work. One unique approach, called *strategic process management (SPM),* results in effective cross-functional process improvement teams with fewer problems of the type discussed here.

A strategic process is one of a handful of large-scale, critical processes that are fundamental to the competitive stance and survival of an organization. Taken together, these processes define what an organization does, and they are almost always cross-functional. A generic list includes these:

- Designing and developing new products and/or services.
- Producing products.
- Generating leads and making sales.
- Receiving and fulfilling orders.
- Billing and collecting money.
- Providing service and support.

SPM creates a cascading infrastructure that builds a series of interrelated teams from executives to front-line workers. Some teams are formed specifically to handle process management issues. Others such as management teams or department teams, may already exist. These teams take on process management responsibilities in addition to their regular duties.

There are three parts to the infrastructure: an executive team, strategic teams, and spin-off teams.

The *executive team* is almost always composed of top management. The executive team determines (1) what the strategic processes are in the organization, (2) which one(s) are the first priority for change, (3) what the priority issue is for the process(es) selected, (4) which

Strategic Process Management Team Structure

```
┌─────────────────────────┐
│     Executive team      │
│          ┌──────────────┴──────────────────────┐
└──────────┤──────────►   Strategic team         │
           │              ┌──────────────────────┴──────────────────┐
           └──────────────┤──────────►   Spin-off teams             │
                          └──────────────────────────────────────────┘
```

functional groups make up a particular process, and (5) who should be on the strategic team.

Once established, the *strategic team* clarifies the issue and turns it into a specific objective. Then the team prepares a broad, low-detail map of the entire process, creates long-term measures to track progress toward the objective, and analyzes the overall process to find the vital few areas where change will lead to the greatest gains. Finally, spin-off teams are launched to tackle each of these hot spots.

The *spin-off teams* work on developing specific ways to improve their subprocess. Once they develop improvements and modifications, they take their recommendations to the strategic team for review and sign-off. Depending on the size and scale of the change, their recommendations may have to be approved by the senior management team as well. Once approved, the change will be implemented on a full scale and established as a standard procedure.

With the knowledge and control that SPM gives organizations, teams can begin making major improvements, confident that their problem-solving efforts will achieve the intended results. In addition, instead of rushing in and problem solving or starting major innovations before they truly understand the process, organizations can make more knowledgeable decisions about where to focus change, whether or not to undertake sweeping changes (in the case of reengineering), and how best to proceed.

Today, cross-functional teams are increasingly employed as an effective tool for making organizations more functional and competitive. Bringing together people from different functions offers a fertile environment in which creative solutions can be readily formulated and developed. But, managers and executives should never lose sight that this unique team environment is a hybrid. Like a delicate orchid, it has its own singular set of problems that need to be addressed.

PUTTING IT ALL TOGETHER

12

(6) **PROFILE OF A
SUCCESSFUL TEAM
ROLLOUT**

*The question that remains is whether businesses can make the needed
fundamental changes on an organizational-wide basis. . . .We believe that
the outline of a New American approach to management is being defined
by companies that are users of employee involvement and total quality
management practices . . . [and that this] can play a major role in helping
firms be winners.*

Edward E. Lawler III

As with any complex operation, from swinging a golf club to managing
a team environment, it helps to be able to picture what it looks like when
everything comes together. Consequently, we thought it would be useful
to profile the management style of an executive who has successfully
instituted a team environment in his or her organization.

Bill Johnson is the plant manager of the Distribution Systems
Division of ABB Power T&D in Florence, South Carolina, a leading
manufacturer of low- and medium-power voltage circuit breakers.
Johnson is not your typical executive. For one thing, he has been on a
fast career track. At 28 he was quality assurance manager of the
Switchgear Systems Division of ABB Power Distribution in Sanford,
Florida (now ABB Power T&D). At 29 he was operations manager of
the same division. At 30 he became plant manager of the company's
power circuit breaker manufacturing facility in Florence, replacing the
general manager's position. Johnson's résumé is also unusual in the
wealth of management experience he acquired early on as an officer on a
nuclear submarine and in his various positions with ABB Power T&D.

On first encounter, Johnson is disarmingly boyish. His roundish
face is accented by a thin mustache, and his somewhat stout, 5'9" frame
might encourage you to cast him as the manager of the football team or

the new hire in the marketing department. But, behind the boyish charm is a quick, native intelligence tempered by a compassionate disposition and a powerful, intuitive grasp of human nature. You sense that Johnson could read you the riot act and still remain the kind of person you'd like to go out with after hours to bowl a couple of frames and grab a beer or two. A natural athlete, he was captain of his high school football team and throughout his schooling assumed a variety of leadership positions.

Johnson earned a B.S. in ceramic engineering from Alfred University and then went through the Navy's nuclear engineering school, a particularly rigorous program for which only 1 percent of all applicants qualify. Following this, he earned an M.B.A. from Rollins College. He is committed to the doctrine of empowering others and does so assertively, with a clear sense of his own role and responsibilities.

By presenting this interview, we are not suggesting that Johnson's approach is a precise model for how one *should* manage in a team environment. Obviously, his management style reflects his own unique persona. Furthermore, this interview should not be read simply as a profile of a successful individual but of a successful team rollout as seen through the eyes of the top executive. The interview provides you with a sense of the complexity of teams and the diversity of problems that any manager or executive is likely to encounter. It also points to the kind of mindset and management skills that are effective in motivating and sustaining teams.

INTERVIEW WITH BILL JOHNSON, ABB POWER T & D

The interviewer's questions and comments are in italics. All other comments are those of Bill Johnson.

Where was the company initially?

We had a very serious situation. This facility had lost a significant amount of money over the last five to seven years—very negative numbers. They'd brought in a couple of people to turn the organization around, but it wasn't happening. I was fortunate in that I was the quality manager for the Switchgear Division before I was the operations manager in Florida, so one of the things that I got to do was to come up a couple of different times and audit the entire system. That gave me an idea of where the holes were.

How did the previous managers try to turn it around?

They had eight-hour staff meetings and tried to muscle through their improvements, plus they paid some consultant thousands of dollars to come in, but overall, they didn't have much success. [Figures detailing the extent of the dramatic turnaround that has taken place since Johnson took over the helm and introduced teams are presented at the end of this interview.]

What was your first day like?

I'll tell you I was a bit nervous. I was 30 years old and walking in to be in charge of a $25 million operation. All these people were looking at me. Business had been real bad. We had just eliminated the general manager and the operations manager's position, changed our entire staff, and everyone was thinking, "What's going to happen now, and who the hell is this young guy?" So I stood up there in front of everybody, and the first thing out of my mouth is, "All I got to say is—there'll be no more short, fat jokes." Everybody cracked up, and it really broke the ice. At that point I said, "My name is Bill Johnson. I met some of you before, and here's what we're going to do."

At any rate, management consolidated the Florida facility and this facility into one unit and put me in here and called me the site manager. I have all the functions—marketing, QA, HR, engineering, manufacturing, and so on—and I report to the general manager in Florida.

You're in quite a responsible position for someone who just recently turned 31. Where did you get your experience?

I went to Alfred University, where I got my B.S. in ceramic engineering, and while I was there I enlisted in the N.U.P.O.C. program, which is the Nuclear Propulsion Officer Candidate Program. After attaining my B.S., I spent five years on nuclear submarines.

That must have been quite a learning experience.

Oh, yeah. You learn a lot of things on a submarine. Imagine coming on board, you're only 22, and all of a sudden you're in charge of a guy who's probably in his 40s. He has 20 years' experience. He knows his job. He's been doing it a long time—almost as long as you've been alive—and you're now his boss. You have to figure out very quickly how you're going to be of value and a service to *him,* even though you're his superior. Same with the other chiefs on the sub. They really don't need you. You're an officer, but to them you're just part of the hierarchical structure, even though you're a nuclear engineer.

What you have to figure out is how do you talk to those people? How do you listen? And how do you react to what they're telling you? You found out very quickly that the successful officers were the ones who could listen to what these chiefs had to say and find ways to take some of their work load away. In most cases it was their paperwork. Coming out of college, you were very good in doing paperwork, and they just didn't like doing it. On the other hand, you'll need to get this guy to teach you what he knows because the next guy coming in is going to be a junior chief, and you as the senior officer are going to have to teach him.

You certainly were in an ideal position to learn a lot about people.

No question, when you're in a black tube for three months with 150 men, you learn a whole lot about psychology whether you want to or not. You learn about how people get motivated. You have to learn to care for people because you're in a life-or-death situation. I was in a couple of floodings and a couple of fires. I saw a couple of people get killed. Those are all things that shape you as a person.

It certainly introduced me to a whole set of managerial skills that other kids right out of college are seldom exposed to. They come into a company, they're junior engineers, they work their way up, so they're always the youngest and least experienced person.

One thing I learned that I apply here is that you need to touch people's spirits. It's an opportunity to take that human being and really make them into a person who, when he comes home, his spouse says, "Wow, what happened to *you* at work?" And he says, "You won't *believe* what we're doing today." That's when people are alive. Those are the joys in this position you look for because if you get caught up in the other stuff, it's going to be a long day.

You've been here only two years, but you appear to have established a team environment that's not only delivering the numbers but having a powerful impact on those who work here. What were some of the things you first noticed when you took over the job?

The first and most obvious thing was the lack of trust. That's an ingredient that a lot of managers don't recognize is lacking when they say,

"We're going to do self-directed work teams." I mean, you're asking a lot of people to open up their hearts and minds, and if you don't have some sort of infrastructure or some idea of how you are going to support that trust, these people all of a sudden will be saying, "I went 50 percent, and you didn't even come halfway."

You're saying that the manager or executive needs to take the first step?

That's right. Remember, you're the one they watch, so you have to pay attention because whatever you do will have an impact on them. If I'm dealing with a problem and I'm on the floor and people ask me how I am, I always say "terrific," no matter how I feel. You have to do this, otherwise people start reading all kinds of false messages into how you present yourself. You also have to be very careful in the kinds of questions you ask because people will be quick to read things into your questions that aren't there. If I *do* have a problem that concerns them directly, I always break it to the team and not to any single individual.

What were some of the first things you did when you took over this job?

The first thing I did when I came into this office, I had a stack of manager's reports sitting in the corner of my desk, all having to do with how people were performing. So I called the entire staff into my office. They all crowded in, and I took this garbage can with a shredder on top, and put it in the middle of the room, and I asked, "Which one of you gave me this report?" One of them said, "I did." So I said, "I don't need that any more," and fed it into the shredder which dropped it in the can. We went through the whole stack of reports, and finally I had one little piece of paper. I held it up and said, "Whoever gave me this piece of paper, this is what I need. But I don't need it every day. I only need it once a month. Now the rest of you go out and do something that adds value to the organization and stop worrying about telling me what you're doing."

By the way, my strategy fits on one Excel spreadsheet that says "these are the goals and this is what we want to do."

So you eliminated the middle management layer. This must have changed the climate dramatically.

Oh, it did. There was a time when if a person went to HR to complain, they'd get back to their machine, and one of the supervisors would be in their face saying, "We have a problem between you and me. You obviously have an attitude problem," which eventually led to, "I'm going to make your life miserable, and it's just a matter of time before you have to go."

We found out who those people were and confronted them and asked them to leave. Then I assembled the entire workforce together and said, "As far as I'm concerned, I'm looking at the replacement for those people. Today is day one of your new lives. This is what you've asked for for 15 years. Now you've got it. So let's get on with it." People felt like the shackles were lifted. They could talk. They could tell you what the problems were, and it's been positive ever since.

What else did you do in those first weeks?

In the managers meeting I alluded to a minute ago, I also told my staff that "by the end of the year I think there will be about half as many as you, because I can't manage this many people and do it effectively. I don't know who you are. I don't know which ones will be left. I'm just telling you, this is probably what's going to happen." There were 13 managers on staff when I got here, and by the end of the year I had 6.

Didn't that put a damper on things?

Not really. It's a funny thing about responsibility. There are a lot of people who don't want it, so rather than standing there and taking it on, they'll just leave. We've had more people leave than we've had to let go. It's amazing what happens when people realize they're going to be held accountable. We've had more people just say, "This isn't for me. You guys are working too hard, and you're expecting too much."

If you were to guess, what percentage of people in an organization are cut out to be on a team?

I'd say initially, before any training, about 30 percent.

How would you characterize those who are suited for teams?

One way I'd characterize them is that they respond to a vision. Martin Luther King didn't say, "I have a strategic plan." He said, "I have a vision." If you don't have people with vision, it's very difficult to implement teams because teams are a very long-range thing.

Does that apply to all teams?

Well, perhaps not all. You tell a project team, "Come up with this cost reduction idea, get it done, and you've got three weeks." Then they do it, resolve it and it's done. You don't need much vision there because it's all spelled out. But self-directed teams are a much longer-range proposition. You can't expect the average worker to understand what the process is all about and really buy into it without some sort of vision or help because it takes them a while to understand it.

One thing I should mention is that you can't just talk vision; you also have to translate it into their terms. Keep in mind there are a lot of people who have been doing the same things the same way for 15 years. If you want them to buy into the change, you've got to let them know how it's going to affect their lives and their security, *and* you have to do it in terms they understand.

You can't say, "If you guys reduce this cost, the return on investment for the company is going to be 12 percent. Isn't that great?" They'll look at you like you just spoke in gibberish. So you say, "That means that next July we'll be able to give everybody 4 percent raises instead of 3 percent." "Oh," they'll say, "we can do that." Or you say, "We're not going to have to lay off 20 people if we can get the numbers." They can relate to that.

How do you go about preparing people who are fairly unsophisticated to have a level of understanding about the business?

We have plant meetings once a month, and I also have weekly round-table meetings with all employees. In talking concepts, I try to use a lot of word pictures. For example, if I'm explaining inventory to people—I don't care whether it's a manager or a guy on the floor—I say something like, "You just got your paycheck. And your paycheck is $500. Now you go to the grocery store, and you know you need toilet paper, so you buy $500 worth. And you bring all that home, and you got a whole bathroom full of toilet paper. Now, does that make sense to you?" "Well, no," they say. "Then," I answer, "why would we do it at work and buy $500 worth of screws when we only need $2 worth?"

I'll do the same kind of thing with cash flow: "You just spent $500 on toilet paper," I tell them. "So how much cash do you have left over to buy groceries? You say there's nothing left? Then you can't buy groceries, correct? Well, guess what. If we spend all our money on inventory, we don't have a whole lot of cash left over to pay your salary. That's what cash flow is all about." Now the concept is not so foreign to them.

You can explain an income statement and balance sheet by comparing it to your checkbook and savings account. I might say something like, "You guys transfer money to your savings and checking accounts, right? Well, we do the same thing. We take money out of the balance sheet and put it into our income statement. Now when you take money out of savings, that's bad because it doesn't leave you very much. Right? Well, at times that's not very good for a company either."

It's amazing how many people, even those who call themselves professional people, have no clue to how a business is run and what it really takes. What's a line of credit? A lot of them can't answer things like that. So every week I have a staff meeting, and we talk about the P&L statement. We may talk about the same thing 10 different times. Until everybody gets a real good understanding, it's important to talk about it, and if they're bored, so be it.

Do you present the information yourself?

It depends. I do some of it, and sometimes it's done by a plant accountant we have here.

What are your staff meetings like? How would you characterize them?

Our staff meetings aren't the free-for-alls that a lot of staff meetings are. We always start out by asking everybody to say something positive about what's happened to them individually or to the team during the week. So somebody might say, "Well, John did a good job in helping me out with this last purchase order." And I'll write that down. We'll go around the table like that. Then I'll come back to my office and take a little card, and in response to what John did, I'll write on it, "I really appreciate your helping Jill out this week with the purchase order. Keep up the good work." And I'll sign it "Bill" and have it delivered over to John in assembly.

It took people in the plant six months to figure out how I knew all this stuff. At first everyone thought I was kind of goofy. "This is really corny," they'd say. But after a while they could see that it made people feel good, and it helped start to change the culture toward "let's look at all the good things." I wanted my staff to understand that there are more good things going on than bad things. Sure, the bad things require our attention, but in order to approach those bad things with the proper attitude and the proper problem-solving approach, people need to be thinking positively. So let's look first at all the good things we're doing.

I'll bet that 90 percent of the executives in other companies don't think about creating this kind of a positive climate. Do you think it's because they don't know how to do it or that they don't think of doing it?

Either. Or both. When I was in the Navy, one of the things I saw was all these young sailors, and nobody kept them informed. They were just expected to be mindless robots doing the same jobs over and over.

The other interesting thing was that nobody told their wives anything. You had these women at home, and they had absolutely no clue what their husbands did all day. They had no clue when the ship was leaving. They had no clue who the officers on the ship were and what was going on. So one of the things I did when I went to work in Florida was to send a letter to all of my staff's spouses. I just said, "Hey, Mary, I just wanted to write this letter about John. John does a great job as the manager in fabrication, and I really appreciate all the time you give him to spend at the plant. I know I ask a lot of him, but I think his career is important. I think that if he continues his education, I expect him to be the plant manager some day. So once again I just want to say 'thanks' for all your support," and I sent a box of chocolates with it or flowers or something. I've had husbands come in and say, "Man, I can go to school now and my wife's not hassling me about it any more."

I've also gotten letters back from the wives. There was one manager I had to send out of town for a couple of weeks, so I had a bouquet of flowers delivered to his wife with a note that said, "I know I took him away from you for a long time, but it was important." A couple of days later I got a note back from his wife that said, "I really appreciate it. I was having a bridge club meeting that day, and the flowers just looked beautiful on the table. Many thanks."

I guess the moral of the story is that managers don't realize there's a whole family behind the person who works for them that has to be supported. That's how you get your superheroes; you motivate the entire person, but you can't do that if you don't motivate the family. When you finally realize that, it's like pouring octane into people's tanks. Most managers just ignore it because it's too controversial or too sensitive or too intimate, but I don't think so. I think people appreciate it.

I can see this working well in a facility of 138 people like this. But how can you be this personal in a larger facility?

You can't, not in the same way. That's why you have to develop your staff. You should be able to project these same values to the people under you, and then they should be able to translate that to the people under them.

But in addition to that, you still want to develop some sort of intimate relationships with the next level below them. The wonderful thing about direct reports and staff reports is that you always hear just their side of it. But there are always a whole lot of different sides to the argument. If you have personal relationships at the next lower level, you can get feedback from other directions.

Suppose you sense that people don't want to be in teams?

I'm sure some day I'm going to go into a facility and want to introduce teams, and somebody is going to say, "You just can't do it with this group." Then you have to ask yourself, "Do I really want to be here?" I don't care if you're the boss or who you are. If the people don't want teams, you might as well forget it.

Do you get any static from people who hope you don't succeed because if you did, it might pose a threat to them?

It happens, and it really underscores the need to fight for the teams. There are three groups of people you have to manage. The first is your boss, the second is your direct reports, and the third is your peers. Out of all of these the most important are your peers. Your direct reports will do pretty much what you want them to do, but your peers have the same direct access to your boss. They're really the people who make or break your career because they have the power to stonewall you or make some of your projects not successful.

What do you do if your peers give you a hard time?

You're always going to have your critics. You just can't let them get to you. I think you simply have to ignore their criticism and say, "Listen, these are the results I'm getting." You've got to know and believe in yourself and believe in the values and in the culture you're creating.

What kind of response do you get from your management?

By and large, I think they're cautious about teams. A lot of time they don't understand how you can get this level of commitment from people.

Admittedly, it is a major paradigm shift for executives who have spent their corporate lives in a traditional hierarchical setting. It's like asking them to change their religion.

True. That's why I still have to live and die by the results, so heaven help me if the results turn soft. But I have enough faith in these people that they won't let us down.

It always seems to get back to trust, doesn't it? In this case, you have to trust in the process and in your employees.

Sure. I risk my career on it every day. But in many ways I consider it a safe bet because I'd much rather bet my career on 138 people than on the abilities of just one person, namely, myself. I'll guarantee I'm going to make more mistakes than 138 people collectively because I make hundreds of decisions a week. If I'm right on only 90 percent of them, I'm still going to make a lot of mistakes, so to minimize that number, I give everybody access to the information so everybody has the power to make sound business decisions. Of course, whether they choose to grasp that power is up to them.

Information is something that a lot of managers like to keep to themselves.

That's why they have all the power. But getting the employee to take on that power is a personal decision that each and every person has to make. I can't make somebody reach for it. I can simply make the information available to them.

In general, how do people respond to this opportunity?

I'd say probably 70 percent of the people grab the information. The other 30 percent just want to be good faithful soldiers. They don't want to be the platoon leader. They don't want to be the general of the army. They just want to come to work and feel good about it and draw a paycheck.

They'll do whatever you ask them to do. You have to have those kinds of people. The trick is figuring out which ones are which because it's real easy to get fooled. We've been fooled a lot of times.

I have a belief that if you allow people to do what you expect them to, they'll fulfill everything you asked them to do and more. Those that do become the leaders. But you've got to look at all the signs. You've got to watch the body language and the way they interact. You have to eat lunch with them, you have to spend time with them. You've got to get to understand them because we all communicate in very different ways. Some people can't put a sentence together to tell you what they want. You have to be able to figure it out from their actions.

We have this young kid who's maybe 26 years old. He took over the job of team leader three or four months ago. He's been just an absolute surprise. A dark horse. I think it's because he didn't have any preconceived notion of how it's supposed to be done. He just does it. You have to find those people and allow them to be successful. And you never want to lower your expectations. People tend to jump for that bar, so you always have to keep your expectations high.

You make a good point, and that is, you need to be a good observer.

Right, which means spending a lot of time on the floor. I'm on the floor all the time. I guess less than a week after I got here I knew everybody's name in this facility, and that was important to people.

I can see where that would have a big impact on people. It's really symbolic. What other kinds of symbolic things do you do?

One thing I like to do, we might have an executive VP or somebody visiting in here, and of course, everybody wants a shop tour. I'll say, "Listen, Thomas, this is Mr. Executive VP." I always put the employee first who's adding value. Then I get out of the way. I don't stand there and say, "Well, he does this and this and this." I move aside and let Thomas do the talking. So Thomas gets a chance to showcase his area. People end up being really proud of their area and what they do.

Is it a different problem motivating salaried people?

There *are* key differences. We've been putting in salaried teams over the last three months to support the work teams on the floor. The problem is, you can't say, "If you work real hard, you're going to be the engineering manager" or some other title. That's all gone.

Then how do you motivate people?

There are things like gain-sharing, which we're looking at. But primarily, you do it through trust and nurturing and caring. Yesterday I walked by a guy in marketing, and I looked at his face and could see something was wrong. So I said, "Is everything okay?" He said, "Why do you ask?" I said, "You just don't look right." He said, "Yeah, my dad's sick. I just put him in the hospital last night." It's just watching for those kind of things. A series of little events like that, and eventually he'll start reciprocating. He'll start caring about the orders coming because he knows that's something that's important to *me.* But this is not something you create in six months. You're really looking at the long haul when you start talking about professionals.

Do you have as many salaried support staff as you did before?

That's the other remarkable thing. We've cut back 50 people since I've been here. We're down from 188 to 138, and yet, when you compare the two employee surveys we did—one in February '94 and the other in November '94—you'll see that in almost all the questions, the positive responses have made quantum leaps upward. Keep in mind we had laid off a lot of people by this time, but the difference was people knew what was coming. People could plan their lives. They felt like they were being treated like human beings and not like an afterthought.

We also provided employee relocation assistance. Jill (Jill Heiden, human resources manager) has been in this area for twenty-some years, and she has a tremendous network of people in businesses and throughout the communities. She's served on every major board of directors for every nonprofit organization in this town. And she's been able to secure jobs for many individuals that we've had to lay off.

That kind of support is not only important for the people you let go, it's also important for the survivors. You've got to work hard with the survivors because whatever you do can have a long-term impact on them. It's not like a pay raise where people forget about it after two weeks. They say things like, "You remember a year ago when you laid that person off? That really made me mad."

Let's move on to a little different topic. What's it like communicating in a team environment? Do you do things differently?

I have a production meeting, and all the team leaders are in it. Mostly, I just sit there and listen. If there's anything I need specifically, or if I feel

they're getting lost, I'll ask them questions. I say, "Why isn't that breaker done yet?" and let them talk. Then I might say, "Well, I don't understand that. Why don't you have parts?" I try and help them define
problems and discourage them from always falling back on pet solutions. You do that enough times and before long, the next time you come
to the meeting, you only have to ask three questions. And then the next
time it's only two. The amazing thing is that they're smart, and they realize, "He just wants to find out if we know what the root cause of the
problem is." It's your line of questioning as a manager that determines
how your culture is going to be.

*So you have these weekly production meetings in which you talk about
schedules and stuff. Then you have your monthly meetings. Is that an
entire facility meeting?*

Yes. I break it up into three groups, just because of the logistics of it. We
can't fit them all in the cafeteria. We go over all the financials for the
division and for the site; we go through what the actual numbers are and
what the reported numbers are because the reported numbers are different from the actual numbers. Then we go over any specific problems that
I see. Maybe we'll explain what cash flow is. Maybe we'll explain what
a balance sheet is. I just love it. That's where you're really doing your
work. You're breeding that culture. You're showing people how you
want things done. Then we might have some videos from corporate that
we show.

After that, they usually beat me up for 30 minutes or so with questions like "What are we going to do?" and "How are we going to do
this?" and "Are we going to have another layoff, and how will it be
determined?"

*What about giving feedback on personal performance? How do you han-
dle that?*

I try and provide it for everyone on my staff every six months, whether
it's time for their review or not. I say, "These are where I feel your
strengths are, and these are your opportunities for improvements." It
tends to take a lot of the anxiety out of the work environment because
people don't have to go the full year without knowing where they stand.
It's like "if that's all the things I need to improve, I can do that."

I'm trying to get my staff to do the same thing with their next layer
down. I try to show them, "If you can surround yourself with people that

know exactly what you want, you can stop doing stuff that doesn't add value and find yourself a whole lot more time to do some of the things that do add value."

Is there anything you need to do for self-directed work teams over the long haul to make sure they continue at the same high level?

Teams are a lot like Maslow's hierarchy of needs. When you start putting in self-directed work teams, people only really care about shelter and food and whether they're going to have a job and things like that. But then they very quickly get used to the new model. As their needs become more sophisticated, the teams start wanting to be able to discipline their people. Then they start asking, "When are we going to start with the hiring decisions." Then they start asking, "How are we going to be compensated for this?" Very quickly, they start figuring out that they are the key resource to this thing that makes it work. So just like you, they want to be challenged, recognized, and rewarded.

What about a compensation plan? What are you doing about it?

Our reward structure right now is pitiful at best. We're relying on the pat and the free dinner here and there. I think at some point it's management's responsibility to start saying, "If these people are giving more than they gave before, we need to go to a new level of responsibility and accountability for them."

We're also starting to look at gain-sharing and things like that, but you have to be careful not to do that too quickly because you can destroy everything you've built up. You can do that very quickly with money. You have to have a very good set of metrics.

Some of the changes you made happened very quickly. For example, you had a design team that did the work redesign in the plant and determined the team configuration. How long did it take to complete the redesign?

I got here in October, and we had the entire factory—103 pieces of equipment—moved by the end of December. Was it pretty? No. Were all the electrical drops where they should be? No. But did we meet our production load? Yep. Actually, we shipped more breakers in December than we did in September, October, or November.

How did you manage to do that with all the turmoil?

I didn't let people take their foot off the gas pedal. I said, "Production level will be met. I realize this is a big thing, but it can be done." If you get people believing it can be done, the next thing you know, it happens. I know that sounds simplistic, but it's really amazing what people can do if you just let them. But you also need to be very clear about what you want.

What do you mean?

If you tell them, "Move all the equipment," you're going to get all the equipment moved, but your production level will fall off. On the other hand, if you simply say, "Make sure you meet your production level," you'll meet your production level, but you'll only get three pieces of equipment moved. But if you say, "I want the production level met *and* the equipment moved," guess what? It happens. So you have to be very clear what you ask people to do. Of course, that's what you get paid for, to be able to judge those things and also having enough knowledge to put the right people where they're doing the right things.

You mentioned earlier that in the process of moving to teams, you ended up laying off—what was it?—about 50 people. How do you go about this? How do you choose who goes?

First off, you don't look at people. When you ask me how do I determine who I lay off, the answer is, I look at what processes aren't creating value for us. Then we reengineer those processes. If somebody falls by the wayside, you simply have to take that cut.

What do you say to people when they ask how they can protect themselves from layoffs?

I talk about cross-training. I say to them, "The days when my father and your fathers were working for a company for 30, 40, 50 years just don't happen any more. The rate of information is doubling every five years. The amount of computer power and things that are happening is absolutely phenomenal. If you think that you can stand at a punch press machine for the next 50 years and punch those parts out—if you think that somebody isn't going to figure out a better way to do that—you're not very bright. We have one of the finest technological colleges in the state five minutes from here. You can go learn all kinds of skills that the company pays for 100 percent. And if you want job security, you have to go out and continue your education. Go to night school once a week. Learn, cross-train, become a team leader, make yourself invaluable to the organization."

But what do you say to an engineer who has the same concern? I read a recent study that said that 80 percent of what engineers do can be transferred to the teams. In fact, at a division of Exxon we work with, they've eliminated all but about three engineers from a staff of maybe 45. People always think you eliminate the supervisors, but it's really that engineering corps that you end up downsizing.

If a work redesign makes some engineers superfluous, we put them on our task teams. There are always plenty of big task cost reductions, so we put them on our most important projects. Give them those kinds of assignments. You can keep people busy for a hundred years doing some of that stuff, and yet they still are valuable to the organization. They're doing meaningful things. We have some guys who have been here for 25 years that no longer have anything to do with day-to-day production. Yet they're the people who are looking at what parts we're going to bring back into production. How are we going to cost reduce these parts, deal with certain vendors? Things like that. It's nice for them because they're out of that day-to-day rat race and stress of meeting the production load, but they still feel valuable to the organization. They're still very integrated with the team.

Are the teams less dependent on the engineers than they were before?

Yes, they're much more independent. If they have a question, they don't just take a piece of paper to an engineer. They get all the information and write it all down and put together what they think they should do, then take it to one of the engineers who's on the floor playing a supportive role. It's different from what you'd see in a traditional facility.

So they recommend solutions and then go to the engineer to check it out.

Sure. The person who's making the widget is the one who really knows. You don't need an engineering degree for that. Now, you may have to change the blueprints and get it approved, and if it's UL, there are all the different idiosyncrasies you have to deal with. That's where the engineer can help out.

In fact, I heard a talk a while back by an entrepreneur who had over 200 companies. His gross profits for the year were $700 million. One of the things the guy said is that the average Japanese worker will have about 150 suggestions a year on how to improve his work, whereas the average American worker comes up with 1.4. But that's not the amazing thing. The amazing thing is that the average Japanese management implements 96 percent of the 150 suggestions, whereas the average American management implements 14 percent. That's where I'm trying to teach the people—"The reason that management doesn't implement your solution isn't because it's not right or we don't think it's important. It's just that when you dump the problem on our lap, we all have other things to do, too. So generate a solution, and it makes it much easier for us to implement it for you." Today we have a much higher hit rate of things being done. And that's all happened because of the teams. None of this was happening before we installed the teams.

We also have a complete quality data tracking system that the teams input all the information into. That gives us all of our statistical information. How many defects per unit, what's our six sigma level, and all those kinds of things.

Did you have those systems in place before you went to teams?

No. We put those in as well.

Do you have facilitators outside the team that people can go to when they have problems?

We just have my staff. The way I look at it, why put in another level of communication and filters? My door is always open, and people feel very comfortable walking into my office or seeing me on the shop floor and saying, "I need to talk to you about something." Or they'll go to Jill. Or Dan [the manufacturing manager]. Basically, I guess that's it.

You talked about how you got started, but where do you see it going from here?

I see shifting as many of these roles and responsibilities to the teams on the floor as we possibly can. That's the direction we're headed. In July of last year we took a major step in allowing the teams to do their own performance evaluations. That was the first one. They've done another one since.

We've put a task team together, a subcommittee of the employee council, and they wrote their own reviews after reviewing other companies' benchmarking. They wrote the way they wanted the reviews to look and the questions they wanted to ask, and this determines the merit increase they get.

They also rated themselves. In January they did their first full evaluation of their own review. Ninety percent of the facility was thrilled. They expected exactly what they got.

The other thing was, you can make that a very complicated process. Before we did this, a consultant we work with brought in a guy from California. He was a very intelligent man and all that, but the problem is that the process he wanted required hundreds of hours of evaluation—two hours per individual for every single person. With every individual, it's not only two hours for their review, but everybody on the team is out for two hours. So if you have a team with 10 people, that's 200 hours *off of the floor.*

His process was very elaborate and, I'm sure, effective, but the problem is, it's not practical. You just can't do that. By having the teams do their own evaluations, we got what I think are just as good results, and without that huge loss of time.

The cross-training model—Jill is working at that right now with the team, developing a much more flexible workforce than we have currently: one that is, basically, anybody can do anything.

When you're ready to move on, what control will you have over who comes in? It seems obvious that you've been successful in introducing teams to a large degree because of your personal vision and strengths. I know that you're building a staff that can champion the teams. Yet, once you move on, those teams will be very vulnerable to the next executive who comes in.

You're right. I will have some input into who comes in here. But what I tell these people is that there are no guarantees in life, even if I handpick a successor. I've hired enough people and have been fooled by enough people in the interviewing process to know that at best, you're flipping the coin on somebody. Even if I handpick somebody, who knows what he's going to do when he hand picks the next one?

So I tell people, "The only way you can be successful long term is to continuously produce the results that make those guys look good. Make them be afraid to change it. If they're afraid to change it because the results might fall off, they'll leave you alone. But the minute your results start falling off, then all of a sudden they'll feel obligated to do something to produce a different outcome because that's their job. What you have to do is to stay a step ahead of them and produce the results. If you do that, you'll see that most of these executives leave you alone."

I also have an obligation to educate my management because if I don't try to make them understand, it's these people here who will suffer.

I think you've really captured the flavor of what it is to manage in a team environment. Any last comments?

Just this. Once you've created an environment where your leaders can rise to the top, people you didn't even know were there will begin to surface. That's when it really starts to blossom. That's when you'd better be holding on because the train is going full bore down the tracks. You better hope you've gotten on the right train and that you're going in the direction you want because there are no magic cords to pull to stop it. It's not like in the movies. It's a freight train moving at 100 miles an hour, and you hope there's nothing on the tracks. If there is, you hope it's something bad, because it'll be obliterated by the time you get there. The momentum can be just incredible.

SUMMARY OF RESULTS

As a consequence of the team initiative, the following improvements were recorded at the ABB Power T&D plant in Florence, South Carolina. The time frame covers the 15-month period between October 1993 and December 1994.

- *Productivity.* 11.3% improvement in hours per breaker.
- *On-time delivery.* 97% improvement.
- *On-time production.* 20% increase in breaker production while head count decreased from 188 to 137.
- *Safety index.* Received 1994 Safety Award from the Occupational Safety Council for best safety record in South Carolina for all manufacturers of electrical and electronic equipment. The plant also received awards for reducing its accident rate by over 40% between 1993 and 1994 and for being at least 75% below the accident rate for the average of all industry in South Carolina.

- *ISO certification.* Completed in May of 1995.
- *Yields.* First-pass yields increased 375%.
- *Inventory.* 60% reduction in inventory, 105% increase in inventory turns.

HIGHLIGHTS FROM EMPLOYEE SURVEYS

Please rate how satisfied you are with the chance to use your skills and abilities.

Date	Very good	Good	Fair	Poor	Very poor	Favorable Response
11/3/94	32%	50%	15%	2%	1%	82%
2/11/94	18	54	18	10	0	72
1993	12	36	38	11	2	48

Please rate how satisfied you are with the sense of accomplishment your job provides.

11/3/94	32%	49%	18%	1%	1%	80%
2/11/94	16	52	23	10	0	67
1993	7	40	39	9	5	47

Please rate how satisfied you are with the variety of tasks in your work.

11/3/94	29%	56%	14%	0%	0%	66%
2/11/94	15	56	20	9	0	70
1993	13	39	36	10	1	52

I am given all the authority I need to perform my work in the most efficient way.

Date	Strongly Agree	Agree	Agree and disagree	Disagree	Strongly disagree	Favorable Response
11/3/94	24%	46%	25%	4%	1%	70%
2/11/94	12	45	34	9	0	57
1993	14	42	28	12	4	56

I am given all the authority I need to make work-related decisions.

11/3/94	25%	46%	24%	4%	1%	71%
2/11/94	14	41	34	11	0	55
1993	13	35	30	16	7	48

I feel a commitment to my company/division as more than "just a place to work."

Date	Very good	Good	Fair	Poor	Very poor	Favorable Response
11/3/94	37%	54%	8%	1%	1%	91%
2/11/94	31	44	19	5	1	75
1993	21	43	23	8	5	64

The changes at my company/division have mostly had a positive effect on me personally.

11/3/94	32%	46%	19%	4%	0%	77%
2/11/94	19	48	26	6	1	67
1993	11	31	34	13	8	42

My company/division management is clearly customer focused and committed to quality.

11/3/94	39%	47%	13%	1%	0%	86%
2/11/94	31	49	17	3	0	80
1993	13	35	31	15	7	48

A team rollout will generally produce fewer problems if all team members share similar beliefs and values. Before the ABB Power T&D rollout was actually begun, the following declaration was developed by management and workers at the Florence plant and signed by everyone in the facility. Today, this document is on permanent display on the plant floor.

THE ABB STANDARDS OF BUSINESS CONDUCT AND COMMITMENT TO PROFESSIONAL BEHAVIOR

BUSINESS CONDUCT

As employees of the ABB Power T&D, whether management or nonmanagement, we accept the responsibilities and expectation to comply with relevant laws, obligations and company policies applicable to decisions and conduct in the workplace. These standards of business and conduct are outlined in a booklet we have received and carefully studied.

PERSONAL BEHAVIOR

As employees of the company, whether management or nonmanagement, we accept the responsibility and expectations to daily demonstrate the following behavioral traits:

1. Our actions and words will reflect respect and dignity in all our communications.
2. We will choose our words carefully and avoid any words that can be perceived as unprofessional, out of place, or that create an uncomfortable feeling (e.g., slang, cursing, derogatory type words and comments).
3. We will seek first to listen and understand, then to be understood in all communications processes.
4. We will be committed daily to achieve the principle of fairness with the understanding that when we value correct principles, we have truth, a knowledge of things as they are.
5. We will be committed daily to achieve the principle of integrity and honesty, which creates the foundation of trust, which is essential to cooperation and long-term personal and inter-personal growth.

Developed by 1992 Action Planning Team Representatives

13

⑥ HOLDING THE COURSE

The future may show that moving to high performance work organizations is not so much an organizational as a societal change—one that pays enormous dividends because it provides a better quality of life.

Edward E. Lawler III

Questions Addressed in This Chapter

- Are you developing realistic expectations?
- Are you willing to stand up for the million-dollar moments?
- How do you foster long-term support for teams?
- How do you weigh the debits and the assets?

Every person who steps into the unknown has a moment when doubts surface. It happens for the bungee jumper making that first leap from the bridge into the ravine below. It happens for the surgeon who pauses, scalpel in hand, before committing to a radical new procedure. It happens for the astronaut who sits atop a missile pointed toward the darkness of outer space. It happens for the individual in wilderness survival training who, tired and discouraged, huddles under a makeshift shelter while an evening rainstorm beats mercilessly down.

The doubt may last only a moment, or it may persist for the duration of the journey. But the question is always the same. "Do I go on, or do I turn back?"

Philosopher/consultant Peter Koestenbaum, author of the book *Leadership: The Inner Side of Greatness,* observes that one thing that great leaders are able to do is bear up under continuous anxiety and stay the course, even though they don't know for certain how things will turn out.

What keeps them going? In part, the answer has to do with their personal qualities. The most salient of these include

- Courage.
- Faith in oneself.
- Realistic expectations.
- Confidence in others.
- Love of challenges.
- Commitment to a vision.
- Staying power.
- Strong conviction.
- Sense of humor.

Consider the harried executive who's had a day she'd just as soon forget. The numbers are down. There's dissention on the floor. Peers are sabotaging her team's best efforts to succeed. A sense of control is slipping like sand through her fingers.

It's at black moments like these that the inevitable question arises: "Exactly how much am I willing to invest before I see results?" Things can look very confused after the launch, and as teams continue to be mired in chaos, doubts creep in. This is where the mettle of the executive is put to the test. If he or she can resist the urge to cut and run, transformation is possible. To stay the course, however, the executive must draw on the kinds of personal resources in the preceding list.

ARE YOU DEVELOPING REALISTIC EXPECTATIONS?

Without question, people hold high and sometimes unrealistic expectations of what teams will be able to accomplish and how long it will take to see results. Many executives anticipate a straight linear progression and become upset when things get "messy."

In a survey conducted for Zenger Miller by the American Institutes for Research, Inc., 4,500 potential respondents, most of whom worked in human resources and quality assurance departments, were asked what five benefits they expected from teams and how successfully these benefits were realized. In the best of cases there was a 4 percent differential between expectation and realization; in the worst case, the difference was as high as 21 percent.

Top Five Expected Benefits from Teams

Factor for Teams	Percent Expecting Benefit	Percent Reporting Benefit
1. Increased customer participation	81	72
2. Improved quality of products/services	79	63
3. Improved productivity	78	57
4. Increased customer satisfaction	76	57
5. Improved employee skills	66	62

Considering all the different pressures and issues that affect teams, it is perhaps amazing that perceived benefits are as high as they are. What the numbers clearly show is that expectations of team performance are seldom fully realized.

People who make their living in creative professions—writers, designers, research scientists—know that in shifting from one paradigm to another, there is always a time when everything appears mired in chaos. They expect this to happen. Giving up the old way—whether the old way represents an organization structure or an artistic idiom—requires disassembling the existing system. The parts, which were organized and interrelated, now just sit about. Nothing seems to work.

The creative individual puts up with the chaos because he or she perceives it as an integral part of the process. While the worst of it is going on, the creative person may drink too much coffee, chew pencils, or go on long walks, but he or she knows that only from this chaotic state can new paradigms emerge. It is not surprising, then, that in countless studies done though the years on the creative personality, one of the most common characteristics is the ability to tolerate a period of chaos while a new *gestalt* takes hold.

The harried executive can learn a useful lesson from the many published descriptions of the creative process: it is helpful to anticipate that things will get worse before they get better. If the executive *is* realistic, he or she is better prepared to tolerate the ups and downs during the difficult transition time.

ARE YOU WILLING TO STAND UP FOR THE MILLION-DOLLAR MOMENT?

Probably the largest challenge to the executive is having to fight for the team's interests in the face of opposition and doubt. These are the million-dollar moments when it's time to cinch in your belt and take a stand. There may be opposition and disagreement from peer groups and senior management, there may be self-doubts. At such moments you will have to tap into your deepest convictions and beliefs.

What are these moments like?

Perhaps the most common moment involves cutting costs. Executives are charged with increasing profitability. When squeezed, trimming personnel is tempting. "After all," the reasoning goes, "if the team can meet its quota with 11 people, couldn't it do the same with 10 by working a little more efficiently, thereby saving the department $40,000 a year?"

Perhaps not. People lose sight of the fact that a team is a dynamic unit. It develops its own balance, its own homeostasis. To lop off one part is to throw this balance off kilter. You need to consider what the impact will be on those who stay behind. Will people feel that they are being penalized for their successes? In more segmented functions, the impact of personnel cuts is likely to be absorbed with minimal upheaval, but a team is different. A team is a work *family,* and cutting family members is always demoralizing.

In addressing the need to reduce costs, cutting people is the easy way out, because downsizing is standard operating procedure. It's the tried and true option and, therefore, unlikely to draw criticism from above. But how will it impact *you,* the executive or manager? Can *you* live with the feeling that you've let the team down? What about the impact on the team survivors? Will they conclude that though they're being asked to support the organization, the organization is not really committed to supporting them?

A more effective strategy, one that supports the team, is to bring the problem back to the team members. Let *them* look for solutions. "We have to cut $40,000," you might say. "What can you come up with?"

It takes guts for an executive to say to his or her superior, "I'm not just going to make cuts. I'm going to work with the team." It's risky because, even though an executive may throw the problem back on the team, it may still not work out. But there's a difference. If people eventually have to be cut, at least the team members know that they were given an opportunity to address the problem *first* and that even their best efforts fell short. This is much different than never having been given this chance in the first place.

FOSTERING LONG-TERM SUPPORT FOR TEAMS

If teams are to gain long-term support, they must ultimately work their way into all corners of the organization. When that happens, a critical mass is created, and the organization's beliefs and values make a quantum shift in a new direction.

What generally happens in many companies, however, is that the establishment is willing to go along with teams at the micro level until they challenge the organization's fundamental ideas. Then the team initiative hits the wall. Because the team concept has not yet gained full acceptance, when teams come up against an entrenched corporate culture, it's no contest—the establishment wins every time.

Often this resistance is expressed in terms of exclusivity. You'll find facilities in which people believe that teams will work with technicians but not with engineers, or in Kentucky but not in Detroit. Managers will say things such as, "Teams won't work for us because my people are more technical," or "My requirements simply are too complex for teams." People can be quick to believe that they're above these kinds of changes. They can be just as quick to refuse to allow the diffusion of teams in their area.

Unfortunately, there are no guaranteed answers to how support can be ensured. For teams to truly exist in a supportive environment, cultural changes must reach well beyond the organization. These changes need to take place where a person's thinking is originally formed—in homes and schools. The tenets of mutual support and cooperation—a basic win-win philosophy—must begin replacing the traditional win-lose approach fostered by aggressive competition.

Not that competition isn't appropriate in the proper situation. A football team could never win without a strong competitive spirit, nor could a company succeed in local or world markets. Just as the football teams with the most wins have not only outstanding individual talent but also a strong team spirit, so too *within* the organization there needs to be a radical shift in thinking if team spirit and cooperation are to become the prevailing philosophy.

WEIGHING THE DEBITS AND ASSETS

In the end, everything always seems to come down to the numbers. How do you weigh the gains of the team initiative against the costs? What results can you expect to see in the early days of the team environment and what gains later on?

In the first six to nine months, it is unlikely that the team initiative will show positive results at the bottom line. More likely, the opposite will be true since a thousand nagging problems are being worked through. There will, however, be early signs to reassure the anxious executive. Most of these will be in the area of changed employee attitudes.

One of the first likely changes will be an increased level of collaboration as team members look for ways to support one another. Regular team meetings will promote common interests, and employees whose purview was previously limited to their own work area will begin to look beyond their department toward concerns that impact the larger organization. The executive may also notice that people seem to be more involved, more alive, more satisfied. Employees will be *coming* to work, rather than just *showing up*. These intangibles are the softer gains. More tangible benefits will manifest themselves only after the teams have been up and running for a while. Signs that teams are maturing include these:

- Increased productivity.
- Reduced cycle times.
- Higher levels of customer satisfaction.
- Increased volume of work, often with fewer people.
- Increased communication.
- Streamlined decision making.

Only at this point does the trip into the unknown begin to directly impact the bottom line. How long the executive can operate on faith before the positive signs appear obviously depends on many factors. This is never an easy call, but when things get rocky, the executive might take heart from the misbegotten mission of *Apollo 13*.

When Astronauts Lovell, Haise, and Swigert set out for the moon, they had no guarantees that they would make it or even that they would return. They knew only that they had prepared as best they could, that all exigencies anyone could think of had been anticipated, and that they had the best infrastructure to support them.

En route, an oxygen tank exploded in the service module, crippling the vessel's power and life-support systems and threatening to maroon the astronauts in space. The three astronauts saved the day by using the descent engine of the lunar module to accelerate the crippled command module around the moon and back to earth. Once in the vicinity of earth, they reentered the command module and guided it to a safe landing.

The lesson is simple. Don't be afraid to go for broke simply because you can't anticipate every problem, and don't allow yourself to become paralyzed if the situation gets tenuous. Mistakes are okay; you can recover. It's within bounds to let chaos rule while you help get the situation under control. Just remember that choosing not to pull the plug doesn't mean that you've forsaken your capacity to make a decision. You're simply making an intelligent choice about when such decisions need to be made. Keeping up your confidence in the team process— being a true believer—leaves you open to be surprised, perhaps even startled, by the dramatic results that can be realized.

TOOLS AND TECHNIQUES

⑥ INTRODUCTION TO TOOLS AND TECHNIQUES

This section provides a variety of tools and procedures for evaluating the organization's readiness to expand existing teams, planning and implementing the rollout, and for managing team interactions. The 18 tools and techniques described here address issues at all levels (executive, manager, facilitator, and team) and at all team stages (beginning, evolving, and mature). They help in chartering new teams, characterizing existing teams, identifying team needs, and enhancing feedback and communication.

The tools include checklists, assessments, questionnaires, guidelines, and methods for measuring team development and productivity. Many of these techniques have helped organizations solve team problems and strengthen teams at various stages. Others can help justify the investment in teams. Many tools address problems common to all teams and their support personnel; others focus on issues specific to particular teams, such as self-directed, cross-functional, or problem-solving teams.

The tools and techniques include the following:

- Employee Involvement Assessment, Parts 1 and 2
- Predicting Organizational Orientation toward Teams (POOTT)
- Signaling Commitment to Values: An Assessment
- Checklist for Managing and Planning the Transition to Teams
- The Team Charter
- Planning for the Team's Development
- Team Personality Identification
- Evaluating Team Morale
- Phases of a Developing Team
- Diagnosing a Stuck Team
- Peer Review
- The Team Leader/Facilitator Evaluation

- Interviewing Candidates for the Team Manager
- Assimilating a New Manager into a Team Environment
- Mature Team Index
- Advanced Team Training
- Prescription for Organizational Improvement
- The Process for Deciding When to Redesign

Each tool or technique follows this format:

- *What.* A brief description of the tool, its purpose, and its importance.
- *When.* Cues, time lines, or guidelines as to when the tool is best used or is most applicable.
- *Who.* Identification of the job type. role, or person who would be involved in using or taking responsibility for applying the tool.
- *How.* Directions for using the tool along with any necessary preparation, materials, and ground rules.
- *What's next.* Expected outcomes or results, follow-up activities, and possible next steps.
- *Forms.* Examples, when appropriate, of specific forms to use or adapt when using the tool.

If, like the champions and managers of teams in most organizations, you need ways to solve problems, manage changes, provide better team support, and identify new directions for stronger teams, these tools can help. They offer proven ways to meet and solve the short- and long-term challenges of working with teams.

⑥ EMPLOYEE INVOLVEMENT ASSESSMENT

WHAT

An Employee Involvement Assessment is a systematic exploration undertaken to determine whether the organizational climate and business conditions favor expanded levels of employee involvement. When multiple types of teams operate within an organization, the assessment can be used to determine which type of team is most appropriate. The assessment will provide a much clearer sense of how ready the organization is to move to teams and the employees current level of involvement.

The Employee Involvement Assessment covers the potential costs of teams, the potential benefits, any special opportunities or problems, and recommended action steps. It also may be used to recommend the next steps for organizations that are already prepared to move ahead with teams.

WHEN

Organizations with a pocket strategy that want to expand the scope of teams can use this tool to decide whether expanded employee participation would benefit the business. When the tool is used after teams have been launched, it can reflect the progress made and the readiness to expand team responsibilities.

For organizations exploring the appropriateness of teams, an Employee Involvement Assessment can be initiated when management is considering teams as a useful approach to achieve productivity gains or when multiple types of teams are functioning in various sections of an organization that wants to expand its team initiative.

WHO

An Employee Involvement Assessment is conducted under the auspices of the executive championing the team initiative. The study is carried out by an internal change agent—someone who can ask hard questions and maintain an objective attitude. Everyone in the organization can provide the data, or a representative sample can complete the assessment. The leadership team should also complete the assessment and share its findings.

HOW

There are four steps in the Employee Involvement Assessment:

1. Designing the study.
2. Collecting the data.
3. Analyzing the data.
4. Presenting the results of the analysis.

These steps are usually carried out by the internal change agent or an external consultant.

1. **Designing the study.** From the point of view of the teams' champion, the most critical aspect of the design is to make sure the study will generate a fair sampling of data and opinions. Often the internal change agent determines the key respondents for the assessment. These may include the people in the organization who are considering moving to teams, as well as key managers, supervisors, actual or potential team members, and representatives from key support areas.

2. **Collecting the data.** The assessment survey form asks questions that cover several key areas: control of operations, decision-making power, customer feedback, hiring practices, skills, access to information, rewards and recognition, organization structure, work redesign, and employee involvement. People can complete the assessment individually or in small groups. The change agent or consultant collects all completed forms and aggregates the data.

3. **Analyzing the data.** The data analysis indicates the types of teams that may be most appropriate to the business and the organizational climate. The data will suggest one of the following four types of teams:

a. Traditional or departmental work groups.
b. Participative improvement teams.
c. Shared leadership teams.
d. Self-directed teams.

4. **Presenting the analysis.** Champions and key supporters of teams gather to discuss the findings and determine the next steps. The Employee Involvement Assessment often helps sell a particular course of action, form the basis for initial planning (including the selection of team sites), and spark discussion of other forms of employee involvement.

WHAT'S NEXT?

In most cases, the next step is to make a go/no go decision regarding teams. If the decision is to go ahead, the next step will be the process of launching teams. If the decision is a no-go, the key champions should (1) begin discussion of what can be done to make the organization more receptive to and compatible with teams and/or (2) consider other more limited forms of employee participation until more people become comfortable with teams. Unless the possibility of moving to teams has been kept securely under wraps, deciding to do nothing at all could be demoralizing.

EMPLOYEE INVOLVEMENT ASSESSMENT, PART 1

WHAT LEVEL OF EMPLOYEE INVOLVEMENT DO WE HAVE?

The 10 items that follow compose a "diagnostic" assessment tool that will help you analyze and understand the level of employee involvement most prevalent across your organization today. Every item consists of four essentially parallel descriptions, each relating to a different level or degree of employee involvement. The results will give you a clearer indication of where you are starting from and assist you in making a realistic plan of where you need to go.

Instructions

For each item, read the four descriptions carefully and circle the number of the column that most closely describes your organization's current reality. In making your decision, try to take an *overall* view of the organization rather than focus on the division, department, or area that is most advanced in terms of employee involvement.

When you have completed all items, fill in the scoring section.

Which of the following practices are most prevalent in the organization now?

Item 1

1	2	3	4
Managers, with limited input from employees, decisions, set goals, control schedules, determine how jobs are to be done.	Managers get input from team members before planning team activities and making critical decisions.	Managers share responsibility with team members for planning, decision making, problem solving, and coordinating with other teams.	Team members are responsible for team make activities, budgeting, scheduling, evaluating and performance, and interacting with customers and vendors.

Item 2

1	2	3	4
Employees identify problems in their work area and pass them to management. Managers make decisions, and employees implement final solutions.	Employees participate in problem-solving teams formed by managers to address specific issues. Teams make recommendations within narrow, well-defined boundaries. Suggested solutions are subject to approval and changes by management.	Employees and managers work together to address team and organizational issues.	Employees directly address team and organizational issues with minimal input from managers who focus their time and energy on strategic issues.

Item 3

1	2	3	4
Customer issues and complaints are channeled through individual departments or passed down from above. Correct responses are defined by policy. Direct customer contact is generally limited to sales, service, and order/fulfillment personnel.	Customer feedback is solicited periodically, often via surveys or response cards. Results are reported to all employees. Managers assign appropriate groups of employees to target specific emerging or identified problems and to recommend preventive actions or improvements.	Customer and supplier data are actively solicited. Customers are involved in new product development and process improvement.	Team efforts are driven by the needs of both external and internal customers. Teams pool and share information as it relates to the efforts of other teams. Customers are an integral part of the team process.

Item 4

1	2	3	4
Managers make hiring decisions based on individuals' technical skills.	Employees are hired for technical and interpersonal skills. Team members sometimes have input on hiring but do not make final decisions.	Employees are hired for technical and interpersonal skills and for commitment to team values. Both team members and managers interview candidates. Hiring decisions are made jointly.	Employees are hired for technical and interpersonal skills and for commitment to team values. Teams often conduct interviews and make final hiring decisions.

Item 5

1	2	3	4
Training focuses on technical skills related to specific job functions.	Employees receive additional training in interpersonal and problem-solving skills.	Employee training includes skills traditionally targeted only at managers, such as meeting leadership and influencing others.	Cross-training is common. Employees learn technical, interpersonal, and administrative skills. Team members are also trained in leadership.

Item 6

1	2	3	4
Managers provide information regarding decisions that employees are then expected to support.	Managers provide information about the organization's performance when they deem it necessary.	Managers provide the team with the best information available on customers, competitors, and the organization's performance.	Employees have direct access to customers and to information on competitors and the organization's performance.

Item 7

1	2	3	4
Rewards and recognition are based on the individual's performance and contribution.	Small rewards and recognition are given based on work done on problem-solving teams.	Rewards and recognition are increasingly based on team performance as well as individual performance.	Employees are rewarded and recognized for satisfying the customer through the work of teams. Various systems encourage employees to work toward team goals.

Item 8

1	2	3	4
The organization is structured by function and resembles a tall pyramid with many layers. It is designed for efficient management control.	The organization structure is functional, with multiple layers; cross-functional, problem-solving, and task teams create a horizontal overlay.	The organization structure is slightly flat although multiple layers remain. Processes and customers have been integrated into the structure to some degree. The organization is designed to respond more quickly and flexibly to changes in customer requirements.	The organization and its teams are focused on and built around customers and processes. The structure is relatively flat with few layers. The organization is designed to anticipate changes in customer requirements and to adapt quickly.

Item 9

1	2	3	4
Work is designed by experts and managers. Employees who perform the work have little or no input.	Employees are asked to make recommendations regarding more effective ways for work to be designed.	Managers and employees work together to design more effective ways to perform the work.	All employees are actively involved in designing more effective ways to perform their work. Team members make the ultimate decisions on design.

Item 10

1	2	3	4
Involvement activities may include • Suggestion systems. • Press conference meetings to voice concerns and request information.	Involvement activities may include • Safety committees. • Departmental problem-solving groups. • Temporary cross-functional quality improvement teams (process improvement teams). • Task forces operating with management direction.	Involvement activities may include • Permanent cross-functional teams responsible for work processes (process management teams). • Functional employee teams with management responsibilities. • Task forces functioning with minimal management involvement.	Involvement activities may include • Self-directed work teams. • Representatives from many teams on short-term task forces. • Several teams working together to integrate processes and enhance customer service.

SCORING

To score your assessment, enter the total number of responses you had in each column and multiply. (For example, if you circled number 2 for six of the assessment items, you'd score 12 points.) Then add your individual column scores for a grand total.

Total in Column 1 = _____ × 1 = _____

Total in Column 2 = _____ × 2 = _____

Total in Column 3 = _____ × 3 = _____

Total in Column 4 = _____ × 4 = _____

Grand total = _____

Your total score indicates the degree to which your organization (as you perceive it) currently exhibits the characteristics of each of four levels of employee involvement described on the following pages. This assessment can also serve as a discussion tool by helping to clarify and highlight how you and others perceive the current development of the organization.

**Traditional or
Departmental Work Groups**

Informed, efficient
implementation of
management decisions

**Participative
Improvement Teams**

Broad base of experience
brought to bear on
complex problems

**Shared Leadership
Teams**

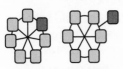

Greater cross-functional
coordination and
expansion of the capabilities

**Self-Directed
Teams**

Highly flexible, highly
responsive operations
of all members of the
organization

To become more familiar with some of the typical activities, behaviors, and organizational requirements that characterize each level of employee involvement, read the team descriptions that follow. This will help you to identify the current level of participation and assist you in deciding whether this is appropriate to your goals and objectives.

Traditional or Departmental Work Groups

Typical Involvement Activities
- Managers regularly schedule meetings in which they brief employees on routine operations.
- In special meetings, managers announce new developments.
- "Press conference" meetings allow employees to voice their concerns and/or request information about events.
- Managers use roundtable discussions to seek employees' views on problems and issues before making a decision. Managers may base subsequent decisions on employee input or may choose to disregard it.

What Executives Do
- Set the direction for the organization.
- Monitor organizational performance.
- Stay in touch with the external environment and the marketplace.
- Become increasingly visible to all employees.

What Managers Do
- Set goals, control schedules, and determine how jobs are to be done.
- Make most decisions and develop solutions for most departmental and cross-functional problems.
- Concentrate on the performance of the team and spend minimal time coordinating the efforts of teams with the rest of the organization.
- "Sell" ideas to employees and ask for their support.

What Employees Do
- Receive information regarding decisions that they are expected to support.

- Provide input on certain issues.
- Work at jobs that are specialized and narrowly defined.
- Primarily relate one-on-one with the leader rather than to one another.
- Identify problems in their work area and pass them along to management for a solution.

Organizational Requirements

- A willingness to spend time informing employees about critical issues.
- An employee suggestion system that includes a mechanism for acknowledging input.
- A willingness to provide training for managers in the skills of listening, presenting information, and receiving feedback.
- The ability to respond constructively when employees sense a discrepancy between the expected and actual influence they have on decisions.

Advantages

- Managers have access to the opinions and views of employees.
- Decisions can be made quickly since group consensus is not required.

Pitfalls

- If employees' input is not acted upon, they may feel that the time taken from their regular tasks was wasted.
- Employees may resent having their ideas taken over and implemented by others.
- Responding quickly to changes in customer expectations and demands can be difficult.

Participative Improvement Teams

Typical Involvement Activities

- Task forces (e.g., a safety committee) are used to address a particular issue. Selected employees (often from more than one department) are asked to find a solution to a particular pre-defined problem rather than simply offer a broad range of ideas.

- For a departmental quality or problem-solving effort, employees within a function are asked to solve a particular problem relating to the department's effectiveness.
- Temporary cross-functional quality improvement teams involve employees from different departments in solving a specific problem or improving a process related to the interaction between departments.

What Executives Do

- Articulate why the organization is using teams and what support executives will give.
- Develop plans for the rollout of teams.
- Respond to the requirements of teams with appropriate resources and support.
- Increase the amount of information shared across the organization.
- Spend increasing amounts of time with customers.

What Managers Do

- Form quality improvement and problem-solving teams.
- Get input from team members before planning team activities and making critical decisions.
- Encourage team members to work cooperatively with one another.
- Focus primarily on the performance of the teams but also coordinate their teams' interaction with other teams in the organization.

What Employees Do

- Provide input on a wide array of issues.
- Interact with one another to fulfill team responsibilities.
- Perform specifically defined jobs but also participate in tasks that "enlarge" or "enrich" their day-to-day activities.
- Participate in problem-solving and improvement teams formed by managers to address specific issues; make recommendations within narrow, well-defined boundaries.

Organizational Requirements

- Clear "boundary guidelines" for cross-functional teams and task forces so that these groups know what resources are at their disposal and what limitations are placed on their decision-making authority.
- A willingness to train employees in a problem-solving process and in the use of problem-solving tools.
- A willingness to reschedule and redistribute work to create time for employees to take on problem solving without neglecting their usual tasks.

Advantages

- Teams permit the application of just the right mix of expertise to a problem.
- Teams tap employee creativity.
- This level of involvement requires no alteration of the existing management system.
- The involvement helps managers and employees gain an understanding of other departments and the overall organization.
- The involvement improves organizationwide coordination and productivity.
- Employees feel they have some influence on policies and procedures that go beyond their own departments.

Pitfalls

- Employees can feel squeezed between the demands of their regular work and their problem-solving activities.
- People can end up on too many teams, thus taking too much time from their regular work and negatively affecting productivity.
- If teams are working on ill-defined problems or operating without problem-solving or meeting-leading skills, the process can drag on without a solution.
- As more people from different parts of the organization work together, "turf issues" can flare up, strengthening barriers between departments instead of eliminating them.

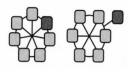

Shared Leadership Teams

Typical Involvement Activities

- Departmental or functional teams gradually take on specific management responsibilities: budgeting, scheduling, and interteam negotiations.
- A team is created for a long-term project or task. Team members take responsibility for team formation, implementation, evaluation, and disbanding when the project is finished. Managers are involved as coaches only.
- Members of departmental or functional teams work together on an ongoing basis to identify and implement solutions to problems in their work area.
- Permanent cross-functional teams are responsible for the work processes that cross their functions (process management teams). They set goals, monitor progress, and standardize and improve the way work is done across departments.

What Executives Do

- Exemplify values consistent with teams.
- Demonstrate a commitment to enhancing their own team-related skills.
- Model team-oriented communication and shared leadership behaviors on their own teams.
- Delegate operational decisions and share strategic decision making.
- Initiate the analysis of strategic processes.
- Share accountability for and ownership of cross-functional processes.
- Challenge existing systems and encourage examination of the organizational structure.

What Managers Do

- Share responsibility with team members for planning, decision making, problem solving, and coordinating with other teams.

- Spend a great deal of time on large organizational issues that affect team performance.
- Provide information to the team about customers, competitors, and the organization's performance as a whole.
- Take on more of the tasks from the next level up.

What Employees Do

- Make group decisions by reaching consensus.
- Directly address team and organizational issues.
- Perform broadly defined jobs.
- Develop and implement innovative ideas.
- Take responsibility for improving work flow, quality, and productivity.

Organizational Requirements

- The readiness to adopt a new definition of leadership.
- A willingness among all members of the organization to take on more of the responsibilities of the level above them.
- Training for team leaders in consensus decision making, group conflict resolution, and strategic thinking.
- Training for team members in decision making, planning, and promoting team development.
- Executive commitment to support the expanded role of team leaders and team members.
- Executives willing to share some of their responsibilities.
- The willingness of executives and management to share information extensively.

Advantages

- Although the traditional management structure may not have changed, employees have far more ownership of their work.
- By including employees, the organization taps into a broader base of knowledge and experience to solve complex problems.
- As teams make more day-to-day decisions, front-line leaders have the time to do more global thinking and long-range planning.
- As everyone in the organization takes on more of the responsibilities of the level above, people at all levels expand their capabilities.

Pitfalls

- Supervisors and managers may not be prepared or willing to share decision making with employees.
- Expanding the capabilities of teams needs to be a gradual, managed process. If the process goes too quickly or is not carefully planned, the team can get in over its head and fail.
- As teams take on more and more of the tasks of the manager, the manager needs to take on more of the tasks of the next level up. If all levels in the organization are not willing to share activities, front-line and middle managers may feel squeezed out.
- Teams and individuals in the organization will evolve in their capabilities and attitudes at different rates. Contention and confusion can occur between advanced teams and less advanced teams or among individuals with different levels of commitment to the success of team strategies.
- Teams may be asked to make decisions based on insufficient information.
- Performance measurement and reward systems may not fully or adequately support the team effort.

Self-Directed Teams

Typical Involvement Activities

- The members of a functional or departmental work team are responsible for setting team goals, budgeting, scheduling, and interacting directly with customers and vendors. The manager's time and energy are focused on strategic issues.
- Several teams from different parts of the organization work together to better integrate their work processes and provide enhanced customer service.
- Representatives from many teams form a short-term project team to deal with a specific issue, such as new product development.

- One team helps select and train members for a new team being formed to handle a new product or service.

What Executives Do

- Spearhead the effort for work redesign and organizational restructuring.
- Encourage the continuing development and growth of teams so that the initiative does not lose momentum.
- Represent teams to headquarters to ensure ongoing financial and policy support.
- Challenge organizationwide systems that do not support teams.
- Set a clear expectation that all managers will support the expansion of teams and be accountable for the success of teams.
- Continually coach and encourage managers to expand team boundaries.

What Managers Do

- Rarely get involved in day-to-day operational decisions and activities but are still accountable for team performance.
- Work on strategic planning and provide teams with resources, information, and guidance.

What Employees Do

- Take responsibility for the team's activities: budgeting, scheduling, evaluating performance, and interacting with customers and vendors.
- Work together to set goals and plan how to accomplish them.
- Work with other teams.

Organizational Requirements

- *A willingness to change.* Everyone must be willing to learn and practice a new role. All employees will need support in dealing with their concerns and fears.
- *A willingness to share information.* To manage themselves, self-directed teams need good information, including financial information.
- *Time and resources.* Success depends on long-term planning, prompt access to resources, and sometimes the physical redesign of plants and offices.

- *A commitment to training.* Work teams stand or fall on training that replaces the outmoded skills and behaviors of the traditional workplace.

- *Operations conducive to work teams.* Successful work teams commonly perform a complex but repeatable task that is complex enough to require many skills yet manageable enough to allow rotation of cross-trained members. Ideal operations that increase employee decision making and yield increased day-to-day productivity.

- *Access to help.* Organizations need experienced help throughout the transition to self-directed teams. Veterans of team development can provide assurance that ups and downs are normal. While organizations ultimately find unique design solutions for their teams, they can learn from the successes and mistakes of others.

- *Union participation.* Unions and top-level management must work cooperatively together to institute changes necessary for the organization's long-term health and productivity.

Advantages

- Quality is enhanced when teams assume more responsibility because they commonly develop a deep sense of ownership in their work. As a result, they're more likely to find and implement new ways to improve quality.

- Flexibility is ensured because self-directed teams have the skills, information, and motivation to move easily from job to job. Consequently, the company as a whole can respond quickly to changing conditions in the organization and marketplace.

- Commitment grows because self-directed teams breed increased employee involvement in meeting organizational goals. Commitment tends to remain high, too, since team members develop a strong sense of owning their piece of the business.

- Productivity also increases. Many operations moving to teams report 20 to 40 percent gains in productivity within 18 months.

- Streamlining results as self-directed teams create new options for flattening the organization. The organization needs even more skilled leaders than before, but leadership is spread across the organization instead of stacked up in vertical chains of command.

- Customer satisfaction is maintained and enhanced through the quick response time and improved quality of self-directed teams.

Pitfalls

- Communication of information can become a substantial task since there is a need to know at every level of the organization.
- The cost of training, planning, restructuring, and obtaining outside help for three to five years of concentrated effort can make the transition too expensive for the organization.
- Fear of change can result in tremendous resistance from unions, managers, and employees alike. This resistance can overwhelm an organization that is not prepared for the team effort.
- An oversimplified view of what it takes to install self-directed work teams can lead to early failure. The organization may well be worse off than before because employees may feel that they were given a chance and failed.
- Supervisors may not have been given appropriate new roles and responsibilities and may not be actively involved in the transition.

EMPLOYEE INVOLVEMENT ASSESSMENT, PART 2

WHAT LEVEL OF EMPLOYEE INVOLVEMENT DO WE NEED?

The goal of this assessment is to clarify the connection between employee involvement and your organization's ability to respond effectively to key competitive challenges.

Here you'll take a second look at each of the items from the previous assessment and, based on what you've read about the levels of employee involvement, identify the level most appropriate and/or likely to help your organization rise to the challenges it is facing. This assessment will help you decide where you have to move next.

Instructions

As before, read the four descriptions for each item carefully and circle the number of the column you believe best answers the following question:

Given the competitive challenges we face, what level of employee involvement will we need to have at the end of three years?

When you've completed the assessment, score your responses. Deliver your assessment as instructed by the person administering it.

Given the competitive challenges we face, what level of employee involvement will we need to have at the end of three years?

Item 1: Control of Day-to-Day Operations

1	2	3	4
Managers, with limited input from employees, make most decisions, set goals, control schedules, and determine how jobs are to be done.	Managers get input from team members before planning team activities and making critical decisions.	Managers share responsibility with team members for planning, decision making, problem solving, and coordinating with other teams.	Team members are responsible for team activities, budgeting, scheduling, evaluating performance, and interacting with customers and vendors.

Item 2: Accountability for Decisions and Solutions to Problems

1	2	3	4
Employees identify problems in their work area and pass them to management. Managers make decisions, and employees implement final solutions.	Employees participate in problem-solving teams formed by managers to address specific issues. Teams make recommendations within narrow, well-defined boundaries. Suggested solutions are subject to approval and changes by management.	Employees and managers work together to address team and organizational issues.	Employees directly address team and organizational issues with minimal input from managers who focus their time and energy on strategic issues.

Item 3: Customer Feedback

1	2	3	4
Customer issues and complaints are channeled through individual departments or passed down from above. Correct responses are defined by policy. Direct customer contact is generally limited to sales, service, and order/fulfillment personnel.	Customer feedback is solicited periodically, often via surveys or response cards. Results are reported to all employees. Managers assign appropriate groups of employees to target specific emerging or identified problems and to recommend preventive actions or improvements.	Customer and supplier data are actively solicited. Customers are involved in new product development and process improvement.	Team efforts are driven by the needs of both external and internal customers. Teams pool and share information as it relates to the efforts of other teams. Customers are an integral part of the team process.

Item 4: Hiring Practices

1	2	3	4
Managers make hiring decisions based on individuals' technical skills.	Employees are hired for technical and interpersonal skills. Team members sometimes have input on hiring but do not make final decisions.	Employees are hired for technical and interpersonal skills and for commitment to team values. Both team members and managers interview candidates. Hiring decisions are made jointly.	Employees are hired for technical and interpersonal skills and for commitment to team values. Teams often conduct interviews and make final hiring decisions.

Item 5: Skills

1	2	3	4
Training focuses on technical skills related to specific job functions.	Employees receive additional training in interpersonal and problem-solving skills.	Employee training includes skills traditionally targeted only at managers, such as meeting leadership and influencing others.	Cross-training is common.Employees learn technical, interpersonal, and administrative skills. Team members are also trained in leadership.

Item 6: Access to Information

1	2	3	4
Managers provide information regarding decisions that employees are then expected to support.	Managers provide information about the organization's performance when they deem it necessary.	Managers provide the team with the best information available on customers, competitors, and the organization's performance.	Employees have direct access to customers and to information on competitors and the organization's performance.

Item 7: Rewards and Recognition

1	2	3	4
Rewards and recognition are based on the individual's performance and contribution.	Small rewards and recognition are given based on work done on problem-solving teams.	Rewards and recognition are increasingly based on team performance as well as individual performance.	Employees are rewarded and recognized for satisfying the customer through the work of teams. Various systems encourage employees to work toward team goals.

Item 8: Organizational Structure

1	2	3	4
The organization is structured by function and resembles a tall pyramid with many layers. It is designed for efficient management control.	The organization structure is functional, with multiple layers; cross-functional, problem-solving, and task teams create a horizontal overlay.	The organization structure is slightly flat, although multiple layers remain. Processes and customers have been integrated into the structure to some degree. The organization is designed to respond more quickly and flexibly to changes in customer requirements.	The organization and its teams are focused on and built around customers and processes. The structure is relatively flat with few layers. The organization is designed to anticipate changes in customer requirements and to adapt quickly.

Item 9: Work Design

1	2	3	4
Work is designed by experts and managers. Employees who perform the work have little or no input.	Employees are asked to make recommendations regarding more effective ways for work to be designed.	Managers and employees work together to design more effective ways to perform the work.	All employees are actively involved in designing more effective ways to perform their work. Team members make the ultimate decisions on design.

Item 10: Involvement Activities

1	2	3	4
Involvement activities may include • Suggestion systems. • Press conference meetings to voice concerns and request information.	Involvement activities may include • Safety committees. • Departmental problem-solving groups. • Temporary cross-functional quality improvement teams (process improvement teams). • Task forces operating with management direction.	Involvement activities may include • Permanent cross-functional teams responsible for work processes (process management teams). • Functional employee teams with management responsibilities. • Task forces functioning with minimal management involvement.	Involvement activities may include • Self-directed work teams. • Representatives from many teams on short-term task forces. • Several teams working together to integrate processes and enhance customer service.

Plot your score on the scale below.

INDIVIDUAL SCORING

As before, enter the total number of responses you had in each column and multiply. Then add your individual column scores for a grand total.

Total in Column 1 = _____ × 1 = _____

Total in Column 2 = _____ × 2 = _____

Total in Column 3 = _____ × 3 = _____

Total in Column 4 = _____ × 4 = _____

Grand total = _____

Record the group's scores

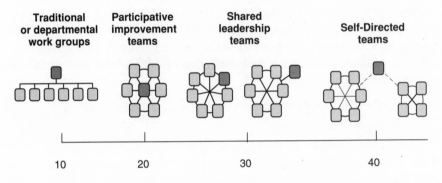

| Traditional or departmental work groups | Participative improvement teams | Shared leadership teams | Self-Directed teams |

10   20   30   40

Even though the movement to teams in your organization might have been in progress for some time, you'll find this scene a good reality check as to what you've accomplished and where you need to go. This book will offer ways you can take some bold steps forward.

⓺ PREDICTING ORGANIZATIONAL ORIENTATION TOWARD TEAMS (P.O.O.T.T.)

WHAT

The P.O.O.T.T. inventory is based on research conducted by Darlene Russ-Eft. Her empirical examination of factors that predict a team orientation within an organization was based on executive interviews, focus groups, and paper-and-pencil questionnaires gathered from 10 organizations. Questionnaire data from 81 managers and 364 associates indicated that five factors provide the best prediction of a high team orientation in an organization:

1. Relationships among organizationwide management.

2. Innovation on the job.

3. Control of work by the immediate manager or supervisor.

4. Group cohesiveness.

5. An open group process within work groups.

The P.O.O.T.T. helps determine how effectively teams could be incorporated into a particular area of the organization. The inventory examines all five dimensions. The higher the overall rating on the Team Orientation Inventory, the easier it will be for the organization to implement teams in that area.

WHEN

A P.O.O.T.T. inventory is initiated when an organization is expanding its team initiative to additional areas beyond an initial pocket strategy. Once the P.O.O.T.T. rating is determined, management decides whether an expansion of the initiative or a full transition to teams is worth the time and investment. Ratings obtained for separate areas can be used to compare the level of team orientation in different parts of the organization. If management is committed to moving ahead with teams, the lower responses on the P.O.O.T.T. can be guideposts to potential pitfalls.

WHO

A P.O.O.T.T. inventory of the area being considered for teams should be conducted under the direction of the area's management. Often an internal consultant administers the instrument, analyzes the data, and presents the report. Potential team members and team leaders, current managers and supervisors, and executives complete the instrument.

HOW

There are four steps to conducting a P.O.O.T.T. inventory: designing the study, collecting the data, analyzing the data, and presenting the results. These steps are usually carried out by the internal consultant. Data gathered should assess the degree to which certain conditions exist for each of the five factors examined. Topics to address in each area are as follows:

1. Organizationwide management
- Management treats people fairly.
- Management keeps people informed.
- Management keeps informed about how employees feel.
- Management helps people develop their skills.

2. Innovation on the job
- People are encouraged to do things differently.
- People are constantly trying new ideas.
- Management regards variety of tasks and methods as important.

3. Control of work by management and supervisors
- Manager plans the work.
- Manager knows what work is being done.
- Manager sets high performance levels.

4. Group cohesiveness
- People feel part of the team.
- Team members are involved in making decisions.
- Team spirit is obvious.

5. Open process within the group
- Team members willingly contribute ideas.

- Team members give one another feedback.
- Team members' opinions are listened to.

WHAT'S NEXT?

A high score on the instrument indicates that a particular area or site is suitable for teams. Once an area is identified, an implementation plan must be developed. Management should continue to use assessment to monitor the organization's progress and to identify potential pitfalls.

TEAM ORIENTATION INVENTORY

Section 1

This set of questions focuses on groups in this organization. For this questionnaire, think of your "work group" as the set of people with whom you work most closely on a day-to-day basis.

If you are a member of only one work group, the questions will be easy to answer. If you are a member of two or more work groups, you will need to decide which group to think about when answering the questions. For this part of the questionnaire, keep this one group in mind.

1. The following are statements that may or may not describe your work group. How much do you agree or disagree with each statement? *(Circle your choice.)*

	Strongly disagree	Disagree	Slightly disagree	Neither agree nor disagree	Slightly agree	Agree	Strongly agree
I feel I am really a part of my work group.	1	2	3	4	5	6	7
If we have a decision to make, everyone is involved in making it.	1	2	3	4	5	6	7
There is a lot of group spirit.	1	2	3	4	5	6	7

Add the numbers circled to get a total score for this section   Section 1 Total

Section 2

2. The following statements could be used to describe how work gets done in a work group. How much do you agree or disagree with each statement? *(Circle your choice.)*

	Strongly disagree	Disagree	Slightly disagree	Neither agree nor disagree	Slightly agree	Agree	Strongly agree
We tell each other the way we are feeling.	1	2	3	4	5	6	7
I look forward to being with the members of my work group each day.	1	2	3	4	5	6	7
In my work group, everyone's opinion is listened to.	1	2	3	4	5	6	7

Add the numbers circled to get a total score for this section   Section 2 Total

Section 3

3. The following statements could be used to describe a job or an organization. How much do you agree or disagree with each statement? *(Circle your choice.)*

	Strongly disagree	Disagree	Slightly disagree	Neither agree nor disagree	Slightly agree	Agree	Strongly agree
Doing things in a different way is valued.	1	2	3	4	5	6	7
New and different ideas are always being tried out.	1	2	3	4	5	6	7
Variety and change are particularly important.	1	2	3	4	5	6	7

Add the numbers circled to get a total score for this section   Section 3 Total

Section 4

This part of the questionnaire focuses on your immediate manager or supervisor.

4. The following statements describe managers and supervisors in organizations. Please indicate whether you agree or disagree with each of the statements as a description of your immediate manager or supervisor.
(Circle your choice.)

My manager	Strongly disagree	Disagree	Slightly disagree	Neither agree nor disagree	Slightly agree	Agree	Strongly agree
Plans work in advance.	1	2	3	4	5	6	7
Keeps informed about the work being done.	1	2	3	4	5	6	7
Maintains high standards of performance.	1	2	3	4	5	6	7

Add the numbers circled to get a total score for this section

Section 4 Total

Section 5

This part addressed organizationwide management in your organization.

5. The following statements describe the overall management in an organization. Please indicate whether you agree or disagree with each of the statements as a description of your organization's management.
(Circle your choice.)

Organizationwide management	Strongly disagree	Disagree	Slightly disagree	Neither agree nor disagree	Slightly agree	Agree	Strongly agree
Keeps everyone informed.	1	2	3	4	5	6	7
Is always fair.	1	2	3	4	5	6	7
Helps people develop their skills.	1	2	3	4	5	6	7

Add the numbers circled to get a total score for this section

Section 5 Total

Add the section totals to get a total score

Section 1   [ ]

Section 2   [ ]

Section 3   [ ]

Section 4   [ ]

Section 5   [ ]

Total   [ ]

Note: For the person administering this assessment: Add the totals from all Team Orientation Inventories completed and divide by the number of respondents to get an average score for the group or the area of the organization.

Compare the average score to the scoring ranges:

Score of 17–34

Address organizational issues related to all five factors that predict team success.

Score of 35–79

Proceed with caution. The organization has to improve in all dimensions before teams can be successful.

Score of 80–112

Plan the implementation. The organization is ready to move ahead.

⑥ SIGNALING COMMITMENT TO VALUES: AN ASSESSMENT

WHAT

Signaling Commitment to Values: An Assessment examines current behaviors, norms, and daily practices that reflect the values of the organization. By describing these practices, an internal change agent can gauge the level of commitment, identify mixed signals, and coach managers and executives on leadership behaviors needed to build teams successfully.

This tool describes behaviors in a traditional environment and the related behaviors in a team culture. Pairs of behaviors can be considered end points on a continuum. Modified approaches can be identified as middle points that indicate progress in moving toward a team-based organization.

WHEN

A coaching session using this tool may be needed when

- A new team is getting started and wants to be sure there is solid management commitment before it begins.
- A team is demoralized and wants to give up.
- A team needs help developing systems, procedures, and work practices to support the transition.
- Team leaders are not sure that building effective teams is worth the frustration.
- People are opting out of participating on a team.
- Executives, managers, and supervisors are unsure how to reinforce their commitment to building a team culture.
- Executives and managers want to accelerate the team development process.

WHO

The internal change agent or consultant usually takes responsibility for determining when one of these coaching sessions is needed. The internal change agent also sets up and facilitates the meeting. Key executives, managers, and supervisors are invited to assess their behaviors and identify changes.

HOW

The following steps are usually performed by the internal change agent.

On-the-Job Observation

1. Observe the team and the organizational environment to assess congruence between stated values and behavior.
2. Listen to the team members. Listen particularly for evidence of frustration or feeling constrained by systems. Focus on comments that suggest lack of management support, unclear expectations, and uncertainty about the impact of teams. These cues are helpful in determining congruence between what's being said and what's being done.
3. Identify executives, managers, and supervisors whose actions the teams are watching closely. Individually or in small groups, meet with these leaders to assess their values.

Session Intervention

4. Prepare an agenda. A sample agenda might look like this:
   - Individuals complete the Signaling Commitment to Values assessment.
   - Individuals post their responses on the master assessment chart.
   - Trends are noted on the individual charts.
   - Those involved discuss the assessment (see the sample discussion questions that follow).
   - Action plans are identified.

Follow-Up Coaching

5. Follow up after the session by meeting with each participant individually to provide specific guidance and coaching.

Sample Discussion Questions

- *How often are more traditional values being demonstrated?*
- *What impact do these values and behaviors have on the teams?*
- *Why are these values still being practiced?*
- *What is necessary to create a change in leadership behavior?*
- *What emerging values were identified?*
- *Why are these values being practiced?*
- *What education, training, or personal coaching would assist leaders in demonstrating these new values?*

WHAT'S NEXT?

The change agent or internal consultant continues to listen to the teams, notice incongruent behaviors among managers and in the organization, and repeat the session intervention until the emerging values are integrated into the culture.

SIGNALING COMMITMENT TO VALUES: AN ASSESSMENT

Consider how values are demonstrated every day at your organization. On the lists below, check any items that you believe accurately describe the thinking, assumptions, and behaviors that are widely demonstrated in your organization today.

Signaling Traditional Values	Signaling Emerging Values
☐ Most information is "management property.	☐ Most information is freely shared at all levels.
☐ Training should focus on technical skills.	☐ The need for continuous learning mandates interpersonal, administrative, and technical training for all.
☐ Jobs are tightly defined; cross-training is viewed as inefficient.	☐ Jobs require broad skills and knowledge; cross-training is the norm.
☐ Risk taking is discouraged.	☐ Measured risk taking is encouraged and supported.

Signaling Traditional Values	**Signaling Emerging Values**
☐ People should work alone.	☐ People should work together.
☐ A large, hierarchical structure is most effective.	☐ A small, flat structure is advantageous.
☐ Rewards are based on individual performance.	☐ Rewards are based on individual and team performance.
☐ Compensation is the primary motivator.	☐ Motivators include involvement, recognition, benefits, awards, personal growth, and pay.
☐ Managers determine the best methods.	☐ Everyone is responsible for improving methods.
☐ Achieving control is management's most important job.	☐ Anticipating change is management's most important job.
☐ Accountability rests with functional groups and employees.	☐ Executives and managers accept and share accountability for managing cross-functional processes.
☐ Executives and managers set priorities, define processes, and review results.	☐ Customers set priorities, drive design, and measure effectiveness.
☐ Suppliers are adversaries.	☐ Suppliers are partners.
☐ Product quality is the major key.	☐ Service quality is as critical as product quality.

⑥ CHECKLIST FOR MANAGING AND PLANNING THE TRANSITION TO TEAMS

WHAT

The Checklist for Managing and Planning the Transition to Teams assists an organization in determining what activities are in place to support the move to teams. The tool covers four basic areas that need to be addressed in an effective plan:

- Structural issues
- Training
- Communication
- Implementation

Although actions that address these four elements make up the overall plan, the planning prework is organized into time frames, each with its own primary focus: explore, prepare, implement, and maintain.

The checklist prepares the organization's change agents to focus on those action steps with the greatest urgency and payoff. It also mobilizes the organization to invest whatever resources are necessary to ensure that teams are effective.

WHEN

The Checklist for Managing and Planning the Transition to Teams is most helpful and appropriate in two situations:

1. *When an organization is in the explore phase and is learning about teams,* the checklist can be used to estimate the time required and the types of resources essential for the successful launch of a go-for-broke team initiative.
2. *After an organization has launched teams with a pocket strategy or in a separate section,* this checklist helps identify the elements needed to establish a strong infrastructure to support the expansion of the team initiative into the wider organization.

WHO

Champions of the change effort who are responsible for establishing an effective infrastructure to maintain teams and to expand the initial teams will complete the checklist. In addition, it may be appropriate for people who will support the change initiative to complete the checklist. These additional people might work in areas such as accounting, human resources, planning, and engineering.

HOW

There are two applications for collecting information and sharing it with the people who are charged with moving the team initiative forward.

Application 1: Launching a Team Initiative

The champions and leaders of the change effort and the people who will be essential in supporting the launch and growth of teams meet to complete the checklist in a group setting. The group begins by identifying listed items that have been completed. It is important for the group to reach consensus on these items. The group's facilitator needs to press for specific examples of each completed action item.

Once the entire inventory has been reviewed, the group can focus on uncompleted activities in the explore phase before moving on to the prepare phase. This concentration of energy enables the organization to reduce its cycle time in implementing teams.

Application 2: Expanding the Scope of the Initial Team

Representatives from sections of the organization where a pocket strategy or a separate section strategy is in place meet to (1) share their first-hand experience with teams and (2) cite examples of activities on the checklist that have been completed. The group then determines the priorities and next steps for the remaining items.

By completing the remaining items on the checklist, the group defines ways that the teams can expand in scope and spread more extensively throughout the organization. This inventory also highlights the steps needed to sustain the gains of teams to date.

Unless steps are taken to broaden the impact of teams, the original teams will be more vulnerable and may be prevented from achieving their full purpose.

WHAT'S NEXT?

When the organization has completed the checklist and reached consensus on the current transition phase, activities to expand the teams can be planned. At this point, the tool serves as a guide that focuses attention on what remains to be done and reduces the cycle time for completing the launch of initial or expanded teams.

During and after the launch, executives can use the checklist as a concrete example of the leadership behaviors they must demonstrate to support the team initiative. The checklist also provides a way to identify and communicate to the entire organization what is being done to increase employee involvement in planning, processes, and wider issues.

CHECKLIST FOR MANAGING AND PLANNING THE TRANSITION TO TEAMS

| | Check the appropriate column | | | |
| | We have done this | | | |
	Well	Fair	Poorly	Not Addressed
Strategic Prerequisites				
Clarify the vision, mission, values, and strategic imperatives of the organization.	☐	☐	☐	☐
Establish critical business measures.	☐	☐	☐	☐
Explore				
Learn about the benefits of teams.	☐	☐	☐	☐
Determine levels of employee involvement needed to meet the organization's strategic goals.	☐	☐	☐	☐
Assess stakeholder readiness.	☐	☐	☐	☐
Learn what is involved in the transition.	☐	☐	☐	☐
Determine the scope of redesign.	☐	☐	☐	☐
Create a Case for Action.	☐	☐	☐	☐
Prepare				
Communicate the vision.	☐	☐	☐	☐
Link the use of teams to strategic imperatives and current organizational improvement efforts.	☐	☐	☐	☐
Identify business measures teams are expected to impact.	☐	☐	☐	☐
Define the role of the leadership team in planning and supporting the implementation of teams.	☐	☐	☐	☐

	Well	Fair	Poorly	Not Addressed
Define a rollout strategy: pocket, separate part of the organization, or entire organization.	☐	☐	☐	☐
Identify systems that will have to be changed to support teams.	☐	☐	☐	☐
Identify work redesign needed to establish teams.	☐	☐	☐	☐
Charter design implementation teams.	☐	☐	☐	☐
Conduct work redesign.	☐	☐	☐	☐
Develop guidelines for sponsoring and chartering teams.	☐	☐	☐	☐
Define the team's purpose as it is linked to strategic business imperatives.	☐	☐	☐	☐
Define the roles and responsibilities of team members, team leaders, facilitators, managers, executives, and sponsors.	☐	☐	☐	☐
Establish sponsorship accountabilities for launching, monitoring, supporting, and disbanding teams.	☐	☐	☐	☐
Develop measures, goals, parameters, and success criteria for teams.	☐	☐	☐	☐
Define and provide resources necessary to support a team's mission.	☐	☐	☐	☐
Determine the decisions to be made by teams.	☐	☐	☐	☐
Define monitoring and communication methods with the teams.	☐	☐	☐	☐
Provide resources for the team transition.	☐	☐	☐	☐
Identify rollout dates.	☐	☐	☐	☐
Formally communicate plans for organizational change.	☐	☐	☐	☐
Identify what will be done by teams when they reach maturity.	☐	☐	☐	☐
Educate executives for their new responsibilities; identify ways to model the vision and values of the organization.	☐	☐	☐	☐
Evaluate employee understanding of the vision, goals, and objectives.	☐	☐	☐	☐
Begin initial awareness training.	☐	☐	☐	☐

Implement

	Well	Fair	Poorly	Not Addressed
Charter and launch teams.	☐	☐	☐	☐
Deliver technical, administrative, and team skills training , as needed , to all levels of the organization.	☐	☐	☐	☐
Develop guidelines for sharing information, answering questions, and discussing issues and concerns.	☐	☐	☐	☐

	Well	Fair	Poorly	Not Addressed
Establish mechanisms for direct feedback to teams on their performance.	☐	☐	☐	☐
Develop new skills for leaders in the team organization.	☐	☐	☐	☐
Assess the effectiveness of communication efforts.	☐	☐	☐	☐
Reassess the accountabilities of teams as resources change.	☐	☐	☐	☐
Develop plans to continue to innovate and to improve systems and processes.	☐	☐	☐	☐
Maintain a high level of executive involvement.	☐	☐	☐	☐
Fine tune and revise the overall plan.	☐	☐	☐	☐

Maintain

	Well	Fair	Poorly	Not Addressed
Align key systems and processes: budgeting, evaluation, compensation, measurements, information systems, and strategic and long-range planning.	☐	☐	☐	☐
Track estimated costs for training and meetings, cost savings due to improvements, and increased market share due to customer satisfaction or new product introductions.	☐	☐	☐	☐
Examine executive behaviors and signals that show continued commitment to and expansion of employee involvement.	☐	☐	☐	☐
Continuously improve redesigned processes.	☐	☐	☐	☐
Disband and reward temporary teams that have achieved their objectives.	☐	☐	☐	☐
Assess overall progress.	☐	☐	☐	☐
Examine and refine the vision, values, mission, and strategic imperatives to ensure that they are still appropriate.	☐	☐	☐	☐
Examine critical business measures.	☐	☐	☐	☐
Assess the level of employee involvement needed to achieve new strategic imperatives.	☐	☐	☐	☐
Fine tune and revise the overall plan.	☐	☐	☐	☐

⑥   THE TEAM CHARTER

WHAT

A Team Charter defines the performance expectations for the team. It is a formal document that communicates to the team (and to other departments that need to support the team) the central issues and standards that govern the team's formation and its work. Specific areas that must be addressed in a Team Charter are these:

- The organizational rationale for teams.
- The definition of the team and its makeup.
- The purpose of the team's work.
- The responsibilities of the team.
- Measures for the team's outputs or work.
- Criteria the team will use to make effective decisions.

WHEN

When new teams are launched or existing teams are refocused on new tasks, the Team Charter is part of the initial communication to clarify the team's makeup and its work. Prior to the first team meeting, the team's sponsor works with key executives, managers, and supervisors to draft the charter. As the team is about to begin its work, the charter clarifies some of the initial questions team members need answered.

WHO

The team sponsor drafts the initial charter based on the organization's Case for Action (reason the organization needs to change). The team leader, manager, and supervisor meet with potential team members to complete the charter. Team members need to identify any concerns or issues regarding their new assignment and obtain answers to any questions they have.

HOW

There are three phases to working with the Team Charter. First, the team sponsor gathers specific information to clarify the team's role within the organization. Then the sponsor conducts a series of three chartering discussions before the team begins its work. During the team's developmental phases, the sponsor schedules follow-up discussions with the team to ensure that it is on track and its needs are being met. The team sponsor often manages these discussions and the team chartering meetings with assistance from a team facilitator.

Before the Team Starts

1. Using the Team Chartering Worksheet as a guide, the team sponsor gathers information on the organizational issues and determines the non-negotiable team boundaries. Then the sponsor meets with potential team members to discuss their input and suggestions for the charter.
2. The sponsor drafts the Team Charter based on information from the worksheet and team members.
3. The sponsor schedules a series of three meetings with the team manager, supervisor, facilitator, leaders and potential members to discuss, modify, and ratify the draft of the Team Charter. Breaking the discussion into three sessions held on different days allows incubation time that helps everyone comprehend the scope and responsibilities of the team.

Discussion of the charter should cover the information included on the Team Chartering Worksheet. The topics are best handled in three two-hour meetings. This gives team members time to think about the topics and how they will be impacted by the information

Meeting 1.   Organizational case for action
   • Reasons for establishing teams
   • Types of teams that will be most appropriate

Meeting 2.   Team purpose, scope, and training

Meeting 3.   Team decisions and boundaries

The team sponsor communicates the content of the ratified Team Charter to key support people: executives, managers, and supervisors. The sponsors of several teams share their information to develop team-specific training and developmental plans. Then the sponsor arranges for appropriate resources to assist the team.

WHAT'S NEXT?

Because the Team Charter outlines developmental opportunities for the team, issues the team needs to have clarified, and training for team members, it allows the team to be launched with minimal confusion and frustration.

After the launch, the Team Charter serves as an instrument for comparing the accomplishments of the team with its purpose and goals as recorded in the charter. This allows the team sponsor to determine through follow-up meetings whether the team is still focused on its purpose and whether that purpose is linked to the organization's Case for Action. In addition, the charter continues to serve as both a guide for the team and a gauge of its results.

TEAM CHARTERING WORKSHEET

Team sponsors and/or facilitators gather information to complete the following questions and then share the information with their teams.

Organizational Information

1. What is the vision of the organization?

_____

_____

_____

2. What is the mission of the organization?

_____

_____

_____

3. What are the strategic goals of the organization?

_____

_____

_____

4. Why are we using teams here (as communicated in the organization's Case for Action)?

_____

_____

_____

Team Information

5. Who is the team's sponsor?

_____

6. What is the team's mission or purpose?

_____

_____

_____

7. How does that mission fit into the mission of the larger organization?

_____

_____

_____

_____

8. What are the goals/expectations for this team?

_____

_____

_____

9. If goals/expectations don't already exist, what is the time
frame for developing them?

_____

_____

_____

10. How will the team be measured?

_____

_____

_____

11. What is the time frame for results?

_____

_____

_____

12. Where can the team go to get the information it needs?

_____

_____

_____

13. What resources will be available to the team (people,
materials, equipment, budget)?

_____

_____

_____

14. What time commitment will participation on this team require
from each team member?

_____

_____

_____

15. What are the responsibilities and the role of the team sponsor?

_____

_____

_____

16. What are the responsibilities and the role of the team leader?

_____

_____

_____

17. What is each team member's specific role? Long-term responsibilities?

_____

_____

_____

18. What training will the team members and leader be expected to attend?

_____

_____

_____

19. How will the team be monitored?

_____

_____

_____

20. What process will the team use to communicate with the larger organization?

_____

_____

_____

21. What are the limits on the team's authority to make decisions?
   - Decisions the team can make by itself.
   - Decisions the team can make with input from leadership.
   - Decisions the team can request (recommendation authority only).
   - Issues out of the scope of the team's charter.

_____

_____

_____

_____

_____

_____

_____

_____

_____

_____

_____

_____

22. Who approves decisions that are outside the team's limits?

_____

_____

_____

23. When will this team disband?

_____

_____

_____

Key Themes and Insights

_____

_____

_____

_____

_____

_____

_____

_____

_____

_____

_____

_____

_____

_____

_____

_____

_____

_____

⑥ PLANNING FOR THE TEAM'S DEVELOPMENT

WHAT

Planning for the Team's Development documents the learning opportunities for three key team roles: team leader, team members, and team facilitators. This tool describes a process for involving team representatives in preparing a team development plan and increasing the team's motivation to address developmental areas in a timely fashion.

WHEN

Teams need training when they take on new roles or responsibilities. It's important to prepare a development plan when these situations arise:

- Forming a new team.
- Changing a team's composition.
- Starting a new team assignment or project.
- Modifying the work processes that affect a team.
- Expanding the set of team responsibilities.
- Changing the team's purpose.
- Working with a team that is not meeting its goals.

WHO

Initially, an internal consultant may work with the team to draft its first development plan. Subsequent plans can be created without the internal consultant as long as the team is comfortable with the process of conducting the developmental discussions.

HOW

If possible, intact teams should prepare their own development plans. The following process encourages the team to step back and get a big picture of its purpose and its members' experience. This process can be adapted to meet an organization's specific requirements, but it is best to follow this approach as closely as possible, especially for the initial plan.

Discussion Process

Have team members form groups of three. In each group, members should take one of the following roles so that all three roles are assigned.

- **Interviewer.** Asks questions about developmental areas
- **Interviewee.** Responds to the interviewer with information from the interviewee's current role
- **Recorder.** Completes the Development Plan Record form with information from the interviewee

Allow 20 minutes for the discussion. Then have participants switch roles and repeat the interview, using the process described below. At the end of three rounds of development plan discussion, each participant will have assumed all three roles.

Part 1

The interviewer leads the discussion and asks the interviewee the following (or similar) questions:

- How would you describe your current responsibilities?
- What are your preferences for these responsibilities?
- What two or three developmental opportunities do you see as most critical now?

The recorder notes the answers on the Development Plan Record form.

Part 2

The interviewer asks the interviewee to list all the skills required in his or her new role. These skills should be separated into three categories:

- *Technical skills* necessary to perform the breadth of the process.
- *Administrative skills* required to understand how to supply and gather the data the team needs, including business performance information.

- *Communication skills* needed to resolve team issues, conduct effective meetings, and negotiate resources.

Once the skills are listed, the interviewer instructs the interviewee to

- Determine which skills are most critical at this time to his or her success.
- Rank these critical skills from 1 to 5, with 1 being the most critical.

The recorder completes the Development Plan Record form (or a similar one), summarizes the information for the group, and turns in the form to the team leader at the completion of the session.

WHAT'S NEXT?

When all discussions have been completed, the team leader or facilitator compiles the list of critical skills for training and development. Working with the appropriate resources, the team leader or facilitator communicates the team's priorities for skills development and schedules the training for the most critical skills as soon as possible.

Forming networks of team leaders, facilitators, and team members helps the teams share learning and skills development throughout the organization. To ensure maximum benefits, team leaders or facilitators should next establish ways to share learning and development processes so that each team can benefit from the skills and applications of others.

DEVELOPMENT PLAN RECORD

Circle the interviewee's role: Team Member
                                     Team Leader
                                     Team Facilitator

Part I

List the interviewee's current responsibilities and opportunities for development.

Current responsibilities_____

_____

Preference for current responsibilities_____

_____

Two to three development opportunities_____

_____

Part II

- For each area below, list all the skills the interviewee says are required for the new role.
- Of the skills listed, circle the ones the interviewee believes are most critical now.
- Record the interviewee's ranking of the most critical skills from 1 to 5, with 1 being the most critical (highest priority).

New Technical Skills Required

_____Rank_____
_____Rank_____
_____Rank_____
_____Rank_____
_____Rank_____
_____Rank_____

New Communication Skills Required

_____Rank_____
_____Rank_____
_____Rank_____
_____Rank_____
_____Rank_____
_____Rank_____

New Administrative Skills Required

_____Rank_____
_____Rank_____
_____Rank_____
_____Rank_____
_____Rank_____
_____Rank_____

- Summarize aloud the most critical (highest priority) skill requirements for the group's review and agreement.

⑥ TEAM PERSONALITY IDENTIFICATION

WHAT

Knowing the team's personality is especially important when (1) adding new people to the team, (2) problem solving, (3) or resolving interpersonal issues. This is because incompatabilities in individual styles can have a negative effect on team performance.

The following tool measures the personality of the team as a whole. It is based on the big five personality factors, a well-accepted personality structure that has emerged in the personality literature. The big five factors are

1. **Extroversion** (sociable, talkative, and assertive).
2. **Agreeableness** (good natured, cooperative, and trusting).
3. **Conscientiousness** (responsible, dependable, persistent, and achievement oriented).
4. **Emotional stability** (relaxed, stable, and secure; or from the negative pole: tense, insecure, and nervous).
5. **Openness to experience** (imaginative, artistically sensitive, and intellectual).[1]

WHEN

Team Personality Identification can be used to determine the best membership for the team. When new people being considered for the team complete the instrument, the team gets a focused profile of the candidates. Also when the team wants to improve understanding among team members or improve group cohesiveness, Team Personality Identification can provide the basis for a team-building session.

---

1. For more details on the "big five" factors, see M. R. Barrick and M. K. Mount, "The Big Five Personality Dimensions and Job Performance: A Meta-Analysis," *Personality Psychology* 44 (1991), pp. 1–26; J. M. Digman, "Personality Structure: Emergence of the Five-Factor Model," *Annual Review of Psychology* 41 (1990), pp. 417–40; and L. R. Goldberg, "An Alternative of 'Description Personality': The Big Five Structure," *Journal of Personality and Social Psychology* 59 (1990), pp. 1216–29.

It is useful to explore the personality types of team members several times in the team's history, such as

- When an existing team is interviewing candidates for the team.
- When the team is learning to work more effectively as a unit and wants to learn more about how team members operate in different situations.
- When a team is establishing ground rules and wants to understand more clearly how to work with other team members.
- When a new team leader starts working with the team.

WHO

Team members complete the personality instrument. The internal change agent, facilitator or team leader coordinates the process.

HOW

The internal change agent, facilitator, or the team leader administers the Team Personality Survey to team members. After team members complete the instrument, the person administering it aggregates the results, leads a discussion to share the team's personality types with team members, and conducts a team-building session. These sessions help team members understand how a teammate reacts to information and what his or her style is for working in a team environment.

Activities conducted in a team-building session could include these:

- Share individual profiles and develop team profile.
- Discuss the impact on the team of the team profile.
- Develop guidelines to discuss personality issues with team members.

WHAT'S NEXT?

After the team has identified its personality traits, members can use the information to develop or modify ground rules, procedures, and other team business. The personality information can be shared when team members need to assess new ways to work more effectively with one another.

Once a team has used this tool to identify the personality of the team as a whole, team members or the team leader can administer it to candidates applying for openings on the team. The results can help the team select compatible candidates for further evaluation or interviews.

TEAM PERSONALITY SURVEY

Directions: Circle the option that you agree with most. Avoid choosing the Not Sure category when possible.

1. As a team, we usually don't enjoy taking the time to talk with others about social events or parties.

   a. True

   b. Not sure

   c. False

2. When joining with other groups, our team doesn't seem to fit in.

   a. True

   b. Not sure

   c. False

3. Our team feels that

   a. Most jobs don't have to be done as carefully as others.

   b. Some jobs don't have to be done as carefully as others.

   c. Any job should be done thoroughly if it is done at all.

4. When something upsets our team, we usually don't get over it easily.

   a. True

   b. Not sure

   c. False

5. Our team finds it difficult to be comfortable in a disorganized setting.

   a. True

   b. Not sure

   c. False

6. As a team, we'd prefer spending time

   a. Working to get the job done.

   b. Not sure.

   c. Having fun at a party.

7. There's usually a big difference between what other groups say they'll do and what they actually do.

   a. True

   b. Not sure

   c. False

8. Our team generally doesn't feel responsible for things that happen around us.

  a. True

  b. Not sure

  c. False

9. Team members tend to be too sensitive and worry too much about something they've done.

  a. True

  b. Not sure

  c. False

10. Our team likes to follow well-tried ways rather than think up new ways to do things.

  a. True

  b. Not sure

  c. False

11. We tend to be shy about making friends with new people.

  a. True

  b. Not sure

  c. False

12. Our team generally is unwilling to help other groups.

  a. True

  b. Not sure

  c. False

13. Our team members are not known for being perfectionists.

  a. True

  b. Not sure

  c. False

14. If others act as if they dislike our team members

  a. Team members usually feel hurt and spend too much time talking about the situation.

  b. Team members don't tend to get upset at all.

  c. Team members may discuss the problem in a constructive manner and try to find a solution.

15. As a team, we are people who

   a. Are always doing practical things that need to be done.

   b. Not sure.

   c. Will brainstorm and think up new things.

16. We tend to be reserved and keep our team problems to ourselves.

   a. True

   b. Not sure

   c. False

17. We find that it's wise to be on guard because people outside of the team might take advantage of our team.

   a. True

   b. Not sure

   c. False

18. We don't always try to do our work just right the first time.

   a. True

   b. Not sure

   c. False

19. When one thing after another goes wrong, our team

   a..Feels as though it cannot cope with the problems.

   b. Goes on as usual.

   c. Spends time solving problems.

20. As a team, we tend to be sensible and down to earth.

   a. True

   b. Not sure

   c. False

21. Our team doesn't like to be in the middle of a lot of excitement and activity.

   a. True

   b. Not sure

   c. False

22. In dealing with other groups, it's better to

   a. "Play your hand close to the chest."

   b. Not sure.

   c. "Put all your cards on the table."

23. When we are frank and open, others try to get the better of us.

   a. True

   b. Not sure

   c. False

24. When two team members get angry at each other, it usually bothers all team members.

   a. True

   b. Not sure

   c. False

25. Work that is familiar and routine makes team members feel

   a. Secure and confident.

   b. Not sure.

   c. Bored and restless.

Scoring Guidelines

Transfer your answers from the questionnaire to the following key. Use this key to identify the category to which your answers correlate.

Extroversion	a	b	c
1	☐	☐	☐
6	☐	☐	☐
11	☐	☐	☐
16	☐	☐	☐
21	☐	☐	☐

If you checked mostly *a*s on items 1, 6, 11, 16, and 21, your team tends to be *low* on the Extroversion Scale. If you checked mostly *c*s, your team is *high* on the Extroversion Scale.

Agreeableness	a	b	c
2	☐	☐	☐
7	☐	☐	☐
12	☐	☐	☐
17	☐	☐	☐
22	☐	☐	☐

If you checked mostly *a*s on items 2, 7, 12, 17, and 22, your team tends to be *low* on the Agreeableness Scale. If you checked mostly *c*s, your team is *high* on the Agreeableness Scale.

Conscientiousness	a	b	c
3	☐	☐	☐
8	☐	☐	☐
13	☐	☐	☐
18	☐	☐	☐
23	☐	☐	☐

If you checked mostly *a*s on items 3, 8, 13, 18, and 23, your team tends to be *low* on the Conscientiousness Scale. If you checked mostly *c*s, your team is *high* on the Conscientiousness Scale.

Emotional Stability	a	b	c
4	☐	☐	☐
9	☐	☐	☐
14	☐	☐	☐
19	☐	☐	☐
24	☐	☐	☐

If you checked mostly *a*s on items 4, 9, 14, 19, and 24, your team tends to be *low* on the Emotional Stability Scale. If you checked mostly *c*s, your team is *high* on the Emotional Stability Scale.

Openness to Experience	a	b	c
5	☐	☐	☐
10	☐	☐	☐
15	☐	☐	☐
20	☐	☐	☐
25	☐	☐	☐

If you checked mostly *a*s on items 5, 10, 15, 20, and 25, your team tends to be *low* on the Openness to Experience Scale. If you checked mostly *c*s, your team is *high* on the Openness to Experience Scale.

REFERENCES

Barrick, M. R., and M. K. Mount. "The Big Five Personality
Dimensions and Job Performance: A Meta-Analysis." *Personality Psychology* 44 (1991), pp. 1–26.

Digman, J. M. "Personality Structure: Emergence of the Five-Factor Model." *Annual Review of Psychology* 41 (1990), pp. 417–40.

Goldberg, L. R. "An Alternative 'Description of Personality': The Big Five Factor Structure." *Journal of Personality and Social Psychology* 59 (1990), pp. 1216–29.

⑥ EVALUATING TEAM MORALE

WHAT

Team performance is impacted by how well team members get along and how enjoyable and satisfying it is to be on the team. Therefore, knowing how the team is feeling about itself can give you vital clues about how to intervene if performance is lagging. Morale is eroded when any of the following conditions are present:

1. **Meaninglessness**—The team experience is not personally meaningful to team members.
2. **Powerlessness**—Team members do not experience having control or authority over outcomes.
3. **Social isolation**—Team members view relationships as impersonal and unfriendly.

The Team Morale Instrument helps identify events affecting the team members so that steps can be taken to improve low team morale.

WHEN

When problems arise with the team, The Team Morale Instrument can be effective in helping to identify and diagnose what must be overcome for the team to progress. At regular intervals (probably quarterly), the team needs to collect information on how members feel about working together. If the team membership changes or the team is struggling with a difficult issue, the team may choose to use the Team Morale Instrument more often or in response to the particular situation.[1]

---

1. For more details on these concepts, see J. Doherty, "Psychological Morale: Its Conceptualisation and Measurement: The Doherty Inventory of Psychological Morale (DIPM)," *Educational Studies* 14 (1988), pp. 65–75; and A. G. Neal and H. T. Groat, "Social Class Correlates of Stability and Change in Levels of Alienation: A Longitudinal Study," *Sociological Quarterly* 15 (1974), pp. 548–58.

WHO

Team members complete the Team Morale Instrument (see page 266). The internal change agent, facilitator, or team leader coordinates the evaluation.

HOW

The internal change agent, facilitator, or team leader administers the instrument to team members. Once the instrument has been completed, the person administering it collects the information, analyzes it, and process the data according to the scoring guidelines on page 267. Then the change agent, facilitator, or team leader conducts a discussion to share the results with the team members.

WHAT'S NEXT?

Based on the results of the evaluation, the team conducts a problem-solving session with the change agent, facilitator, or team leader. If team morale is particularly low, the team should contract with the facilitator or change agent for specific interventions that will assist the team and help members solve whatever problems are blocking team efforts. After a successful intervention, the team may want to use Evaluating Team Morale again to document improvements.

TEAM MORALE INSTRUMENT

Directions: Read the statement and circle the number that best reflects your feelings.

	Never				Always
1. Sometimes I think that our work is meaningless.	1	2	3	4	5
2. Our team seems to have little influence over others.	1	2	3	4	5
3. Other people don't seem to have time for us.	1	2	3	4	5
4. Sometimes our team is just drifting.	1	2	3	4	5
5. Our team members have little control over what we do and how we do it.	1	2	3	4	5
6. Sometimes I feel that our team is an outsider in this organization.	1	2	3	4	5
7. Sometimes I feel that our work isn't worth doing.	1	2	3	4	5
8. Others seldom listen to our ideas.	1	2	3	4	5
9. We often feel left out of things.	1	2	3	4	5
10. Our work really doesn't help anyone.	1	2	3	4	5
11. Our team has little authority over what it does.	1	2	3	4	5
12. We tend to be left out of organizational meetings.	1	2	3	4	5
13. We get little recognition for our work.	1	2	3	4	5
14. Our team rarely gets involved in making important decisions.	1	2	3	4	5
15 Hardly anyone seems to remember that we are here.	1	2	3	4	5

Scoring Guidelines

Transfer your answers from all the questionnaires to the following key. Add all team members' scores for each statement and enter the total for each statement in the appropriate box. Total the scores for each morale dimension and divide by the number of respondents to get a mean score for the team.

Meaninglessness

1

4

7

10

13

Total

Mean (divide by the number of respondents)

Powerlessness

2

5

8

11

14

Total

Mean (divide by the number of respondents)

Social Isolation

3

6

9

12

15

Total

Mean (divide by the number of respondents)

Interpretation of Results

16 or higher

A mean score of 16 or higher indicates that overall team morale for a particular dimension is satisfactory or high and is not having a negative impact on the team's performance or group cohesiveness.

5–15

A mean score in this range suggests that the team needs help to overcome problems in a particular dimension. The team should contract with the facilitator or change agent to isolate specific items or issues contributing to the low morale. Once issues have been identified, the facilitator should work with the team to correct the situation so that morale improves.

R E F E R E N C E S

Doherty, J. "Psychological Morale: Its Conceptualisation and Measurement: The Doherty Inventory of Psychological Morale (DIPM)."*Educational Studies* 14 (1988), pp. 65–75.

Neal, A. G., and H. T. Groat. "Social Class Correlates of Stability and Change in Levels of Alienation: A Longitudinal Study." *Sociological Quarterly* 15 (1974), pp. 548–58.

⑥ PHASES OF A DEVELOPING TEAM

WHAT

As teams develop they progress and regress. Phases of a Developing Team is an inventory based on the Tuckman model[1] that allows you to systematically assess how the teams are evolving. With the help of this tool, you can determine the team's developmental state and base any intervention to improve the team's effectiveness on an accurate diagnosis.

WHEN

A few cues that signal the appropriate application of this tool are these:

- A new member has joined the team.
- A new leader has been selected or appointed to the team.
- A member has left the team.
- Team performance goals are not being met.
- Team members feel they are "stuck."

WHO

The team leader is primarily responsible for developing the team. Others who play a part are team members, the team facilitator, supervisor(s), and support departments. All people in these roles should complete the instrument individually and then discuss their responses as a group.

Executives need to encourage and recognize team members for their progress and to offer assistance in addressing organizational barriers. The results obtained from this survey may be helpful in soliciting additional executive support for the teams.

---

1. Tuckman, Bruce W., "Developmental Sequence in Small Groups," *Psychological Bulletin* 63, no. 6 (1965), pp. 384–99.

HOW

Team leaders or facilitators distribute, collect, and tabulate the assessment instruments.

1. Team members, leaders, supervisors, and support departments individually complete the Phases of a Developing Team inventory.

2. Team leaders collect the instruments and compile the scores.

3. The team leader and team members discuss the results from the inventory. In explaining the scores, the team leader should refer to the four phases of team development.

4. The team leader or facilitator debriefs the team by focusing on the inventory and asking questions to analyze the data obtained. Some sample questions for the data analysis include the following:

   a. What phase of development is the team in now?

   b. What trends do you see in the team?

   c. What activities do you need to focus on to improve the effectiveness of the team?

   d. What interferes with the team's ability to improve?

   e. How do you feel about being a member of the team?

5. The team determines action steps to define the activities necessary to accomplish its developmental needs.

WHAT'S NEXT?

Team members and leaders take steps to move the team to the next developmental phase and to improve the team's effectiveness. Team members work with people outside the team and incorporate these people's suggestions for advancing the team. The feedback process is used multiple times to determine whether the activities being pursued are the appropriate interventions.

The team should record its scores for each phase over time and compare the scores after it has completed the instrument multiple times. A graph created to show the scores for each phase should give the team a picture of its overall development.

PHASES OF A DEVELOPING TEAM

Directions: For each item, rate how much time your team spends on this activity. Base your ratings on the majority of the meetings and activities for the previous month. If your team has not worked on this activity, do not rate the item. Identify each activity on a scale of 1–5.

1 = Spend almost no time on this activity.

2 = Spend little time on this activity.

3 = Spend time occasionally on this activity.

4 = Spend time regularly on this activity.

5 = Spend a lot of time on this activity.

FORMING

		1	2	3	4	5
1.	Team members are getting to know the names and background of other team members.	☐	☐	☐	☐	☐
2.	Teams are deciding on their roles and responsibilities based on people's strengths and areas of interest.	☐	☐	☐	☐	☐
3.	Everyone on the team is on his or her best behavior and trying hard to get along with the other members.	☐	☐	☐	☐	☐
4.	Teams are establishing their goals and defining their purpose.	☐	☐	☐	☐	☐
5.	Ground rules are being determined.	☐	☐	☐	☐	☐

Add the numbers checked for each item to get the page score.

Page score ☐

STORMING

	1	2	3	4	5
6. Members are having frequent conflicts with one another.	☐	☐	☐	☐	☐
7. Team members are questioning their ability to accomplish their goals.	☐	☐	☐	☐	☐
8. Team members are discussing how to balance individual and team work loads.	☐	☐	☐	☐	☐
9. Team members are challenging new ideas.	☐	☐	☐	☐	☐
10. Team members are becoming frustrated with their roles on the team.	☐	☐	☐	☐	☐

Add the numbers checked for each item to get the page score.

Page score ☐

NORMING

	1	2	3	4	5
11. Team members resolve their difficulties directly with other team members.	☐	☐	☐	☐	☐
12. Most of the team's time is spent focusing on the work assigned to the team.	☐	☐	☐	☐	☐
13. A person on the team takes responsibility for limiting suggestions to avoid missing a deadline.	☐	☐	☐	☐	☐
14. Members work within the ground rules, roles, and processes agreed to by the team.	☐	☐	☐	☐	☐
15. Team members accept the team leader and are eager to have this person succeed in his or her duties.	☐	☐	☐	☐	☐

Add the numbers checked for each item to get the page score.

Page score ☐

PERFORMING

	1	2	3	4	5
16. The majority of team interactions are efficient and enjoyable.	☐	☐	☐	☐	☐
17. Team measures are frequently achieved by participation from all the team members.	☐	☐	☐	☐	☐
18. Team members suggest innovative alternatives to meet goals in an efficient way.	☐	☐	☐	☐	☐
19. Members can challenge one another without getting personal or defensive.	☐	☐	☐	☐	☐
20. The team seems to be functioning well with little direction or guidance from the team leader.	☐	☐	☐	☐	☐

Add the numbers checked for each item to get the page score.

Page score ☐

Fill in the appropriate page score below.

Forming	Storming	Norming	Performing
☐	☐	☐	☐

SCORING GUIDELINES

Look at the scores for each of the phases. The phase with the highest score corresponds to the team's current level of development. Enter your highest page score in the box, followed by the name of the phase.

☐ _____

(Name of the phase of team development)

After you find your highest score, read the profile below for a description of your team and the performance of its members.

Forming

Early on, team members get to know one another and begin sorting out their roles. They need to agree on their purpose as a team, to set goals, and to establish ground rules. Both you and the rest of the team may feel excited, enthusiastic, or anxious—all at once—and you're all on your best behavior.

Storming

The unsettling but inevitable second phase is marked by conflict among team members, between supervisors or managers and the team, and between the team and the organization. On the positive side, people are asking questions, negotiating trade-offs, and even challenging the team leader. This is a creative and productive time because team members are getting comfortable with new ideas, yet conflict breeds resentment, and team members can become frustrated.

Norming

Gradually, team members resolve many of their difficulties, learn to focus on the work, and enter a norming phase. The problem now is that team members may be so determined to prevent further conflict that they don't share controversial ideas and avoid dealing with delicate situations.

Performing

Finally, team members figure out how to maintain smooth relations and get the job done at the same time. They deal with conflicts as they arise, challenge ideas without getting personal, operate at peak performance, and take pride in their success. At times, the team hardly seems to need a full-time leader. Still the leader is needed to maintain the team's momentum by introducing new challenges.

⑥   DIAGNOSING A STUCK TEAM

WHAT

Diagnosing a Stuck Team helps a team focus on problem areas and monitor its progress so that it can begin to move forward. This process involves collecting information from team members, sharing them summarized data, discussing "low points," and planning changes to assist the team. Repeating this process each quarter until all team dimensions earn high ratings will ensure that the team continues to develop and make gains in achieving its performance objectives.

WHEN

Several cues indicate when a team could use this tool to help it move ahead:

- Team members believe that they are going around and around and rarely moving ahead.
- Team members are looking for excuses not to participate on the team.
- Team members are getting together outside of meetings to talk about the "real issues."
- Team members are uncertain of their responsibilities.
- Team training isn't being applied on the job.

WHO

The team facilitator, the team leader, or a team member, depending on the maturity of the team, can use this process to diagnose current team difficulties. A newer team, however, may not recognize the need to step back and evaluate its progress. With newer teams, an internal consultant may have to recommend and administer this tool.

HOW

The following steps should be completed with all team members present. Most often the team facilitator will assist the team throughout these steps.

1. Team members complete the Team Development Survey.

2. The team facilitator collects the surveys, tabulates the information, and records the results on flipcharts by doing the following:

  a. For each question, put brackets [ ] around the range of responses.

  b. For each question, circle the response chosen most frequently (the mode response).

FLIP CHART A

How We See Our Teams: Mode and Range

	Key:		[ ] = Range of responses selected		
			O = Most frequently selected response		
1.	1	2	[3	4	5]
2.	1	[2	3	4	5]
3.	[1	2	3	4	5]
4.	1	[2	3	4]	5
5.	1	[2	3]	4	5
6.	1	2	[3	4]	5
7.	1	[2	3	4]	5
8.	[1	2	3]	4	5
9.	[1	2]	3	4	5
10.	[1	2	3	4]	5
11.	1	[2	3	4	5]

---

  c. To graphically show those areas where team devlopment may be blocked, plot each mean response by first rotating the above flipchart 45°. On each line, (now a column) there will be a mean score in between the brackets.

The low scoring areas that graphically appear at the bottom of the chart are those that most urgently need to be addressed.

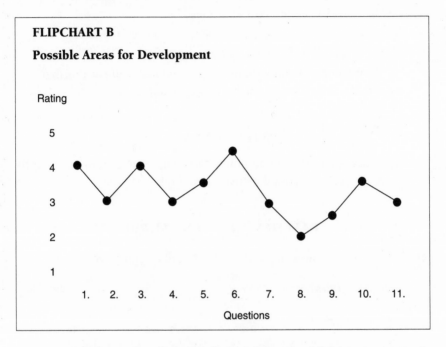

FLIPCHART B

Possible Areas for Development

Rating

d. List on a flipchart the three most repeated responses to each of the two questions at the end of the form.

3. The facilitator uses the following questions to debrief team members on what the analysis reveals:

   a. What are the trends for our group?

   b. What are the lowest scoring issues for our team?

   c. What are the high scoring ideas for our team?

   d. What are some issues for our team to address?

   e. What can we do to improve our behavior as related to issues we need to address?

4. The team summarizes its profile and agrees on next steps.

5. The facilitator or team leader saves the original charts.

6. Three months later, the team repeats the process. The facilitator or team leader graphs the results of the second analysis on the original charts, using a different color to distinguish the two.

7. For this second session, the facilitator or team leader uses these questions to debrief team members:

a. Where has our team improved?

b. What has helped us move ahead?

c. How are we feeling now that we've made progress?

d. What are the current "hot" issues?

e. What are the opportunities for moving ahead even further?

8. The team summarizes its new profile and commits to next steps.

WHAT'S NEXT?

Team members continue to complete this diagnostic tool on a quarterly basis until the scores on all dimensions are high.

TEAM DEVELOPMENT SURVEY

Directions: Circle the number that best describes you or your team.

1.	I **support** the **team's goals.**	Not at all	1	2	3	4	5	Completely
2.	**Leadership** on this team is provided by	A few	1	2	3	4	5	The team
3.	I feel like I am **part of the team.**	Never	1	2	3	4	5	Always
4.	**Disagreement** is	Discouraged	1	2	3	4	5	Encouraged
5.	Team members **confront** each other on **difficult issues.**	Seldom	1	2	3	4	5	Often
6.	Members are **accountable** to one another or the **team's success.**	**Disagree**	**1**	**2**	**3**	**4**	**5**	**Agree**
7.	**Trust** on this team is	Low	1	2	3	4	5	High
8.	Team members **know what is expected** of them.	Disagree	1	2	3	4	5	Agree
9.	Team members are **willing to sacrifice** for the good of the team.	Disagree	1	2	3	4	5	Agree

10. Team members **know which
    decisions** they can make.   Disagree   1   2   3   4   5   Agree

11. Team members **treat one
    another with dignity.**   Never   1   2   3   4   5   Always

COMMENTS

Please use the space below to complete these sentences. Write any additional comments on the back of this page.

The most satisfying part of being on this team is _____
_____

The least satisfying part of being on this team is _____
_____

⑥ PEER REVIEW

WHAT

The Peer Review is a formal process for providing feedback to individuals on the team. The review focuses on what a team member does well and needs to do better, and thus it is sometimes used in lieu of a performance appraisal. Because team members are often most responsive to feedback from their peers, the peer review process typically produces the most efficient and meaningful behavior change.

Most organizations separate peer reviews from compensation decisions. Taking money out of the review process encourages a focus on constructive feedback to improve the team itself—as well as the performance of individual team members.

WHEN

After a team has been working together for at least one year, members are ready to accept feedback from peer review. The team members are also prepared to provide specific feedback in constructive ways. Before participating in a peer review, team members receive training in how to assess the skills and contributions of a team member and how to deliver the feedback. Ensuring that all team members are comfortable with the process is critical to producing the best results for both the team and the person being reviewed.

Peer reviews are usually conducted semiannually, especially when there is a steep learning curve and a strong need to provide developmental guidance. Mature teams are more likely to conduct peer reviews annually. However, they too could benefit from semiannual feedback sessions.

WHO

All members of the team can participate in the peer review or a smaller, select group agreed upon by the team and the person being reviewed can provide the feedback. Often the manager (or someone at the next direct organizational level) participates in the feedback process as well.

Because team members are closest to the work of the individual being reviewed, those who are most familiar with the processes required and best equipped to provide specific, meaningful feedback are the best choices to participate in the review. This means that not all team members must be present. Often three to four people are sufficient to give the feedback. A smaller review group may also enable the person being reviewed to focus more on the feedback offered.

HOW

The peer review process has three principle phases:

Phase 1 Prepare for the Peer Review Session

1. Before the Peer Review Session, meet as a team to discuss the performance of the person being reviewed and to have each team member complete a feedback form. Forms are completed by all team members because often the entire team is not present at the review session. If this is the person's first peer review, a spokesperson should be chosen to summarize the team's feedback and to lead the session.

2. Select a recordkeeper to be responsible for taking notes and summarizing the feedback for the person receiving the evaluation.

3. Appoint a timekeeper to ensure that the session stays within the allocated time. Schedule approximately 60 to 75 minutes for one person's feedback session.

4. Have the individual being reviewed complete a feedback form on his or her performance (see page 282).

Phase 2 Conduct the Peer Review Session

5. The person being reviewed begins the session by sharing his or her self-assessment for the first point on the feedback form. If this is the person's first review session, the spokesperson summarizes the team's feedback on the first item. When the team has more experience with the peer review process, all team members present can take turns providing their feedback on the same point. This process continues until all the points have been covered.

6. Feedback ground rules are reinforced. The person receiving the feedback must listen actively and ask questions only to clarify information. This is not the time to explain a situation—or to challenge the feedback.

Part 3 Conclude the Peer Session Review

7. The recordkeeper (or spokesperson) briefly summarizes the main points covered in the session and states the following:

a. Three ways the team member has contributed to the team.

b Two ways the member could become more valuable to the team.

8. The team member receiving the feedback concludes by doing the following:

a Giving one reason he or she appreciates being part of this team.

b Defining his or her personal developmental goals.

WHAT'S NEXT

The team member works with the facilitator and team leader to address developmental opportunities. Sessions are scheduled to provide the necessary training. During this session, the team member may request specific suggestions for ways to improve in the areas selected for development. Team members can also recognize the team member's progress.

TOPICS FOR PEER REVIEW

Directions: Provide one example for each behavior listed below. If necessary, provide one suggestion for how the person's behavior could be more useful to the team.

Behaviors and Practices	Examples	Ways I Could Improve
• *Initiative.* I am willing to assist other team members without being asked.		
• *Technical competence.* I demonstrate a broad mastery of the majority of skills in the process.		

- *Administrative competence.*
  I am able to use the
  technology and meet
  documentation requirements.

- *Business knowledge.*
  I have an understanding
  of the customer as well
  as business acumen.

- *Leadership.* am able
  and willing to perform
  the leader's responsibilities.

- *Team player.* I support
  team concepts and team
  members.

- *Creativity.* I define
  alternatives to current work
  processes.

- *Innovation.* I provide
  concrete alternatives
  for better ways to accomplish
  work.

Describe three ways you have contributed to the accomplishment of team goals.

_____

_____

_____

_____

_____

_____

_____

_____

Describe two ways you could grow to be more valuable to the team.

_____

_____

_____

_____

_____

_____

_____

_____

_____

⑥ TEAM LEADER/FACILITATOR EVALUATION

WHAT

The Team Leader/Facilitator Evaluation provides a guide for giving feedback to the team leader and or team facilitator. Feedback focuses on the way the leader or facilitator works with the teams, conducts team meetings, clarifies team roles, and champions team efforts.

WHEN

Because team leaders and facilitators are new to this role, they need direction to understand how best to assist the team. Requesting feedback from team members is a key tool in developing that understanding initially and adding to it over time. Most team leaders and/or team facilitators benefit from specific, monthly feedback.

A good time for team leaders or facilitators struggling with their new responsibility to request this evaluation is at the end of a regular team meeting. Evaluation forms can be distributed at that time or soon after the meeting. Instructions for when and where to return the forms should be clarified at that time.

WHO

Team members complete the form on page 286. If the team has both a facilitator and a team leader, a separate form is completed for each person. Otherwise, the team completes the form for the person who has the responsibility to coach the team on tough interpersonal issues, lead team meetings, and oversee the team's development.

HOW

There are two important phases to the evaluation: data collection and action planning.

Data Collection

1. The team leader or facilitator distributes the evaluation form to team members. Forms can be distributed to the entire team or to a sample of team members. Since these forms are completed monthly, it may be helpful to have a different group of team members complete alternate rounds of feedback.

2. One team member collects the evaluation forms and tabulates the responses for the team.

3. The team leader or facilitator also completes the form to provide a self-evaluation for comparison.

4. The team member compares the composite team scores with the team leader's or facilitator's score to determine the gap. The team member plots the gap for the respective month.

Action Planning

5. The team leader or facilitator meets with the team members who participated in the evaluation process. Their discussion focuses on the following points:

   a. Priorities for the team.

   b. Additional support and resources the team needs to have provided.

   c. Gaps that need attention at this time.

   d. Action plans that address issues or concerns.

6. Team members identify ways in which they can partner with the team leader or facilitator to provide what the team needs or to address current concerns.

WHAT'S NEXT?

The team leader or facilitator completes the agreed-upon action items. The following month, steps 1 to 6 are repeated to identify additional action items.

TEAM LEADER/FACILITATOR EVALUATION

Instructions: Rate your team leader or facilitator by circling the most accurate number for each item.

Team leader's name_____ Date_____

This team leader . . .	Never			Always
1. Encourages the team to meet.	1 2 3 4 5
2. Gives credit/praise when it is due.	1 2 3 4 5
3. Is open to new methods and ideas.	1 2 3 4 5
4. Coaches rather than tells.	1 2 3 4 5
5. Treats the team fairly.	1 2 3 4 5
6. Tells the team why decisions are made.	1 2 3 4 5
7. Encourages suggestions.	1 2 3 4 5
8. Keeps team members informed.	1 2 3 4 5
9. Tells the team which decisions it can make.	1 2 3 4 5
10. Maintains confidences.	1 2 3 4 5
11. Involves the team in goal setting.	1 2 3 4 5
12. Is an example of top performance.	1 2 3 4 5
13. Listens to understand clearly.	1 2 3 4 5
14. Praises in public, coaches in private.	1 2 3 4 5
15. Spends time wisely.	1 2 3 4 5
16. Tells team members individually how they are doing.	1 2 3 4 5
17. Follows up with team members.	1 2 3 4 5
18. Makes the team feel important.	1 2 3 4 5
19. Champions team causes.	1 2 3 4 5
20. Coaches the team to come up with its own answers.	1 2 3 4 5
21. Tells the team what is expected.	1 2 3 4 5
22. Handles discipline appropriately.	1 2 3 4 5
23. Spends time with the team.	1 2 3 4 5
24. Uses agendas for meetings.	1 2 3 4 5
25. Is open to feedback.	1 2 3 4 5
26. Helps the team focus on what is important.	1 2 3 4 5
27. Tells the team where the organization is going.	1 2 3 4 5
28. Starts and ends meetings on time.	1 2 3 4 5

TEAM LEADER/FACILITATOR SELF-EVALUATION

Instructions: Rate yourself by circling the most accurate number for each item.

Name_____ Date_____

As a team leader of facilitator, I try to . . .	Never				Always
1. Encourage the team to meet.	1	2	3	4	5
2. Give credit/praise when it is due.	1	2	3	4	5
3. Stay open to new methods and ideas.	1	2	3	4	5
4. Coach rather than tell the team what to do.	1	2	3	4	5
5. Treat the team fairly.	1	2	3	4	5
6. Tell the team why decisions are made.	1	2	3	4	5
7. Encourage suggestions from the team.	1	2	3	4	5
8. Keep team members informed.	1	2	3	4	5
9. Tell the team which decisions it can make.	1	2	3	4	5
10. Maintain confidences at all times.	1	2	3	4	5
11. Involve the team in goal setting.	1	2	3	4	5
12. Serve as an example of top performance.	1	2	3	4	5
13. Listen to understand clearly.	1	2	3	4	5
14. Praise in public, coach in private.	1	2	3	4	5
15. Spend time wisely.	1	2	3	4	5
16. Tell team members individually how they are doing.	1	2	3	4	5
17. Follow up with team members.	1	2	3	4	5
18. Make the team feel important.	1	2	3	4	5
19. Champion team causes.	1	2	3	4	5
20. Coach the team to come up with its own answers.	1	2	3	4	5
21. Tell the team what is expected.	1	2	3	4	5
22. Handle discipline appropriately.	1	2	3	4	5
23. Spend time with the team.	1	2	3	4	5
24. Use agendas for meetings.	1	2	3	4	5
25. Stay open to feedback from the team.	1	2	3	4	5
26. Help the team focus on what is important.	1	2	3	4	5
27. Tell the team where the organization is going.	1	2	3	4	5
28. Start and end meetings on time.	1	2	3	4	5

⑥ INTERVIEWING CANDIDATES FOR TEAM MANAGER

WHAT

Team-based organizations depend on leaders who support and encourage teams. Teams have the most to lose if a manager placed in the chain of command does not support teams. Therefore, team members make eager and insightful participants in the selection process. Teams get involved in selecting a manager by interviewing, as a team, each of the final candidates. After each interview, team members complete a follow-up report, and their data is considered in selecting their next "boss."

WHEN

As teams become more mature, they need to have more control over deciding not only who will be on the team, but also who will manage the teams. Use these guidelines to give maturing teams a role in selecting a new manager for the teams.

HOW

Step 1
Schedule a one-hour team interview between team members and each of the manager candidates.

Step 2
Have team members prepare in advance the questions they will ask each candidate. Encourage team members to determine the sequence of the questions before the interview.

Step 3
Conduct each interview. The team should use the questions members prepared ahead of time.

Step 4

Have team members summarize the interview and submit their information to the appropriate resource.

Team members need to decide who will fill the following roles during each interview:

Interviewee. All team members may participate in asking questions. They should follow a rotation decided in advance.

Timekeeper. This team member should allow sufficient time for the candidate to answer all the questions and for the team to have a brief "conversation" at the end of the interview.

Recorder. This team member notes the answers to the questions the team asks. If anyone asks a question that was not planned in advance, the recorder needs to note both the question and the answer. Depending on time, the recorder may also note the "tone" of the response.

Sample Interview Questions

Here are some examples of the kinds of questions team members may want to ask:

- Describe one scenario in which you were considering a traditional managerial style but deferred to a more team-oriented approach instead.
- When is it most difficult for you to work in a team organization?
- What behaviors are expected of managers who lead a team organization?
- Since you must work with parts of the organization that are not in teams, how do you defend the decision to keep teams in some parts of the organization?
- Why do you think teams are a better way to manage the business?
- When did you decide that you would prefer working in a team organization rather than in a traditional organization culture?
- How would you describe the most important differences between a team organization and a traditional organization?
- How would you resolve differences between two team members? Between two teams?

- Under what circumstances would you not be able to support team decisions?
- What is the most frustrating team situation you've experienced?
- Why would you be a good role model for team members?
- What customer focus information would you share with the teams?
- How would you complete this statement? Teams are a better way because_____

  _____

- What questions or concerns do you have about working with this team?

WHAT'S NEXT?

After the recorder captures the questions and the candidate's answers, the team submits the input to the human resource representative. If multiple candidates are interviewed, the team may be asked to rank the candidates and provide a rationale for the ranking.

⑥ ASSIMILATING A NEW MANAGER INTO A TEAM ENVIRONMENT

WHAT

Assimilating a New Manager into a Team Environment uses a series of meetings to prepare the new team manager and the teams to work effectively together. In this series of small group meetings, questions are asked of the manager, and the manager responds to the team. These meetings allow teams to tell the manager directly what the team needs. The meetings also provide a forum the manager can use to establish realistic expectations.

This tool can also be adapted to orient a new team member.

WHEN

Within the first week of the manager's appointment, a meeting should be scheduled with the teams. Follow-up discussions need to be planned as quickly as possible following the initial meeting.

WHO

The manager may conduct the meeting or contract with a facilitator to lead the session. If possible, the facilitator or manager should obtain a list of questions from the teams prior to the first meeting. The new manager can then review the questions and be prepared to respond to all questions at the first or second meeting.

If possible, all team members should attend the new manager assimilation meetings. When scheduling demands are too complex, representatives from all the teams need to attend the meetings and then share the information with their team members.

HOW

Three formal sessions are scheduled for the new manager to meet with the teams. Each question-and-answer session encourages a mutually supportive relationship by clarifying the hopes, concerns, and expectations of both the teams and the new manager. Primarily, the sessions should produce answers to three basic questions:

1. Who are the teams?
2. What do the teams need from the new manager?
3. How can the teams and managers work together to meet those needs?

Session 1 (90 minutes)

Purpose
To discuss the teams' background and to begin identifying the teams' hopes and concerns for the new manager

Process
There are two primary steps.

1. Each team provides a brief overview of its vision, mission, norms, goals, measures, and success to date.

2. Team representatives ask questions (see sample questions below). The new manager responds now, if possible, or provides answers to the questions at the second meeting.

Sample Questions for Team Representatives to Ask:

1. What do you know about these teams and their work?

2. What is your background for working with teams?

3. What do you need to know about how this team operates?

4. What major problems do you plan to address in the next six months?

5. Which of these do you see as most critical?

6. What are your expectations for this team over the next six months?

7. What questions, issues, hopes, or fears, if any, do you have about working with this team?

8. What are your views on the extent of the teams' scheduling, problem-solving, and decision-making authority?

Session 2 (Approximately two to four weeks later— 60 minutes)

Purpose
To continue clarifying mutual needs and expectations so that an effective relationship can be developed quickly

Process
This session follows up on issues introduced in the first meeting.

1. The new manager responds to any issues raised in session 1.

2. The manager asks any question to further clarify the needs of the teams.

3. The new manager and team discuss ways to attain mutual goals and establish communication expectations.

Session 3 (Approximately two to three months later— 90 minutes)

Purpose
To determine to what extent the mutual hopes, concerns, and expectations have been met and to identify what new issues have surfaced

Process
This session focuses on progress and ongoing needs.

1. Review the original data.

2. Discuss what's working and what needs further improvement.

3. Identify next steps.

WHAT'S NEXT?

As issues develop, team members and the team manager must agree to take the initiative to address concerns promptly. Developing agreed-upon communication expectations based on the methods and time frames used in this tool can be helpful in facilitating this process.

⑥ MATURE TEAM INDEX

WHAT

Identifying mature teams is tricky because maturity is not just based on chronology; it's based on accomplishment as well as the level of group cohesion. The Mature Team Index provides one way to recognize the areas a team has mastered and to identify opportunities for additional growth.

These are characteristics considered in the Mature Team Index:
- Achieving team measures.
- Demonstrating skills.
- Developing as a team.
- Working within the organizational structure.

WHEN

Use this index when you need to understand how well teams are maturing and when they may need stronger training or support. A good time to use the index is 12 months after the team is formed and at 12-month intervals thereafter.

While the easiest marker for team development is time, it's deceiving to assess the maturity of a team by the calendar. If a team has been working together for more than two years and its index rating is low, however, prompt assistance is probably needed.

These are a few common milestones useful in determining when to use the index:

- A team has completed its project or achieved its purpose.
- Team membership has been constant for 18 months.
- Team leadership skills are demonstrated by most team members.
- Team members express satisfaction about their team involvement.
- Team measurements are achieved consistently.

WHO

Team members can complete the instrument individually and then compare their responses to other team members. If the team requests it, the facilitator may gather the data, structure the follow-up conversation, and identify the developmental tools needed.

HOW

There are four phases for this process: gathering the data by having team members complete the instrument individually, comparing individual and team scores, discussing the differences in scores, and preparing both individual and team development plans.

WHAT'S NEXT?

Teams should continue to monitor their development regularly. Encourage teams to meet and discuss developmental needs and the resources available to them. As teams continue to excel, recognize their accomplishments.

MATURE TEAM INDEX

Directions: Team members, team leaders, and the team's manager complete the instrument individually. Individual scores are combined and averaged to determine the team rating on each item.

For each item, circle the answer that describes how often the activity or behavior is demonstrated by the team. The following scale should be used to answer each question:

1 = Never, 2 = Rarely, 3 = Sometimes, 4 = Often, 5 = All of the time

Applying Team Measures

	1	2	3	4	5
1. The team achieves its established measures.	☐	☐	☐	☐	☐
2. The team establishes and meets its "stretch" goals.	☐	☐	☐	☐	☐
3. The team contributes to other teams' ability to meet their goals.	☐	☐	☐	☐	☐

4. The team sets measures that
   support corporate measures.   ☐   ☐   ☐   ☐   ☐

5. The team develops additional
   methods to monitor its performance. ☐   ☐   ☐   ☐   ☐

Add the numbers checked to get the page score.

Page score ☐

Demonstrating Team Skills

	1	2	3	4	5

6. Team meetings are useful
   and practical sessions.   ☐   ☐   ☐   ☐   ☐

7. Team members share responsibilities
   for managing team activities.   ☐   ☐   ☐   ☐   ☐

8. Team members are able to address
   difficult issues with one another.   ☐   ☐   ☐   ☐   ☐

9. Innovative ideas are presented
   with a clear rationale and concrete
   suggestions for implementing the ideas. ☐   ☐   ☐   ☐   ☐

10. All team members competently perform
    multiple team responsibilities.   ☐   ☐   ☐   ☐   ☐

Add the numbers checked to get the page score.

Page score ☐

Working within an Organization

	1	2	3	4	5

11. Management decisions are
    challenged in productive ways.   ☐   ☐   ☐   ☐   ☐

12. New members are quickly accepted
    into the team.   ☐   ☐   ☐   ☐   ☐

13. Questions that ask for clarification and
    that challenge the status quo are
    posed constructively.   ☐   ☐   ☐   ☐   ☐

14. Effective team members are
    recognized in the organization.   ☐   ☐   ☐   ☐   ☐

15. Team performance is rewarded
    according to the team's contribution.   ☐   ☐   ☐   ☐   ☐

Add the numbers checked to get the page score.

Page score ☐

Developing as a Team

                                                       1   **2**   **3**   **4**   **5**

16. Norms are strong, positive, and
    conducive to team growth.   ☐   ☐   ☐   ☐   ☐

17. All team members are given the
    opportunity to expand their skills.   ☐   ☐   ☐   ☐   ☐

18. Team development is regularly
    a topic for discussion.   ☐   ☐   ☐   ☐   ☐

19. Training is an important element
    that is scheduled into the work load.   ☐   ☐   ☐   ☐   ☐

20. New processes are eagerly mastered by
    team members.   ☐   ☐   ☐   ☐   ☐

Add the numbers checked to get the page score.

Page score ☐

Record the scores from each page in the appropriate box and add them to get the total score.

☐   ☐   ☐   ☐   ☐

Applying   Demonstrating   Working   Developing   Total
team   team skills   within   as a team   score
measures   an
                                 organization

SCORING GUIDELINES

Find your total score within the ranges below. Read the brief description.

Total Score of 20–40

Low levels of team maturity are present in the team's practices. Teams with low scores need to invest in communication skills, develop a more effective group process, and improve their performance. The team facilitator or team manager may be helpful in identifying additional resources. The first priority is to improve the team's output and measures.

Total Score of 41–70

Moderate levels of team maturity typically characterize the team's activities. Some of the team members may have high levels of skills and could provide help to other team members who may not be as proficient in either the technical responsibilities or the team process.

Total Score of 71–100

High levels of team performance are consistently demonstrated by the team. Most of the team members are strong performers, and the team is appropriately focused on team development. Two suggestions are suitable for these mature teams: (1) encourage struggling team members to participate in the team and (2) break out some team members to diffuse effective team practices into other parts of the organization.

⑥ ADVANCED TEAM TRAINING

WHAT

Advanced Team Training is a sample curriculum of skills for mature teams. This curriculum assumes that team members have a solid foundation in these three dimensions:

Technical skills. Demonstrated competence in at least half of the tasks the team is responsible for completing.

Administrative skills. Demonstrated competence in completing appropriate forms such as quality reports, attendance sheets, work requests, and assignment schedules, as well as the ability to list three of the team's customers and three suppliers to the team.

Communication skills. Demonstrated competence in participating in meetings, arriving at different types of team decisions, resolving conflicts with team members, presenting new ideas, and solving problems.

Advanced Team Training builds on the foundation competencies essential to effective team participation. It also challenges team members to become familiar with processes and responsibilities outside their current roles.

The following skills are typical of those identified for Advanced Team Training.

Technical Skills

These include the ability to perform additional technical tasks within the team and in supplier and customer teams. This training may also include technical skills for expanded teams.

Administrative Skills

This area covers the ability to perform skills and demonstrate knowledge in the following areas:

- Performing any administrative tasks that have been the responsibility of the manager and are now designated to be assigned to the team.
- Explaining the impact of the teams' performance on company results.
- Determining more than one approach for securing resources, setting schedules, and addressing performance issues.
- Defining customer expectations and identifying the two most common deviations.
- Reviewing financial reports and determining where the team should focus its attention.
- Providing input into operational planning.
- Collecting measurement information.
- Developing action plans to improve the team's performance based on measurement data.
- Compiling information on multiple issues that are impacting the team's performance.
- Balancing short-term production goals with longer-term developmental requirements.

Communications Skills

Team members need the competence to apply the following skills consistently within the team:

- Drawing out quiet team members.
- Launching a new or spin-off team.
- Maintaining a team culture.
- Learning more about the team process.
- Suggesting ways to reconfigure the team in response to changing markets and customer expectations.
- Applying best-practice principles to the team.
- Working across team lines to meet organizational goals.
- Providing support for peer reviews and for handling grievances.

- Conducting "tours" of the facility and emphasizing the unique accomplishments of the team environment.
- Raising difficult issues with team members directly, such as the impact of individual performance on the team, personal developmental concerns, and the root cause for errors in measurement.
- Conducting effective meetings by observing ground rules, the agenda, and time constraints.
- Supporting team members who are struggling with their tasks.
- Turning core values into daily practices.
- Encouraging a diversity of opinions.
- Developing individual presentation skills.
- Hiring a new team member.
- Conducting peer performance reviews (see page 280).
- Assimilating a new manager.
- Identifying boundaries that limit the team.
- Presenting ideas to upper management.

WHEN

Advanced Team Training is appropriate after team members have demonstrated basic competencies. Advanced training is also appropriate when the organization needs to have team members and team leaders expand their current responsibilities.

WHO

With input from team members, leaders, and managers, the internal change agents determine the training required and select the source material for the training. Team members and team leaders determine the training schedule based on priorities and scheduling constraints. Team members, team leaders, and team managers can all be effective training instructors.

HOW

Training is conducted according to the priorities identified for providing expanded competencies. The skills offered should enable team members and team leaders to assume a broader range of responsibilities.

To determine the training required, compare the expanded skill requirements for team members with the team's current competencies. For help in making this comparison, see Planning for the Team's Development on page 269. This tool is useful in getting input from team members and leaders to ensure that any advanced training is on target and meets recognized needs.

WHAT'S NEXT?

Once the required advanced training has been identified, steps must be taken to deliver the training as soon as possible. The process of identifying and delivering training should be a continual one. Skill development will remain an ongoing need for teams as they take on new responsibilities that are transferred to them.

To ensure a team's success, it is critical to establish a mechanism to examine team competencies on a regular basis so that training is provided as needed. Use this tool and Planning for the Team's Development (page xx) to carry out this continuing process.

Foundation Skills for Teams

Team Leader	All	Team Member

Team awareness and role transition
- Provide team leadership
- Building a foundation of trust

Team awareness and role transition
- The advantage of teams
- The basic principles of teamwork

Interpersonal foundation skills
- Giving constructive feedback
- Getting good information from others
- Getting ideas across
- Recognizing positive results
- Managing change

Interpersonal foundation skills
- Giving feedback to help others
- Listening to understand clearly
- Getting a point across
- Participating in group meetings
- Dealing with changes

Team formation and development
- Facilitating meetings to produce results
- Launching and refueling a team
- Expanding a team's capabilities
- Helping the team reach consensus
- Making the most of team differences
- Thinking ahead

Team formation and development
- Keeping the team on course
- Playing a vital role in team decisions
- Developing team plans
- Raising difficult issues with the team

Continuous process improvement
- Quality through the eyes of the customer
- Clarifying customer expectations
- Resolving customer dissatisfaction
- Analyzing work processes and finding opportunities for improvement
- Solving quality problems

⑥ PRESCRIPTION FOR ORGANIZATIONAL IMPROVEMENT

WHAT

Prescription for Organizational Improvement is a method for examining the current level of employee participation, customer focus, and process improvement in a department or function or across the organization. Analysis in these areas yields information about the types of change efforts currently in place. It also identifies opportunities for increasing the effectiveness of any one effort by leveraging and coordinating a variety of other efforts to improve the organization, including the implementation or expansion of teams.

Data gathered in applying the Prescription for Organizational Improvement become the basis for examining the need to integrate various change efforts. By providing an evaluation of any current change activity that is showing success, this tool helps leaders identify areas to concentrate on when revising on-going implementation plans. It also provides critical information needed to expand and sustain team concepts, and it reveals what is needed to promote additional gains.

WHEN

At some point, organizations that have supported several change efforts—and still haven't achieved everything they had hoped to—need to step back and assess just where they stand. In most cases, parts of these efforts will be successful and should be preserved. Other efforts may have reached their goals and have positive results to show. Valuable elements may already be in place—perhaps an effective steering committee, a still-useful capabilities assessment, or a cadre of employees trained in a skill-like problem solving. Other elements, however, may be either missing or inadequate.

When an organization's progress toward change or the return on improvements has slowed or stalled, Prescription for Organizational

Improvement helps the organization refocus and revitalize its change efforts. It helps it identify which efforts to continue, which elements to retain, and which initiatives to modify or conclude.

This tool can also guide the periodic analyses of change initiatives on a regular basis. One year after a change initiative is under way, Prescription for Organizational Improvement can be used to analyze the initiative's successes and shortcomings. Once the analysis is complete, specific information is identified to guide the revision of the team implementation plan and the role of teams in the change effort.

WHO

At the request of the internal or external change agent or the current teams, an analysis is conducted that involves questioning employees, managers, supervisors, and executives in the targeted work operation or department. The change agent also talks with direct support people, including internal suppliers and/or customers of the target operation, and any other support services, such as accounting (receivables and payables), human resources, shipping, and receiving or other departments that work closely with or provide products or services to the target operation.

HOW

The Prescription for Organizational Improvement (see page 307) helps determine to what extent an organization has made progress in the three primary areas for organizational change: employee involvement, customer focus, and process improvement. The data collected, along with their analysis, provide the basis for revising change efforts and developing future implementation plans. The result becomes the organization's Prescription for Organizational Improvement. The steps in the process are as follows:

1. The checklist is most commonly completed by individuals in a group setting. The internal change agent distributes the checklists, collects completed forms, and then analyzes the data for trends.

2. Follow-up focus groups can be used to validate and expand on the information from the paper-and-pencil checklist. Topics for these groups to examine include the following:

    a. Existing and perceived change activity.

    b. Common deviations from the planned change efforts.

    c. Causes and effects of the common deviations.

    d. Potential solutions to the implementation issues.

    e. Current strengths to be maintained.

3. Using the information collected, the change agent develops recommendations for planning that include the following:

    a. What should be maintained?

    b. What should be changed?

    c. What solutions are possible based on information provided by the checklist and follow-up focus groups?

4. The change agent's report is submitted to the group responsible for the change process.

WHAT'S NEXT?

The results of the Prescription for Organizational Improvement are applied by the organization to do the following:

1. Sustain successes, build on components already in place, and identify inadequate or missing pieces.

2. Assess the overall impact of the three types of change initiatives and determine next steps. In other words, determine to what extent the organization is customer focused, process managed, and employee involved.

3. Integrate all change efforts to carry the organization forward.

To do these things the change process team reviews the recommendations and may meet with current teams to agree on amendments to the operational aspects of the team effort. These amendments can include having the teams focus more on process innovation or on customer expectations. Once the expanded plan for change is amended and adopted, the next phase of activity begins.

PRESCRIPTION FOR ORGANIZATIONAL IMPROVEMENT

Directions: The following statements describe characteristics of high-performing organizations in three key improvement areas: the focus on customers, the management of processes, and the involvement of employees. Decide how accurately you believe each statement describes your organization and write the number of the response you select on the line in front of each statement. When you have finished all three sections, go back and total your responses for each section.

5 = Completely accurate statement   2 = Not very accurate

4 = Fairly accurateinaccurate   1 = Completely

3 = Accurate in some respects, inaccurate
      in others

To what extent is your organization focused on the customer?

_____ 1. References to customers, service, and quality have been included in the organization's vision, mission, and strategies.

_____ 2. Surveys, focus groups, and complaint analysis efforts are used regularly to measure customer satisfaction.

_____ 3. Customer data are used to guide the development of products and services.

_____ 4. People from our organization regularly observe how our customers use our products and services.

_____ 5. Customer data are regularly made available to everyone who needs it throughout the organization.

_____ 6. Managers make a point of interacting with customers, even if customer contact is not part of their regular jobs.

_____ 7. Employee performance evaluations include a customer satisfaction component.

_____ 8. The boundaries between our organization and key external customers have blurred.

_____ 9. Our organization has initiated ways to make it easier for customers to deal with us.

_____ 10. We investigate latent needs for products and services, needs that customers may not yet be aware of.

_____ 11. We measure all aspects of any operation that is important to our customers.

_____ 12. We measure how well we meet the needs of our internal customers.

_____   TOTAL

To what extent does your organization manage by key work processes rather than exclusively by department?

_____ 13. Our organization has identified key work processes that involve more than one department.

_____ 14. Each key work process is "owned" by an executive or top manager.

_____ 15. Our organization takes a cross-functional approach to identifying and solving problems.

_____ 16. Cross-functional communication among departments exists at all levels, not just at the top.

_____ 17. People in our organization understand how their work contributes to key strategic goals.

_____ 18. People in our organization know who their internal customers are and how their work impacts these customers.

_____ 19. Our organization maintains procedures for measuring how well processes are performing.

_____ 20. The executive team identifies key measures and cascades them throughout the organization.

_____ 21. There is a high value placed on using hard data to make decisions and resolve disagreements.

_____ 22. People in our organization have the skills to measure work processes.

_____ 23. As part of their normal career path, people in our organization accept permanent or temporary assignments outside their regular function or department.

_____ 24. Managers are expected to adopt a cross-functional perspective when making decisions.

_____   TOTAL

To what extent does your organization involve its employees?

_____ 25. At every level, those closest to the work are making more decisions about how that work gets done.

_____ 26. Most people feel a strong personal commitment to the organization's well-being.

_____ 27. Everyone in our organization is encouraged to take the initiative to make things better.

_____ 28. The organization regularly shares customer, financial, competitor, and performance information with employees.

_____ 29. Throughout the organization, people's roles and responsibilities are expanding.

_____ 30. People receive the support, resources, knowledge, and tools they need to handle their new responsibilities.

_____ 31. Teams are used more and more to identify problems and make improvements.

_____ 32. Teams make decisions about their daily work.

_____ 33. More and more regular work in the organization is being performed by teams.

_____ 34. People receive training in team skills: making group plans and decisions, participating in meetings, solving problems, and resolving differences.

_____ 35. More and more teams work with little or no direct supervision or management.

_____ 36. Managers take the initiative to empower teams.

_____   TOTAL

Interpreting the Results of the Checklist

The purpose of this informal checklist is to serve as a starting point for refocusing and integrating your organization's change initiatives. The information you provide on these pages will be used to plan the next steps for your organization.

In general, a low score in one area indicates where the organization should focus its next change initiative. Conversely, a high score in one area suggests that change efforts would be better focused on one of the other two. (Of course, if a high score comes from recent successes with a particular change initiative, the organization may want to sustain the momentum through further efforts in that area.)

Every organization's situation is different; your scores are only one indicator of what the next steps might be. Perhaps the organization can best use your scores to begin making further explorations.

To begin your analysis, copy your scores in the boxes provided below. Then answer the questions that follow.

Customer Focus   Process Management   Employee Involvement

In those areas with high scores, what has enabled the organization to be successful?

In those areas with low scores, what is preventing the organization from doing better?

What opportunities do you see for undertaking new change efforts?

What possible barriers to success do you see?

⑥　PROCESS FOR DECIDING WHEN TO REDESIGN

WHAT

This process provides a quick way to gauge (1) how appropriate work redesign would be in your organization and (2) how effectively your organization would integrate the work redesign ideas into the workplace. The Process for Deciding When to Redesign helps in evaluating the organization's ability to complete each part of the redesign process and then institute the changes. The basic elements of the redesign process are these:

- Environmental factors
- Technical factors
- Social factors

The Survey to Determine Redesign Readiness on page 312 provides information on the organization and gives guidelines for determining potential success.

WHEN

The two most common times to apply this tool are (1) before teams are configured and team members selected and (2) prior to expanding the team initiative to another part of the organization.

WHO

Internal consultants often work with key leaders in the organization to understand the work redesign process and its outcomes. Then the internal consultant plans a decision-making session during which organization leaders determine whether they will conduct any work redesign analysis. Often, the design team or people representing a diagonal slice of the organization complete the actual analysis.

For an in-depth understanding, review information on sociotechnical systems. One reference is *Designing Effective Organizations: The Sociotechnical Systems Perspective* (John Wiley, New York:, 1988).

HOW

The process includes five steps that help determine whether work redesign is appropriate for the organization.

1. Internal consultants prepare an educational session about the basics of work design and determine who in the organization can appropriately address the issues involved. (See Chapter 3: Should You Redesign the Work Process? pages 43–53 for an overview and examples.)

2. At the educational session, employees, supervisors, and managers who represent a diagonal slice of the organization gather to complete the instrument (see Chapter 3: Should You Redesign the Work Process) and to examine the issues addressed on this survey. The survey can also be completed by those who will attend the decision-making session. Alternatively, the educational session may be used to gather input from people throughout the organization.

3. After the surveys have been completed, consultants average individual scores to determine group scores and then assess the total scores for the group to determine the organization's readiness to redesign.

4. At the decision-making session, internal consultants present the information from the survey and review appropriate options for the organization. Often the leadership team retains the decision-making authority and decides whether to complete the work redesign.

5. If the organization is ready to move ahead, the key leaders determine the possible options for carrying out a complete work redesign (either the fast-cycle method or the design team approach described in Chapter 3).

WHAT'S NEXT?

After determining the potential success of work redesign, the organization can pursue one of three courses of action:

1. Postpone any redesign at this time. Instead, implement changes to create an environment supportive of redesign in the future or continue making incremental improvements.

2. Take specific steps to prepare the organization to effectively conduct and implement a work redesign effort relatively soon. Perhaps more education or an opportunity to tour a redesigned facility would provide the level of detail people need to understand the benefits.

3. Begin selecting employees to conduct the work redesign. Follow through with a communication plan to inform members of the organization about the redesign activities so they will be prepared when asked to supply needed information.

Some organizations involve large groups or teams of employees in the redesign process after the initial assessment of the organization's readiness. For more information on this process, see W. Passmore, Al Fitz, and Gary Frankle, *Fast Cycle, Full Participation Work Systems Design* (Denver: Passmore Associates, 1993)

SURVEY TO DETERMINE REDESIGN READINESS

Directions: Individually complete each item by checking the box that most accurately reflects your response. Be prepared to share your answers with the group during discussion and to use the items to probe more deeply into the redesign process.

OVERVIEW AND ENVIRONMENTAL EFFECTIVENESS

Answer According to the Following Scale

1 = Never   2 = Rarely   3 = Sometimes   4= Often   5 = Always

How appropriate is it for employees to examine:

	1	2	3	4	5
1. The tasks people perform?	☐	☐	☐	☐	☐
2. The way jobs are structured?	☐	☐	☐	☐	☐
3. The technical processes for doing the work?	☐	☐	☐	☐	☐

5. The knowledge and skills people need at work? ☐ ☐ ☐ ☐ ☐

6. How people are formed into work units? ☐ ☐ ☐ ☐ ☐

7. How different units interact? ☐ ☐ ☐ ☐ ☐

8. The layout of the facility? ☐ ☐ ☐ ☐ ☐

9. How work flows? ☐ ☐ ☐ ☐ ☐

10. The way people are led? ☐ ☐ ☐ ☐ ☐

11. How people are rewarded? ☐ ☐ ☐ ☐ ☐

Add the number of each box checked to get a section score.

Section score

TECHNICAL EFFECTIVENESS

Answer According to the Following Scale

1 = Not ever likely

2 = Some ideas occasionally

3 = Many ideas occasionally

4 = Many ideas frequently

5 = All ideas regularly

How likely is it for employees' ideas to be accepted about

	1	2	3	4	5
1. How to control or eliminate variances (errors or inconsistencies) in the standard work process?	☐	☐	☐	☐	☐
2. How to eliminate nonessential work (policies, procedures, sign-offs, steps)?	☐	☐	☐	☐	☐
3. How to eliminate non-value-added work (from the customer's point of view)?	☐	☐	☐	☐	☐
4. What equipment is appropriate?	☐	☐	☐	☐	☐
5. How to make procedures more accurate?					
6. How to improve responsiveness to customer requirements?	☐	☐	☐	☐	☐

Add the number of each box checked to get a section score.

Section score

SOCIAL EFFECTIVENESS

Answer According to the Following Scale

1 = Not likely
2 = Somewhat likely
3 = Likely
4 = Very likely
5 = Always likely

How likely is it that employees will have ideas on:

		1	2	3	4	5
1.	Decisions for how work gets done?	☐	☐	☐	☐	☐
2.	Customers' expectations?	☐	☐	☐	☐	☐
3.	Effective peer relationships?	☐	☐	☐	☐	☐
4.	Opportunities to learn?	☐	☐	☐	☐	☐
5.	Elements that make a job good?	☐	☐	☐	☐	☐
6.	Appropriate rewards?	☐	☐	☐	☐	☐
7.	Sufficient variety of tasks?	☐	☐	☐	☐	☐

Add the number of each box checked to get a section score.

Section score

Fill in the following boxes:

| Overview and environmental effectiveness | + | Technical effectiveness | + | Social effectiveness | = | Total score |

SCORING GUIDELINES

Determine the total score by adding the three section scores together. The highest section score for the group indicates an area where leaders will have the least difficulty implementing redesign. The lowest score indicates areas where leaders will have most difficulty implementing redesign.

Refer to these guidelines to interpret scores.

Score of 27–48

It would probably be better not to undertake work redesign at this time. There is resistance to the results of redesign and insufficient energy to direct toward implementing suggestions.

Score of 49–95

Many of the ideas from the redesign process would be accepted by the leadership. However, there are doubts about the appropriateness of redesign and the ability of the organization to implement changes. If work redesign proceeds and only a few ideas are implemented, employees may become skeptical of management's confidence in them. Before proceeding, verify the authority level of the leadership team to implement the redesign.

Score of 96–140

Most likely the redesign effort will produce significant benefits for the organization in terms of gains in productivity, customer satisfaction, and employee satisfaction. The ideas from the redesign effort will be incorporated into standard organizational practices.

BIBLIOGRAPHY

Ancona, D. G., and D. F Caldwell. "Bridging the Boundary: External Activity and Performance in Organization Teams." *Administrative Science Quarterly* 37 (1992), pp. 634–65.

Ashkenas, R., D. Ulrich, T. Jick, and S. Kerr. *The Boundaryless Organization: Breaking the Chains of Organizational Structure.* San Francisco: Jossey-Bass, 1995.

Bartlett, C., and S. Ghoshal. "Changing the Role of Top Management: Beyond Strategy to Purpose." *Harvard Business Review,* November–December 1994, pp. 79–88.

Becker, F., and F. Steele. *Workplace by Design: Mapping the High-Performance Workplace.* San Francisco: Jossey-Bass, 1995.

Beekun, R. I. "Assessing the Effectiveness of Sociotechnical Interventions: Antidote or Fad?" *Human Resources* 47, no. 10 (1989), pp. 877–97.

Bennis, W. "The Artform of Leadership." In *The Executive Mind,* ed. S. Srivastva. San Francisco: Jossey-Bass, 1983.

Bennis, W. "The Coming Death of Bureaucracy." *Think.* November–December 1966, pp. 30–35.

———, and B. Nanus. *Leaders and the Strategies for Taking Charge: The Four Keys of Effective Leadership.* New York: Harper and Row, 1985.

Bennis, W., and H. A. Shepard. "Theory of Group Development." *Human Relations* 9, no. 4 (1956), pp. 415–38.

Berrey, C., A. Avergan, and L. Moran. *Highly Responsive Teams: The Key to Competitive Advantage.* San Jose: Zenger Miller, 1995.

Berrey, C., and L. Moran. *Ensuring the Success of Self-Directed Work Teams.* San Jose: Zenger Miller, 1995.

Bertalanffy, L. "The Theory of Open Systems in Physics and Biology." *Science* 111 (1950), pp. 23–29.

Beyerlein, M. M., and D. A. Johnson, eds. *Advances in Interdisciplinary Studies of Work Teams,* vol. 1. Greenwich, CT: JAI, 1994.

Bion, W. *Experiences in Small Groups and Other Papers.* London: Tavistock, 1961.

Bridges, W. *Job Shift: How to Prosper in a Workplace without Jobs.* Reading, MA: Addison-Wesley, 1993.

———. *Transitions: Making Sense of Life's Changes.* Reading, MA: Addison-Wesley, 1980.

Burke, W. W. *Organizational Development: A Process of Learning and Changing,* 2nd ed. Reading, MA: Addison Wesley, 1992.

Burke, W. W., and H. A. Hornstein. *The Social Technology of Organizational Development.* La Jolla, CA: University Associates, 1972.

Burnside, R. *Letting Go.* Schenectady, NY: High Peaks Press, 1992.

Cabana, S. "Participative Design Works, Partially Participative Doesn't." *Journal for Quality and Participation,* January/February 1995, pp. 10–19.

Caminiti, S. "What Team Leaders Need to Know." *Fortune,* February, 20, 1995, pp. 93–100.

Campbell, R. *Fisherman's Guide: A Systems Approach to Creativity and Organization.* Boston: New Science Library, 1985.

Carter, D. E., and B. S. Baker. *CE Concurrent Engineering: The Product Development Environment for the 1990s.* Reading, MA: Addison-Wesley, 1992.

Chang, R. *Succeeding as a Self-Managed Team.* Irvine, CA: Richard Chang Associates, 1994.

———, G. E. Bader, and A. E. Bloom. *Measuring Team Performance.* Irvine, CA: Richard Chang Associates, 1994.

Cherns, A. "The Principles of Sociotechnical Design." *Human Relations* 29 (1976), pp. 783–92.

Chisholm, R., and J. Ziegenfuss. "A Review of Applications of the Sociotechnical Systems Approach to Health Care Organizations." *Journal of Applied Behavioral Science* 22, no. 3 (1987), pp. 315–27.

Clark, K. B., and S. C. Wheelwright. "Organizing and Leading 'Heavyweight' Development Teams. Revolutionizing Product Development: Quantum Leaps in Speed, Efficiency, and Quality." New York: Free Press, 1992, 9-28.

Coch, L., and J. French. "Overcoming Resistance to Change." *Human Relations* 1 (1948), pp. 512–32.

Conger, J. A., and Associates. *Spirit at Work: Discovering the Spirituality in Leadership.* San Francisco: Jossey-Bass, 1994.

Croland, D. "The Team That Wasn't." *Harvard Business Review,* November– December 1994, pp. 22–36.

Cummings, T. "Sociotechnical Systems: An Intervention Strategy." In *Current Issues and Strategies in Organization Development,* ed. W. Burke. New York: Human Science Press, 1976.

———, and S. Mohrman. "Self Designing Organizations: Toward Implementing Quality-of-Work-Life Interventions." In *Research in Organizational Change and Development,* ed. R. Woodman and W. Pasmore. Greenwich, CT: JAI Press, 1985.

Cummings, T., and W. Griggs. "Worker Reaction to Autonomous Work Groups: Conditions for Functioning, Differential Effects and Individual Differences." *Organization and Administrative Science* (1977), pp. 87–100.

De Pree, M. *Leadership Is an Art.* New York: Doubleday, 1989.

DuBrin, A. J. *The Breakthrough Team Player: Becoming the M.V.P. on Your Workplace Team.* New York: American Management Association, 1995.

Dumaine, B. "Mr. Learning Organization." *Fortune,* October 17, 1994, pp. 147–68.

Eisenhardt, K. M. "Making Fast Strategic Decisions in High-Velocity Environments." *Academy of Management Journal* 32, no. 3 (1989), pp. 543–76.

Elden, M. "Sociotechnical Systems Ideas as Public Policy in Norway: Empowering Participation through Worker-Managed Change." *Journal of Applied Behavioral Science* 22, no. 3 (1987), pp. 239–55.

Emery, F. "Participative Design: Effective, Flexible and Successful, Now!" *Journal for Quality and Participation* (January–February 1995), pp. 6–19.

———. *Characteristics of Sociotechnical Systems.* London: Tavistock Institute, 1959.

———. *Some Hypotheses about the Way in Which Tasks May Be More Effectively Put Together to Design Jobs.* London: Tavistock Institute, 1963.

———, and E. Trist. "Analytical Model for Sociotechnical Systems." In *Sociotechnical Systems: A Sourcebook,* ed. W. Pasmore and J. Sherwood. San Diego: University Associates, 1978.

———. "The Causal Texture of Organizational Environments." *Human Relations* 18, no. 21 (1965), pp. 21–32.

Exploratory Investigations of Pay-for-Knowledge Systems. Washington, DC: U.S. Department of Labor, Bureau of Labor-Management Relations and Cooperative Programs, 1988.

Frangos, S. J., and S. Bennett. *Team Zebra: How 1500 Partners Revitalized Eastman Kodak's Black and White Film-Making Flow.* Essex Junction, VT: Oliver Wright, 1993.

Galbraith, J. R. *Designing Organizations: An Executive Briefing on Strategy, Structure, and Process.* San Francisco: Jossey-Bass, 1995.

————, and E. E. Lawler III. "New Roles for the Staff Function: Strategic Support and Services." In *Organization for the Future: The New Logic for Managing Complex Organizations.* San Francisco: Jossey-Bass, 1993.

Graham, P. *Mary Parker Follett—Prophet of Management: A Celebration of Writings from the 1920s.* Boston: Harvard Business School Press, 1995.

Grazier, P. "Living with a Self-Managed Team." *Journal for Quality and Participation,* September 1993, pp. 66–69.

Greenleaf, R. K. *Servant Leadership: A Journey into the Nature of Legitimate Power and Greatness.* New York: Paulist Press, 1991.

Greising, D. "Quality: How to Make It Pay." *Business Week,* August 8, 1994, pp. 54–59.

Guzzo, R. A., E. Salas, and Associates. *Team Effectiveness and Decision Making in Organizations.* San Francisco: Jossey-Bass, 1995.

Hackman, J. R. "The Design of Work in the 1980s." *Organizational Dynamics,* Summer 1978, pp. 3–17.

————. "The Design of Work Teams." In *Handbook of Organizational Behavior,* ed. J. W. Lorsch. Englewood Cliffs, NJ: Prentice-Hall, 1987.

Hackman, R., and G. Oldham. *Work Redesign.* Reading, MA: Addison-Wesley, 1980.

Hamel, G. and C. K. Prahalad. *Competing for the Future: Breakthrough Strategies for Seizing Control of Your Industry and Creating the Markets of Tomorrow.* Boston: Harvard Business School Press, 1994.

Harding, J. "What Team Leaders Need to Know." *Fortune,* February 20, 1995, pp. 93–100.

Hartzler, M., and J. E. Henry. *Team Fitness: A How-To Manual for Building a Winning Work Team.* Milwaukee: ASQC Quality Press, 1994.

Herzberg, F. "One More Time: How Do You Motivate Employees?" *Harvard Business Review* 46, 1968, pp. 53–62.

Hoffman, D. "Keeping Teams on Track: What to Do When the Going Gets Rough" *The Process for Deciding When to Redesign.* San Jose: Zenger Miller, 1996.

Holpp, L. "If Empowerment Is So Good, Why Does It Hurt?" *Training,* (March 1995), pp. 52–57.

————. "Self-Directed Teams Are Great, but They're Not Easy." *Journal of Quality and Participation,* December 1993, pp. 64–70.

Huey, J. "The New Post-Heroic Leadership." *Fortune,* February 21, 1994, pp. 42–50.

Hughes, R. "Keeping Teams on Track: What to Do When the Going Gets Rough." *Diagnosing a Stuck Team.* San Jose: Zenger Miller, 1996.

————. "Zero Defects, On Schedule, New Jobs." *At Work,* January/February 1995, pp. 6–8.

Hulin, C., and M. Blood. "Job Enlargement, Individual Differences, and Worker Responses." *Psychological Bulletin* 69 (1968), pp. 41–55.

Hupp, T., and C. Polak, and O. Westgaard. *Designing Workgroups, Jobs, and Work Flow.* San Francisco: Jossey-Bass, 1995.

Hutton, D. W. *The Change Agents' Handbook: A Survival Guide for Quality Improvement Champions.* Milwaukee: ASQC Quality Press, 1994.

Jamieson, K. H. *Beyond the Double Bind: Women and Leadership.* New York: Oxford University Press, 1995.

Johann, B. *Designing Cross-Fuctional Business Processes.* San Francisco: Jossey-Bass, 1995.

Kahn, W. A., and, K. E. Kram. "Authority at Work: Internal Models and Their Organizational Consequences." *Academy of Management Review* 19, no. 1 (1994), pp. 17–50.

Kaplan, R., and D. Norton. "The Balanced Scorecard—Measures That Drive Performance." *Harvard Business Review,* January–February 1992, 71–79.

Katz, A. J., D. Russ-Eft, L. Moran, and L. Ravishankar. *Team Members Speak Out: A New Survey Reveals What Employees Really Feel about Participating on Teams.* San Jose: Zenger Miller, 1994.

Katz, R. *Managing Professionals in Innovative Organizations: A Collection of Readings.* New York: Harper Business, 1988.

Katzenbach, J. R., and D. K. Smith. *The Wisdom of Teams: Creating the High-Performance Organization.* Boston: Harvard Business School Press, 1993.

Kayser, T. A. *Team Power: How to Unleash the Collaborative Genius of Work Teams.* Chicago: Irwin, 1994.

Ketchum, L. D., and E. Trist. *All Teams Are Not Created Equal.* Newbury Park, CA: Sage, 1992.

Klein, J. A. "Why Supervisors Resist Employee Involvement." *Harvard Business Review,* September–October 1984, pp. 125–129.

————., and P. A. Posey. "Good Supervisors Are Good Supervisors—Anywhere." *Harvard Business Review,* November–December 1986, pp. 87–95.

Kotter, J. "Leading Change: Why Transformation Efforts Fail." *Harvard Business Review,* March–April 1995, pp. 59–67.

Kouzes, J. M., and B. Z. Posner. *The Leadership Challenge: How to Get Extraordinary Things Done in Organizations.* San Francisco: Jossey-Bass, 1987.

Larson, E. W., and D. H. Gobeli. "Organizing for Product Development Projects." *Journal of Product Innovation Management* 5 (1988), pp. 180–90.

Lawler, E. E. III. *The New Pay.* Los Angeles: Center for Effective Organizations, University of Southern California, 1986.

————, and S. A. Mohrman. "With HR Help, All Managers Can Practice High-Involvement Management." *Personnel,* April 1989, pp. 26–31.

————. *Strategic Pay: Aligning Organizational Strategies and Pay System.* San Francisco: Jossey-Bass, 1990.

————. *The Ultimate Advantage.* San Francisco: Jossey-Bass, 1992.

————, and G. E. Ledford. *Creating High Performance Organizations.* San Francisco: Jossey-Bass, 1995.

Lewin, K. "Group Decision and Social Change." In *Readings in Social Psychology,* ed. E. Maccoby, T. Newcomb, and E. Hartley. New York: Holt, Rinehart and Winston, 1958.

Lewin, K. *Field Theory in Social Science.* New York: HarperCollins, 1951.

Lipnack, J., and J. Stamps. *The TeamNet Factor: Bringing the Power of Boundary Crossing into the Heart of Your Business.* Essex Junction, VT: Oliver Wright, 1993.

Lippit, G., and R. Lippitt. *The Consulting Process in Action, 2nd ed. San Diego: University Associates,* 1986.

Lippit, R. "The Changing Leader-Follower Relationships of the 1980s." *Journal of Applied Behavioral Science* 18, no. 3 (1982), pp. 395–403.

Louis, M. "Sourcing Workplace Cultures: Why, When and How." In *Managing Organizational Culture,* ed. R. Kilmann, M. Saxton, and R. Serpa. San Francisco: Jossey-Bass, 1985.

Lytle, W. O. *Starting an Organization Design Effort.* Plainfield, NJ: Block Petrella Weisbord, 1993.

Macy, B. A., and H. H. Izumi. "Organizational Change, Design and Work Innovations Meta Analysis." In *Research in Organizational Change and Development,* ed. R.W. Woodman and W. Passmore. Greenwich, CT: JAI Press, 1993, pp. 239–311.

Macy, B. A., P. D. Bliese, and J. J. Norton."Organizational Change and Work Innovation: A Meta-Analysis of 131 North American Field Experiments—1961–1990." Paper presented at the meeting of the National Academy of Management of Miami, August 1991.

McIntosh-Fletcher, D. *Teaming by Design.* Chicago: Irwin, 1996.

Meyer, C. "How the Right Measures Help Teams Excel." *Harvard Business Review,* May–June 1994, pp. 95–103.

Miller, J. B. *The Corporate Coach: How to Build a Team of Loyal Customers and Happy Employees.* New York: Harper Business, 1994.

Mohrman, S.A., and G. E. Ledford, Jr. "The Design of Employee Participation Groups: Guidelines Based on Empirical Research." *Human Resources Management* 24, no. 3 (1985).

Mohrman, S. A., S. G. Cohen, and A. M. Mohram, Jr. *Designing Team-Based Organizations: New Forms for Knowledge Work.* San Francisco: Jossey-Bass, 1995.

Moran, L., J. Latham, J. Hogeveen, and D. Russ-Eft. *Winning Competitive Advantage: A Blended Strategy Works Best.* San Jose: Zenger Miller, 1994.

Nadler, D. A., M. S. Gerstein, R. Shaw, and Associates. *Organizational Architecture: Designs for Changing Organizations.* San Francisco: Jossey-Bass, 1992.

Nadler, D. A., R. B. Shaw, A. E. Walton, and Associates. *Discontinuous Change: Leading Organizational Transformation.* San Francisco: Jossey-Bass, 1995.

Nair, K. *A Higher Standard of Leadership: Lessons from the Life of Gandhi.* San Francisco: Berrett-Koehler, 1994.

Nilson, C. *Team Games for Trainers: High-Involvement Games and Training Aids for Developing Team Skills.* New York: McGraw-Hill, 1993.

Orsburn, J. D., L. Moran, E. Musselwhite, and J. H. Zenger. *Self-Directed Work Teams: The New American Challenge.* Chicago: Irwin, 1990.

Parker, G. M. *Cross-Functional Teams: Working with Allies, Enemies and Other Strangers.* San Francisco: Jossey-Bass, 1994.

———. *Team Players and Teamwork: The New Competitive Business Strategy.* San Francisco: Jossey-Bass, 1990.

Pasmore, W. A. *Creating Strategic Change: Designing the Flexible, High-Performing Organization.* New York: John Wesley, 1994.

————. *Designing Effective Organizations: The Sociotechnical Systems Perspective.* New York: John Wiley, 1988.

————, and J. J. Sherwood, eds. *Sociotechnical Systems: A Sourcebook.* San Diego: University Associates, 1978.

Pasmore, W. A., and K. Gurley. "Enhancing R and D across Functional Areas." In *Making Organizations More Competitive,* ed. R. Kilmann and I. Kilmann. San Francisco: Jossey-Bass, 1991, pp. 368–96.

————. *Optimizing Knowledge Work: Your Key to Competitive Advantage?*

Pasmore, W. A., and R. V. Tenkasi. "The Influence of Deliberations on Learning in New Product Development Teams." *Journal of Engineering and Technology Management* 9 (1992), pp. 1–28.

Paton, S. M. "Implementing Self-Directed Work Teams at USG." *Quality Digest.* February 1994, pp. 24–30.

Pava, C. H. P. *Managing New Office Technology: An Organization: The Sociotechnical Systems Perspective.* New York: John Wiley, 1983.

Pinchot, G., and E. Pinchot. *The End of Bureaucracy and the Rise of the Intelligent Organization.* San Francisco: Berrett-Koehler, 1993.

Purser, R. E. "The Application of Non-routine Sociotechnical Systems Analysis in a Product Development Organization." *Organization Development Journal,* Spring 1991, pp. 73–78.

————, and W. A. Pasmore. "Organizing for Learning." In *Research in Organizational Change and Development,* vol. 6. Greenwich, CT: JAI, 1992, pp. 37–114.

Ray, D., and H. Bronstein. *Teaming Up.* New York: McGraw-Hill, 1995.

Rees, F. *How to Lead Work Teams: Facilitation Skills.* San Diego: Pfeiffer, 1991.

Robbins, H., and M. Finley. *Why Teams Don't Work: What Went Wrong and How to Make It Right.* Princeton, NJ: Perterson's/Pacesetter Books, 1995.

Rummler, G. A., and A. P. Brache. *Improving Performance: How to Manage the White Space on the Organization Chart.* San Francisco: Jossey-Bass, 1990.

Russ-Eft, D. "Predicting Organizational Orientation toward Teams." *Human Resource Development Quarterly,* Summer 1993, pp. 125–34.

Schein, E. H. *Process Consultation: Its Role in Organization Development.* Reading, MA: Addison-Wesley, 1980.

Schindler, J. "Work Teams Boost Productivity." *Personnel Journal,* February 1992, pp. 67–71.

Schuster, J. R., and P. K. Zingheim. *The New Pay: Linking Employee and Organizational Performance.* New York: Lexington Books, 1992.

Senge, P. *The Fifth Discipline: The Art and Practice of the Learning Organization.* New York: Currency and Doubleday, 1990.

Smith, C. G. "Hi-ho, Hi-ho, It's Off to Self-Managed Work We Go." *Journal for Quality and Participation,* October–November 1993, pp. 38–43.

Smith, P.l, and L. Kearney. *Creating Workplaces Where People Can Think.* San Francisco: Jossey-Bass, 1994.

Smolek, J. *Assimilating a New Manager into a Team Environment.* San Jose: Zenger Miller, 1993.

Thamhain, H. J., and D. L. Willemon. "Building High-Performing Engineering Project Teams." *IEEE Transactions on Engineering Management,* August 1987, pp. 130–37.

Thamulds, H. J. "Managing Technologically Innovative Team Efforts toward New Product Success." *Journal of Product Innovation Management* 7 (1990), pp. 5–18.

Tichy, N. M., and M. A. Devanna. *The Transformational Leader.* New York: John Wiley, 1986.

Tobin, D. R. *Re-educating the Corporation: Foundations for the Learning Organization.* Essex Junction, VT: Oliver Wright, 1993.

Tomasko, R. M. *Rethinking the Corporation: The Architecture of Change.* New York: Amacom, 1993.

Trist, E., and K. Bamforth. "Some Social and Psychological Consequences of the Longwall Method of Coal-Getting." *Human Relations* 1 (1951), pp. 3–38.

Tuckman, B. W. "Developing Sequence in Small Groups." *Psychological Bulletin* 63, no. 6 (1965), pp. 334–99.

Tully, S. "Can Boeing Reinvent Itself?" *Fortune,* March 8, 1993, pp. 66–73.

von Glinow, M. A., and S. A. Mohrman. *Managing Complexity in High Technology Organizations.* London: Oxford University Press, 1990.

Walton, R. E. "From Control to Commitment in the Workplace." *Harvard Business Review,* March–April 1985, pp. 77–84.

Waterman, R. H. "P and G—A Learning Organization," *At Work,* July–August 1994, pp. 1–13.

———, J. A. Waterman, and B.A. Collard. "Toward a Career-Resilient Workforce." *Harvard Business Review,* July–August 1994, pp. 87–95.

Weisbord, M. R., et al. *Discovering Common Ground: How Future Search Conferences Bring People Together to Achieve Breakthrough Innovation, Empowerment, Shared Vision and Collaborative Action.* San Francisco: Berrett-Koehler, 1992.

Weisbord, M. R., and S. Janoff. *Future Search: An Action Guide to Finding Common Ground in Organizations and Communities.* San Francisco: Berrett-Koehler, 1995.

Wheatley, M. "De-engineering the Corporation." *Industry Week,* April 18, 1994, pp. 18–26.

———. "Information at Work." *At Work,* November–December 1993, pp. 17–19.

———. *Leadership and the New Science: Learning about Organization from an Orderly Universe.* San Francisco: Berrett-Koehler, 1994.

Whiteside, J. *The Phoenix Agenda: Power to Transform Your Workplace.* Essex Junction, VT: Oliver Wight, 1993.

Whyte, D. *The Heart Aroused: Poetry and the Preservation of the Soul in Corporate America.* New York: Currency Doubleday, 1994.

Wilson, G. *Self-Managed Team Working: The Flexible Route to High-Performance.* San Francisco: Jossey-Bass, 1995.

Zenger, J. H., E. Musselwhite, K. Hurson, and C. Perrin, *Leading Teams.* Chicago, IL: Irwin, 1994.

INDEX

ABOUT THE AUTHORS

ⓑ

Linda Moran

Linda Moran is Director of Strategic engagements for Zenger Miller. Zenger Miller is an international training and consulting firm specializing in training and consulting services to effect broad-scale organizational change. It provides services to over 3,000 major organizations and institutions worldwide, including half of the Fortune 500.

Linda specializes in team effectiveness research and skills building. She manages large-scale organizational change and team implementations for Zenger Miller clients.

As a team leader in developing Zenger Miller strategic consulting business, she conducts research about effective teams. She achieves results by using work redesign, role clarification, task transfer process, and effective team measures. She also assists in developing Zenger Miller's team training systems, which deliver skills needed to operate effectively in a team environment.

Linda came to Zenger Miller from human resource and training positions at the Oyster Creek Nuclear Power Plant and Chubb & Sons, Inc. She received a Bachelor of Science degree from Pennsylvania State University, and a Master's Degree in Organizational Communication from the University of Maryland.

She is co-author of numerous articles and books, including *Self-Directed Work Teams: The New American Challenge* (1990) and the author of numerous articles.

Linda's in-depth experience and original research into the leading-edge field of self-direction have created a high demand for her consulting and speaking services across the country. She is a regular presenter at such conferences as International Work Team Conference 1991–1995; ASQC, 1992, 1994; AQP, 1992; ASTD, 1989; and many local chapters of these organizations. In addition, she is frequently quoted in *Quality Digest, Training, Training and Development,* and *Journal of Quality and Participation.*

Ed Musselwhite

A proven executive, Ed Musselwhite was President and CEO of Zenger Miller, Inc., a research-based consulting, education, and training company with over 3,000 client organizations worldwide, from 1991 to 1996. He is currently working with Times Mirror, Zenger Miller's parent company, in the development of a new start-up organization.

A graduate of Northwestern University's School of Business, he began his career with IBM in 1964 in sales and marketing management. His interest in team effectiveness began in those early days of business teaming, and his work with teams today, particularly executive teams, displays a unique practicality, maturity, and insight toward team effectiveness issues.

Ed left IBM to become a co-founder and Executive Vice President of Deltak, Inc., an international computer systems engineering and programmer training company. The company eventually grew into a $100 million organization.

Based on his business successes, Ed formed his own executive consulting organization in 1977. His clients included General Electric, Rockwell International, Metropolitan Life, Fireman's Fund Insurance, IBM, and Stanford University.

Ed joined Zenger Miller in 1982 as the company's Vice President of Research and Product Development. Under Ed's leadership, Zenger Miller's growing list of competencies, products, and services focused on improving organizational and individual performance, won industry awards for quality, and helped rapidly expand the company's client base worldwide. Zenger Miller was acquired by Times Mirror in 1989 and Ed was named President of Zenger Miller in 1991.

Ed is a co-author of the best-selling business "how-to" books, *Self-Directed Work Teams: The New American Challenge,* published in 1990, and *Leading Teams: Mastering the New Role,* published in June 1993. Ed was a contributing author to the *Harvard Business Review* case study, "The Team That Wasn't," published in the *HBR* November–December 1994 issue. He is a much-sought-after speaker on subjects of organizational change, management effectiveness, and team development.

John H. Zenger

John H. Zenger is Chairman of Times Mirror Training, Inc., which includes four professional training companies in North America: Zenger Miller, Learning International, Kaset International, and software/courseware developer Allen Communication; and three international training operations in Europe, Asia-Pacific, and Latin America.

Mr. Zenger co-founded Zenger Miller in 1977. The international firm, headquartered in San Jose, California, specializes in the areas of leadership, employee involvement, customer focus, and process improvement. In addition to their consulting business, Zenger Miller is distinguished as one of the largest management training companies in the world with offices throughout the United States and Europe. Times Mirror acquired the company in 1989.

Prior to forming Zenger Miller, Mr. Zenger was Vice President of Human Resources at Syntex Corporation, an international pharmaceutical company. Prior to that, he was Executive Vice President of a consulting company and taught at the graduate schools of business at the University of Southern California and Stanford University.

Mr. Zenger is the author of *Not Just For CEO's: Success Secrets for the Leader in Each of Us* and *Producing More with Less: 20 Actions Any Leader Can Take to Boost Productivity* (to be released 9/96). He is the co-author of *Self-Directed Work Teams: The New American Challenge, Leading Teams,* and *Keeping Teams on Track: What to Do When the Going Gets Rough.* He is a frequent speaker at business and trade conferences and has authored numerous articles about training and its role in strategic business issues. In 1994 he was inducted into the Human Resource Development Hall of Fame.

Mr. Zenger earned his Bachelor of Arts degree in psychology from Brigham Young University, graduating magna cum laude in 1955. In 1957, he earned a Master's degree in business administration from the University of California, Los Angeles, and received a Doctorate in business administration from the University of Southern California in 1974.

John C. Harrison

John C. Harrison has a 30-year career as an advertising copywriter, scriptwriter, speech writer, and author, and is a regular contributor to Zenger Miller's custom product development staff. As a former Associate Director of a nonprofit organization, he continues to edit a newsletter and conducts workshops in public speaking.

Thank you for choosing Irwin Professional Publishing for your business information needs. If you are part of a corporation, professional association, or government agency, we invite you to consider our newest option: Irwin Professional Custom Publishing. This allows you to create customized books, manuals, and other materials from your organization's resources, select chapters of our books, or both.

Irwin Professional Publishing books are also excellent resources for training/educational programs, premiums, and incentives. For more information on volume discounts or Custom Publishing, call 1-800-634-3966.

Other titles of interest to you from Irwin Professional Publishing . . .